MICHAEL BAWTREE

AS FAR AS I
REMEMBER

COMING OF AGE IN POST-WAR ENGLAND

MICHAEL BAWTREE

AS FAR AS I REMEMBER

COMING OF AGE IN POST-WAR ENGLAND

MEREO
Cirencester

Mereo Books

1A The Wool Market Dyer Street Cirencester Gloucestershire GL7 2PR
An imprint of Memoirs Publishing www.mereobooks.com

As Far As I Remember: 978-1-86151-373-1

First published in Great Britain in 2015
by Mereo Books, an imprint of Memoirs Publishing

The address for Memoirs Publishing Group Limited can be found at
www.memoirspublishing.com

The Memoirs Publishing Group Ltd Reg. No. 7834348

The Memoirs Publishing Group supports both The Forest Stewardship Council® (FSC®) and
the PEFC® leading international forest-certification organisations. Our books carrying both the
FSC label and the PEFC® and are printed on FSC®-certified paper. FSC® is the only
forest-certification scheme supported by the leading environmental organisations including
Greenpeace. Our paper procurement policy can be found at
www.memoirspublishing.com/environment

Typeset in 10/15pt Bembo
by Wiltshire Associates Publisher Services Ltd. Printed and bound in Great Britain by
Printondemand-Worldwide, Peterborough PE2 6XD

CONTENTS

Preface

Dedicated to the memory of
my mother and father

PREFACE

As I read over what I have remembered here from my early life in post-war England, I see the old and abandoned workings of a world so utterly different from the one I inhabit in Canada that I am astonished to think that the young boy - the young man - who lived through those times is the person who is writing this now. It is light years away too from the England where a slowly-diminishing number of my dear friends still live.

My parents and their generation, exhausted by the Second World War, were still proud that their country had survived a gruelling test, and looked forward to England's gradual return more or less to its pre-war shape and power. There were troubling signs ahead: swaths were being cut out of the old Empire, and there were tiresome people about who seemed to want some radical transformations in the way their society worked. Like all people as they grow older, they saw changes which they did not feel easy with, and despaired of the rising generation's manners and capacity to hold things together. But over all there was a comfort that they knew what was what, and would continue to be in control of events.

I am still astonished at the care that was taken with me by this generation as I grew up, not only by my aspiring middle-class parents, but by the teachers to whom they passed on responsibility for my education. There was passion in these dedicated people's caring for the children in their charge, as well as unshaking belief in what they were teaching and its verities. They were preparing me and my contemporaries in fact for a future that they could not know, but which they assumed would be recognisable when it showed up. It was not.

What I am glad for is the variousness, the oddity, the humour, the surprises, of the life our family lived. Though my parents pushed me through a formal upper middle-class education of the most conventional kind, they were never entirely part of that social echelon, and their children were in it but never really of it either. We all three of us scattered to other countries as soon as we could, and in the end our parents left too. If we were not jetsam, our Bawtree family was certainly flotsam. As will be seen.

MB
Wolfville, Nova Scotia
December 2014

CHAPTER ONE

'TIS A KING DOWN HERE

Like many Canadians, I was not born in Canada. The light of my first day saw me landing not between sea and shining sea on the North American continent but on a wintry August morning at a cottage hospital in the coaling port of Newcastle, New South Wales, some hundred or more miles north of Sydney. My father, having worked in the office of a coastal shipping firm in Sydney since his arrival there as a British immigrant less than ten years before, had recently been posted as manager of the firm's Newcastle office, and had brought with him his Australian wife of five years and their daughter of three. I was the latest addition, and, to the delight of my parents, I very sensibly restored the balance of the family by arriving as a boy. The year was 1937.

Less than twelve months later, in July 1938, my father became entitled to six months of what was then still called 'home leave', and packed us all into the SS *Strathnaver* for the long voyage around the world to the United Kingdom. I was a little too young to savour the full delights of Colombo, Bombay and Aden, but still enjoy assuring people that Ceylon, India and the Middle East are in the lengthy repertoire of places I have visited.

I am not sure what happened once he was in England, but the joy of returning to his native shores must have overwhelmed my father, whose intense love of the English countryside and its animals and birds had evidently been on agonised hold for ten years, almost without his knowing it. My mother, who had made the visit 'home' in 1927 when fresh out of school, had always preferred England to anywhere else . So within a few weeks of our arrival it was decided not to return to the other side of the world.

And that is why, though born in Australia of an Australian mother, I had no memory of the land of my birth. It flickered into my consciousness only as disconnected images in the stories Mother told us: jacaranda trees and wattle; the cart travelling the lane behind the house in Melbourne to pick up night soil; Christmas dinner of turkey and roast potatoes and plum pudding on the blazing summer beach at Portsea; kookaburras; nearly playing hockey for Australia – but she went to England instead; her grandfather Thomas Westwood, who painted birds for the children, and who had gone to Paraguay in 1893 with a boatload of disgruntled Australian unionists to help found an abortive socialist utopia; camping on the Murrumbidgee River and nearly being washed away in a flash flood. And then the occasional anecdote for which Mother was famous, like the one of the charlady arriving for work one morning and announcing "Today's the day" (or rather, "To-dye's the dye"). "What day, Doris?" asks grandma. A look of astonishment from Doris that her boss should be so ignorant: "Why, they're judging the doilies in the Wagga Wagga show!"

It is not immediately obvious to me even now why, in August 1938, my parents should decide to settle down in Britain, when it was clear to almost everyone else that Hitler was not intending to settle down in Germany. Already in March of that year he had marched into Austria. His subsequent threat to attack

Czechoslovakia had been creating turmoil in France and Britain all that summer, and by September had led to Chamberlain's third visit to Hitler, from which he returned waving his scrap of paper spelling out 'peace for our time'. Perhaps my father believed Chamberlain: perhaps he trusted that all was now well, and that this was an ideal moment to embark on a new life and an ambitious new project in the land of his birth.

Another mystery, which I doubt the family will now ever unravel, is the choice of that project: he decided, of all things, to become a pig farmer. Why? He had never lived or even as far I know worked on a farm. His own father Percy had lived all his life among the villas of north Surrey, and was now settled in a solidly suburban home on Shirley Avenue in Cheam. A staunch Liberal of the old school (he was always proud that he had once shaken the hand of Gladstone), Percy was a director of Ralli Brothers, a major insurance company, and had in fact done everything he could to turn the fifth of his six sons away from his passion for birds and nature and into the steady world of business. Raymond had been accordingly removed from school at sixteen, and dispatched to London, where he was launched into a career as an accountant. It was from his office in Golden Square, Soho, that he had fled to Australia after three years in servitude – though he must have impressed his employers, since I still have the gold watch he was given on his departure:

Presented to
Raymond Francis Bawtree
with best wishes from the staff and firm of
Armitage, Norton, Paton & Co
20.3.28

Perhaps as he sailed to Australia on the SS *Cathay* the following month he had imagined travelling on into the outback and setting up as a grazier. But on his arrival in Sydney without a penny – having spent on board his father's entire allowance of ten pounds, meant to last into his first months in the new country – he had found himself at once snapped up for his accounting skills into yet another office job. Finally, ten years later and back in England, he was free to be a countryman at last – though it was to be not sheep but pigs. This time, Raymond not only managed to fly in the face of his father's judgement, but was even able to persuade his old man to put up £5000 towards the enterprise.

Exactly how things unfolded during the next year I am not sure. I know that Father went off on a crash pig-farming course somewhere in the north of England, and that by the autumn of 1939 we were living in Devon on a 120-acre farm west of Dartmoor, by the banks of the River Lyd, surrounded by pigs. It was not an old house – built perhaps after the First World War: square, grey stuccoed, with a glass-roofed verandah along its southern side. It boasted an ancient wall-mounted telephone in the hall, but no electricity. Set on a ridge in the midst of the Lyd valley, it was encircled by hills dense with oak woods, and connected to the network of tiny Devon lanes – and so to the world – by a long driveway which ran by the 'hams': the fields that lay beside the river. Here my father, with some of his father's money, was soon to build a fattening house. The pigs not yet ready for fattening ran free in the woods, kept in place – most of the time – by electric fencing, and indulging their passion for acorns. This was apparently considered an innovation in its day, and at least a partial answer to the increasingly difficult business of providing the growing herd with fodder: mangelwurzels were grown in various patches around the farm for the same purpose.

One joy for my father, which resulted from having our home in the far depths of the countryside, was that he could take up once again his passionate interest in the identification and behaviour of birds. He disliked being called a 'bird-watcher', preferring to think of himself as an 'amateur ornithologist'. He had a profound knowledge of the birds of England, picking out their calls in the woods with stunning accuracy, and spotting a rare shrike or a hoopoe – or a kingfisher as it flashed along the river. And he began at an early age to record his observations. We were later to say that he preferred birds to people.

But the work of the farm went on. By early 1940, while Hitler was routing the French army and the British Expeditionary Force in Belgium and France, Raymond had built up a herd of over 500 head of Large White pigs: one of the largest pig farms in the West Country, he used to say proudly in later days.

All this had taken place with me as a witness, but an ineffective one. It was only sometime around that same year of 1940 that I began having sensations – of sight, touch, smell and sound – which I could later recall. Lyd Valley House, then, was my first world.

I shared it – apart from various dogs, hens, caged rabbits, a horse or two and of course the pigs – with three other people.

You have already met my father Raymond – or Ray as my mother called him in those days. Just under six feet tall, handsome, strong, big-nosed, huge-handed, with dark hair and moustache, Ray was the powerful force in our family life. We children were just a little afraid of him, and certainly afraid of his anger, although I can only once remember when he spanked me, and that after all was when I had bitten my mother on the arm: a provocation if ever there was one. I still have a picture of him, taken many years later in the sixties, when he had gone back to farming and was managing a herd of someone else's pigs: we see him coaxing a Landrace herd down a sloping field at feeding time, arms wide, hair flying behind him, a prophet on the move – but of course dressed in a tweed jacket and tie, still then the folk costume of English gentlemen farmers. I cannot remember his working clothes in Lyd Valley days, but I imagine they were much the same. He exuded authority within the family, and I suspect that wherever he went he had the same response. There was a patrician air about him which would well have suited a senior ambassador.

Was he in fact a 'gentleman', in the class-conscious English sense? Certainly so in his appearance, good manners, cultured accent and somewhat ponderous delivery: perhaps also in his capacity to speak his mind: as they say, "no gentleman is ever rude unintentionally". He loved his Dickens and his Sherlock Holmes, and was a regular reader of middlebrow novels – when he wasn't poring over his massive copy of *British Birds*, or *The Countryman* magazine, or the *Farmers' Weekly*. But his stock – our stock – was in no way aristocratic. His father Percy was reared a Congregationalist, his Scottish mother a Presbyterian. Many generations of Bawtrees in the eighteenth and early nineteenth century had been engravers of bank-notes at the Bank of England. We were in other words of superior artisan class, and Dissenters – so ineligible for entry to Oxford and Cambridge until the mid eighteen hundreds. No one before my father's generation had university degrees, and of his five brothers only two received higher education, in both cases leading to ordination in the Church of Scotland.

But university education and pedigree were not – are not – necessarily the same thing. Our family tree, lovingly assembled by some cousin in the early twenties, traces our roots back to Sir John de Bautré, of the town of Bawtry in Yorkshire, living around 1460. So perhaps we had gently declined from having money to burn, to simply etching it on copper plates. We did boast two coats of arms:

one was copied from an old tombstone and sported three bull-heads in a triangle; the other was a piece of fun and fakery etched by one of our engraving ancestors. Its family crest showed a lamb grazing under an oak tree: 'baa/tree'. Get it?

And who was this Australian wife Ray had brought back to Britain? She was born Kathleen McEacharn, of a distinguished Scottish-Australian family in Melbourne. Archibald McEacharn had emigrated from the island of Islay in the Hebrides in the 1840s. One of his brothers spawned a long line of sea captains, one of whom, Malcolm, had gone down with his ship in a storm off King Island, on Australia's south-east coast. Malcolm's son − another Malcolm − had been Lord Mayor of Melbourne. My mother's father, Archibald's second son, was James, a Melbourne lawyer and a director of the well-known shipping company MacIlwraith McEacharn, which plied the coastal waters of Australia from the end of the nineteenth century until the 1960s. It was in fact the very same firm which had given my father Raymond his first and only job in Australia.

Kathleen McEacharn − often shortened to 'Kath', a name she hated − was red-haired and diminutive, but fiery and energetic enough to be head girl of Melbourne Church of England Grammar School for Girls, and captain of her hockey team. She also excelled in her studies, and matriculated with high honours − "I came fourth in Geography in the whole of Australia," she told us proudly. Our bookshelves were laden with the beautifully bound school prizes she had won. She was a natural leader, self-willed, gregarious, with a bursting sense of humour, a keen ear for how people spoke, a tremendous gift for anecdote, and a rebellious spirit. Her trip to England in 1927 on the SS *Anchises*, with her mother (also Kathleen) and sisters Sheila and Eila, had started in the highest of spirits. They spent time in Switzerland, and took a house in Menton for four months to improve the girls' French. They met up with their wealthy cousin Neil McEacharn in England, and spent time trying to locate the original home of their mother's family the Westwoods. All in all, they seemed in no hurry to return. But events took a tragic turn: their mother, my grandmother, died suddenly of influenza at their hotel in Kensington in March 1929, leaving the three girls stranded in a foreign land.

Returning to Australia a few months later Kath soon escaped from her bibulous father in Melbourne and settled in Sydney, where she earned a pound or two a week working at a café. Every month her father would send her an allowance, which humiliatingly she had to go and pick up from the local offices of the family's shipping firm. The man who passed her money over the counter was a very junior clerk working in the accounts department: my father Raymond Bawtree. So they met, and soon fell very much in love. They married at a registry office during a lunch break in September 1932, and fifty years later celebrated their Golden Wedding – six weeks before he died.

During their courtship both my parents worked and occasionally acted at the Independent Theatre, a 'little theatre' in North Sydney. The theatre's season for 1931 included a dramatisation of the best-selling novel *The Constant Nymph* by Margaret Kennedy. Captivated by 'Tessa', the rebellious and romantic young 'constant nymph' of the play, Kathleen decided to change her own name, and from that moment until her death was known to everyone except the passport authorities as Tessa, or Tess.

To some extent, then, these two young people were both escapees from stifling home situations and conventional expectations. So it is not surprising that they shared a spirit of adventure, and every so often throughout their lives launched bravely into new and risky situations. Moving off into the depths of Devonshire was their first courageous enterprise. It was not the last.

And then there was Josephine, three years older than I, known in the family as Jo, a name she hated, and which when she was confirmed she changed to Victoria – exchanging, as we said in after years, one empress for another. (This name-changing seemed to run in the family: in his last years my father announced one morning that he had always hated the name Ray, and would henceforward be known as Ben. And so it was – although, in his case as in my sister's, the family was exempted from these whimsies.)

About Jo, I need to start with an anecdote. When I was perhaps five, and she was eight, we were playing one day with the family's wind-up gramophone, and happened by mistake to smash a record – one of those old Bakelite 78s which are now antiques. We ran to Mother in tears, telling her we had broken Daddy's favourite record – I think it was *The Way You Look Tonight*. Mother said he would understand, but we were inconsolable – and I suppose a little scared. Eventually Mother said, "All right, don't worry – I'll tell him I did it". We looked at her with eyes wide open; and simultaneously Jo, still in tears, howled "But you caan't Mummy – it's a lie!" – and I exclaimed excitedly: "Will you really?"

The story is a worse reflection on my moral character than on Jo's, but I always tell it with some modest pride, because it seems to cast Jo as a bit of a prude and me as a bit of a pirate. And perhaps this is not entirely off the mark. From her earliest days, or perhaps from her earliest schooling, Jo had what I felt at the time was an exaggerated moral sense, which for want of other targets she deployed unceasingly against me. I was selfish – the very worst thing you could be; whereas she was *un*selfish – the very *best* thing you could be. I tended to run away when washing up was on the menu. She would come after me shouting my name, find me hiding in the shrubbery, and haul me back to the kitchen and my moral duty. I was low-minded, she was high-minded. There is a photograph of us both from Lyd Valley days: I am holding out a ball to her, obviously begging her to play; she is facing front with a serious face, and thinking about it. That seems to sum up our relationship in those early years.

But it also makes clear that I really wanted her to come play, and that in fact her company and her approval were deeply important to me. As a precocious reader – while I was little more than a baby – she had begun to drink in stories of the Knights of the Round Table, and was always half hoping that Sir Lancelot or Sir Galahad would come cantering through our woods, gather her up and whisk her away to a life of derring-do – as a knight, mind you, not by any means as a maiden in distress. Meanwhile, under her instructions, Mother made swords and shields for us both, armed with which we would march off to a life of chivalric adventure on the pig farm. I was more than happy to serve as a loyal adjutant under her bold leadership. Of course I adored her.

Not far from the house was a little glade dense with knee-high stinging-nettles. One day Jo decided that as a test of our courage we should take up our swords and shields and walk through the nettles from one end to the other, she in her little skirt, I in skimpy shorts. A little while later Mother was astonished to see us running up to the house, our legs red and painfully swollen, but our eyes shining with the glory of it all. Much later I used to wonder whether I remembered this correctly; did she in fact put her loyal adjutant through the test while herself standing at one side to see fair play? But maybe I was being uncharitable.

Our parents were determined from the start that we should be well educated, and that they would undergo any sacrifice to make this possible. They also believed in starting us young. In September 1939, the month the Second World War broke out, Jo was taken early one Monday morning to Launceston, a little town over the border in Cornwall, to be enrolled as a weekly boarder at a small and genteel private establishment called Pendruccombe. It was a girl's school, but attached to it was a day-school kindergarten for boys as well as girls. She was just five. And there she remained until Friday, when she was put on the bus for our local market town, Tavistock, back in Devon. The bus stopped outside the church in the centre of the town, and she would jump out and run into the arms of her parents – I presumably still sucking my thumb in a pram.

Before long she was making the journey by train. Two miles walk from Lyd Valley there was even a station: Lyddaton Halt. The one-carriage Great Western Railway puffer would stop there and pick her up for the ten-minute ride to Lydford, where she would meet up with an older Pendruccombe girl, Jean Bailey, whose mother ran the Lydford Arms, and who would accompany her in the Launceston train and then climb with her up the steep hill to the school. At least once in winter the trek to Lyddaton Halt was made by snow-sleigh, drawn by our superannuated white cart-horse Ditch. We have a photo of this still.

Our little station in fact etched itself into the mythic consciousness of our family from early on. It was little more than a short wooden platform and a diminutive waiting room, painted shabbily in the beige and chocolate brown colours of the Great Western Railway, and sitting alongside the single track branch line which curved off into the woods above our house at Lyd Valley and on to Lydford. My mother would always accompany Jo to the station and see her off. One year, when one of Dad's sows died after giving birth, Mother took the tiniest piglet and brought it up by hand, feeding it from a baby's milk bottle – mine, I expect. She named it Tonk, and Tonk became devoted to her. Even when it had grown into a 300-pound beast, it followed her everywhere around the farm – and of course when she walked to the station it would trot along behind. It must have been mildly odd for the handful of other passengers on the train to see this young woman waving goodbye to her little daughter and then starting back home with the massive Tonk following faithfully in her wake. But when she herself had to catch the train for a day in town there was a serious problem, since Tonk was always clearly determined to join her on the 7.35. Luckily the train's conductor learned to enter into the spirit of the thing. When the train steamed in and Tonk clattered on to the platform, the conductor would step down, offer him an apple, lure him into the waiting room and slam the door. Mother would climb up into the train, and just before the train was due to leave the doughty train man would fling open the waiting-room door, wave his green flag and jump aboard.

One time our grown-up (teenage) cousin Phyllis came for a visit from bomb-blitzed London. After an exhausting day's travel and many changes of train, she arrived at Lyddaton Halt as dusk was falling. She was dressed in her too-smart city clothes, and as she stepped down from the carriage, looking nervously around her at the darkening countryside, one of her red high-heeled shoes fell off and dropped into the gap between the train and the platform. She burst into tears. But all was not lost. Our conductor friend had a word with the engine-driver and he obligingly reversed the train out of the station for a few moments so Dad could climb down and retrieve the shoe. Trains were simpler things in those days.

A year or two later, when the Germans had taken to bombing British ports, Plymouth's harbour installations were one of their prime targets. Lyd Valley House was no more than fifteen miles away, and many was the night that we would stagger – or toddle – down from our bedrooms and take refuge in a cupboard under the stairs, while the crump and crash of bombs would reach us from the coast. The bombers would return to Germany right above our heads, and would often drop their last bombs in our area to lighten their load for the flight home across the Channel. One morning, as Mother was walking up to Coryton to buy provisions, she saw a huge crater, still smoking, just beyond Lyddaton Halt. A local villager passed by and together they looked at the massive hole in the field. The villager spoke confidingly to her: "They do say they was after Providence Chapel".

In those wilds of Devon in the early forties, on the edge of the Moor, life had changed little for centuries, and with the rustic people who lived around us my mother's ear for how people spoke came into its own. One blustery day our farmhand George arrived for work from his cottage up the hill towards Brentor. Mother remarked on the wild weather, and his reply was poetry: "Oo, 'tis a king down here to what it is up over". When one winter old Mr Worth, who farmed across the ford, passed on to his fathers, and was buried in Coryton churchyard, his widow bumped into Mother a few weeks later, when we had been enduring some bitter frosts. "It was good 'e was took when 'e was," she said complacently: "If 'e'd left it another month, they'd never 'ave got 'ee under".

One of Dad's workers was simpler than the others, and was the butt of jokes from the other hands. Returning from Tavistock one afternoon, Dad was surprised to see Lionel ambling along the drive with a paintbrush in one hand, and in the other a can of black paint. He stopped the car, and asked what on earth he was doing. "Oo, George sent me up to old Ditch in the top field. He says those air raid wardles 'ave been aroun' and told us to paint 'im dark coz' of the black-out. Oi'z jus' goin' up there now."

Old Ditch he certainly was. Dad had bought the huge white horse off a neighbouring farmer for five pounds – he was well over twenty-five years old, had been getting feeble and expensive to feed, and was about to be sent to the knackers: a fate Dad would do anything to prevent. So Dad offered him a home. The story repeated itself, and the farm gradually filled up with lame cows, broken-winded horses and unwanted dogs. One day he read that the elephants at Paignton Zoo could no longer be fed and would have to be shot. This horrified him. He started thinking how he could bring them to Lyd Valley and set them to work hauling timber out of the woods. He even read up about how to grow bamboo shoots. But the plan was dropped when he discovered they were not Indian but African elephants – much too lordly to be beasts of burden.

Our own dog in those days, a huge and beautiful Irish greyhound called Biddy, put up with these visitors with amazing tolerance. But the time came when she herself had to be dispatched, having developed a cancerous growth on her stomach. After becoming used to his soft heart, Jo and I were surprised and shocked when Dad took Biddy off for a walk in the woods and calmly shot her with his Home Guard service revolver.

It's hard to unravel my own remembered experiences from the stories passed down in the family from those days, and I am struck now when I realize how much time I must have spent alone with my mother or on my own, once Jo was sent to school. Dad was of course around, and one of my earliest memories – certainly before I was four – was putting on my miniature wellies and running down the hill to visit him in the 'hatting house'. There were no other children in the neighbourhood, and my parents had few friends. In fact I am also struck by the way both my parents had cut themselves off from their upbringings. I cannot remember ever meeting a single friend of Dad's from school or office. He had left for Australia when he was twenty, losing touch with the friends of his youth and early manhood; and by the time he returned ten years later those connections had been broken too long to be re-forged.

Once we were in Devon, of course, we were miles away from any family or old acquaintance at all. As for Mother, she was already half the globe away from her Australian roots. So the two of them had to build their own small world from scratch, which must have required a great deal of self-sufficiency.

I particularly think of Mother – gregarious, talkative and lively, and buzzing with energy to devote to her community – stuck in isolation on a farm in wartime, with no electricity, no central heating, minimal transportation, and for days at a time only a baby boy for company; her husband starting out early for work on the farm, and returning for a quick lunch and then gone again until the end of the working day. Of course it is the lot of millions of farmers' wives everywhere. But it was not a life she was born into, and hardly a fate she would have picked for herself. Her devotion to Father must have been very strong indeed to have led her into such a lonely and unstimulating life-way. The pig farm, after all, was not her dream, but his.

But my sister and I were the beneficiaries of this situation. I remember us often coming to her and whining "Mummy, what shall we _do_?" She was always ready with some suggestion, and got us cutting up paper, or building houses in the woods, or playing firemen, or painting a picture to give to Daddy when he got home. Her imagination rubbed off on us, and forty years later, as I watched her playing for hours with my baby nephew, the way she entered into the spirit of the play was all strangely familiar to me.

We were read to every night, and by the age of four began reading for ourselves. So with almost no social life of any kind, all Mother's intelligence, creative imagination and generosity were directed our way. It's hard not to believe that that is why both Jo and I – and later our younger sister Jenny – all produced books, and nephew Nicholas has become a highly literate environmental journalist.

Money was scarce then, and material things hard to come by. Rationing was soon brought in, not just for food but for fabrics, for clothes, for everything. Mother was nothing if not resourceful, and from her never idle hands came a steady flow of baby's clothes, girls' dresses, curtains, toys and food. What she did not make for us children came from local village jumble sales and junk shops in Tavistock, with the odd treat bought from Spooner's Department Store on our annual visit to Plymouth (I can still remember walking through it after it had been bombed – past mysterious, curtained-off and blackened areas).

For my fourth birthday I had asked for a fort, a crane and a golliwog, and I remember being given all three. The crane was – now I think of it – a crude home-made wooden contraption, freshly painted blood-red. The fort, all green, yellow and brown, was perhaps picked up at Spooner's. And the golliwog, with a fuzz of African hair, yellow trousers and orange jacket, was no doubt passed on from some other blithely imperialist family. I immediately called him Mr Wap and I immediately adored him. From then on he came with me on all my adventures around the farm.

I must have occupied myself busily enough. But I imagine that as I grew a little older I would have longed for Fridays, when Jo would be back and she could direct our play together, in our playroom off the kitchen or outside on the farm. I well remember one afternoon when, fresh from school, Jo decided we should set up a classroom in the woods. We hauled out all our toy animals – teddy bears, rabbits, my sister's dolls, and of course Mr Wap – put them into a sack and dragged them to a glade on the edge of the upper field. We stuck the toy people and animals into the forks of trees or leaned them against tree-trunks, and class began. I remember nothing of the lessons taught, and guess that this was firmly Jo's department. No doubt moral instruction was on the curriculum.

When Dad went by rail to Tavistock, Jo and I would run down to the field below the woods, getting a thrill when by pre-arrangement he would wave a rolled-up newspaper out of his window as the train went by. How much we loved it when our father gave us this kind of attention! Sometimes he would play with us in the garden, and I still have a memory of him appearing from behind the house as an ogre, with a tablecloth over his shoulders and a wicker waste paper basket on his head – Jo and I screaming with terror and delight.

I remember a different sort of scream. When we played down by the river Jo and I used to visit a cave at the water's edge, which tunnelled deep into the hillside. Once, as we came up to it and started to walk inside, a wild-looking man appeared from the back of the cave, striding towards us suddenly and fiercely. The terror of that moment is still with me: we yelled and ran. I seem to remember that a convict had escaped from Dartmoor prison a few days before, and perhaps this was he. Whatever the case, it was many weeks before we ventured down there again. After that time, and for many years afterwards, I would have recurring nightmares of a hideous old man standing at the foot of my bed.

Sometimes we would walk over the fields to visit Mrs Kanoozel, who lived in a small house halfway up the hill to Brentor. I think she was Swiss, but her foreign-sounding name gave rise to the local rumour that she was a German spy. Nor was her good reputation restored by the certain fact that for her health she tossed down half a pint of bull's blood every day. Jo and I saw this with our own wide eyes, and ran back home with all sorts of strange imaginings.

But while we were wandering and playing blissfully in this children's paradise, the pig farm was already in serious trouble. Britain had endured Dunkirk and the capitulation of France, and was being pounded in the London Blitz, and Churchill – now Prime Minister – had still not persuaded the United States to enter the war. Pearl Harbour lay ahead.

Father had already developed a real instinct for the art of pig-breeding, and had invested in several superb sows and two champion pedigree boars which between them had spawned a fine and rapidly-growing herd. Unfortunately, Britain's priorities lay not in fine breeding but in food. As fodder got harder to come by, the herd had to be sold off. Eventually even the boars and sows had to go – and pigs worth perhaps £200 in peacetime conditions had to be sold off for as little as £40 to supply the meat markets of Devon. I can still remember the screams of the pigs being slaughtered in the barn behind the house. No doubt Tonk was among them. It was a frightening sound for a little boy. Only much later did I realize the pain suffered by my poor father, as his bold enterprise was bludgeoned to death. The bright new fattening house lay empty beside the river, mocking his long toil.

Money became tighter still, and though we children were not at all aware of this, we accepted as normal that we had to do without, or make do. Resourcefulness became even more necessary. For a while we bred rabbits, and I remember to this day the smell of the potato sludge being boiled up for them in the scullery. We kept chickens, and had a cockerel which once attacked me in the farmyard, pecking my face and scaring me out of my wits. Farmhand George found me in time and carried me back to the house: Dad marched straight out and shot the cockerel. We no doubt ate him.

We still kept dogs, and to feed them my parents resorted to buying calf heads in the market at Tavistock ('Lots of meat around the eye' as old Mrs Worth used to say). My mother told of a time when they were driving up the steep hill under the viaduct out of

Tavistock on the Brentor road, with a sack full of calves' heads tied to the back of the car, when it came loose and fell on to the road, scattering its contents. My father couldn't get out of the car because the handbrake was useless: the engine's compression was too feeble to hold the weight of the car, and he had to stay put and keep his foot on the brake pedal. So it was Mum who had to get out and chase the bloody heads all over the road, some of them rolling back towards Tavistock.

One year (maybe more often) we grew a crop of barley, and I can still recall a hot harvest day when a magnificent steam engine rolled at a snail's pace up the hill to the field behind the house, dragging its threshing machine behind it; combine harvesters did not reach this part of England from America until a few years later. I remember there being a lot of strange men around to fork the crop into the thresher, and being fascinated by the long driving belt, and being picked up to sit for a moment behind the wheel of the huge, oil-shiny steam engine with its polished brass, green paint and chimney belching smoke. Jo got a piece of barley chaff stuck in her eye, and Dr Lea had to come out from Lifton to extract it. After the operation Dad led the doctor down to the river with me following behind, and they stripped off and plunged in to cool off. It was the same place Dad once rescued one of our dogs that had dived in during the spring floods and couldn't swim to shore.

We had inherited from the previous farmer a patch of double-headed narcissi, an exotic and much sought-after cut flower. In the West Country, warmed by the Gulf Stream, our spring was a week or two ahead of the rest of England, and each April Mother used to get up at four in the morning to gather armfuls of the beautiful blooms and pack them in boxes for Dad to drive to Lyddaton Halt, where they began their long journey to Covent Garden, bringing another few shillings into the kitty.

As a farmer, Dad had extra petrol coupons, which enabled him to keep a vehicle going in the midst of the war. He must have had others, but the only car I remember from those very early days was an Austin 16, which Dad must have picked up for a few pounds when its owner could no longer run the thing. It was a tall and stately four-door black vehicle, a model which Austin had been producing since the early 'thirties. We would run into Tavistock every Friday in the Austin, bringing eggs and rabbit meat for the market, and returning with the week's shopping, including bags of anthracite for the kitchen range and hay for the animals – and of course in term-time with Jo, back from Pendruccombe.

One Friday morning Dad was changing a tyre before we left, and when it was done we piled into the car. He cranked the engine until it sprang into spluttering life, then jumped in behind the wheel and engaged first gear. The engine revved up, but we stayed absolutely still. Dad was mystified – until he remembered he had forgotten to remove the jack, so that the rear wheels were spinning in the air. He always had a great capacity for laughing at himself, and I think it was his laughter, which continued all the way to Tavistock, that made the incident stick in my mind.

We used to eat Friday lunch in town, and to economise Mother would take Jo and me to eat in the British Restaurant. These spartan places were set up all over Britain during the war, providing an amazingly cheap and reasonably nourishing two-course meal for all comers. We sat at long, bare tables, all walks of life together. Our father, though, could not bring himself to eat in such a place, so at lunch time we would separate, and Dad would take himself off to the Bedford Arms, where he would sit in the little saloon bar (men only) and have a pink gin or two before strolling through to the dining-room. The food was not much better than we were getting at the British Restaurant, but it was served by waiters in black tails, on white table-cloths complete with linen napkins and sparkling cutlery.

Once, the car became a bus – when my parents invited all the girls from Jo's school to come and spend a sunny day out in the country. They arrived at Lyddaton Halt by train from Launceston, and were shuttled in at least two trips from the station to the farm, where they wandered down to the river and among the woods, then gathered for a picnic spread, provided of course by Mother. I can still remember all those leggy girls pouring out of the car in their school tunics. I can also remember being babied by them, carried along by each in turn for the walk down to the river. I think I remember not liking this very much.

One day Mother and I went out to the top of the drive to meet a family of London evacuees which had been billeted on us. They had walked up from Lyddaton Halt: a harassed mother dressed in a skimpy floral dress and pushing a pram, with two young children dragging along beside her. Mum and Dad had persuaded us to part with our playroom, which was turned over to the newcomers. I'm not sure now of the living arrangements for the visitors: they must have shared kitchen and bathroom, and it cannot have been easy – either for this sad, bombed-out little family from the East End of London, or for our kind but house-proud parents. In any case, their stay was short. Mother noticed that the baby and children were developing spots over their faces, and called in Dr Lea to examine them. His verdict was almost immediate; they were infected with scabies. He reported this to the authorities, and within a day or two the poor evacuees were trudging down the hill again, presumably on their way to isolation in some clinic or hospital. But scabies is a virulently contagious infection, and we were ordered out of the house so that it could be fumigated for two weeks. The windows and doors of the playroom were sealed with paper tape, and sulphur candles lit to kill the mites. This was a major disruption, but for us children it turned into a wonderful escape. Dad booked us into a hotel on the seafront at Newquay in Cornwall, where we enjoyed the very first of what later turned out to be several seaside holidays. I have faint memories of the beach, and sand-castles, and paddling in pools. But I remember much more strongly the sound of the Home Guard marching along the street outside early each morning – "lef' ri' lef' ri' lef' ri'" – and the one night of an air raid warning, when the hotel manager woke us up and escorted us to a room in the basement. Mother called Jo to sit on her knee. I was deposited unceremoniously on the floor, and looking up to see this arrant favouritism I uttered the words for which I was teased for years afterwards: "How about me?" This still seems to me to have been a fair enough question, but for Jo it was probably just another example of my self-centredness.

Each December in those early years Dad would drive the family to Exeter to see the Christmas pantomime. It was my very first experience of live theatre, and magical for us children; *Jack and the Beanstalk* and *Babes in the Wood* were two I still remember. No doubt it was a matinee we would see, and we would arrive in Exeter in time for lunch at the Royal Clarence Hotel opposite the cathedral, where as part of the day's treats we would eat lunch in the elegant upstairs dining-room. After the show we would return in the dark of early evening, and perhaps my earliest memory – I must have been very young indeed – is of lying in a blanket on the floor of the car as we groped our way back across the snowy Moor in the dark, the road only dimly lit by the shuttered headlights of wartime. One year we arrived home to find that a frozen pipe had burst and a side room storing hay was flooded; I can still vaguely see Dad shifting bales into the hall by the eerie light of candles and a Tilley pressure lamp.

Another year – or perhaps the same year – we had emerged from the theatre and were strolling down the street when my parents caught sight of the billboard outside Exeter's one cinema. It was showing *The Four Feathers*. In one of those moments of unexpectedness which we learned to expect from my father, he decided on impulse that we should all see it – and we did, sitting together in the darkened house not fifteen minutes after we had left our seats at the Theatre Royal. Ralph Richardson's First World War adventure was not obvious fare for two very young children, but I suspect that having sat through the pantomime my parents could not resist enjoying some adult entertainment before returning to remotest Devon. Strangely a few scenes from the film are still etched on my mind: Richardson's opening an envelope and coming on the white feathers accusing him of cowardice; and Richardson again, his face daubed black as he set out to prove his courage.

I have often wondered since whether my father carried a life burden of guilt at having missed serving in the war. As a farmer he was of course in a 'reserved occupation' and exempt from call-up. He joined the Home Guard, and became a captain, spending many bitter nights up in a trench up on Brentor Hill watching for enemy attacks, or down on Brentor Common commanding the searchlight crew – where I faintly remember visiting him and gaping with wonder at the huge lens of the light. He wore his khaki uniform and his captain's pips proudly (we have a studio portrait of him as Captain Bawtree), and was issued with a service revolver – the one he shot the cockerel with, and had taken down to the woods to put Biddy out of her misery. But he was 31 when the war broke out, and watched his three non-ordained brothers serving with distinction – his youngest brother Harold served in Signals in the Desert and at one time was promoted to become the youngest Major in the North African campaign. It seems likely that, at some deep level of my father's consciousness, his perfectly justified avoidance of military action gnawed away at him, along with his other demons. He may well have persuaded himself that there was no way that he could have left Mother alone in the remote countryside with their two children. But then surely there were thousands of men who had to do just that, and many of them never returned.

I still have what must have been the first book I was ever given: *The Magic Pudding: being the Adventures of Bunyip Bluegum and his friends Bill Barnacle and Sam Sawnoff.* It was written by Australian Norman Lindsay, and I remember my parents buying it at Paddington Station while waiting for the train to take us back home after a visit to the grandparents. My father's flowing copperplate hand makes its ownership quite clear:

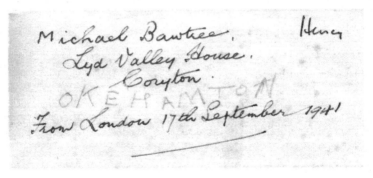

My pencilled addition shows I could obviously print letters at that time – even if my spelling was shaky. Could I read? Only just. But no doubt the book was read to me at first: its mixture of narrative with jaunty poems, and its bold and witty pen and ink drawings, must have captured me then, and were still familiar to me when a few years ago I delightedly came across my copy of the book again in my sister's library.

I am not sure how often we visited our grandparents in those war years; certainly more than once. Perhaps this trip involved my Dad having to confess to his father that the pig farm was in trouble, and that the loan of £5000 was unlikely to be repaid. Of course none of this was known to us, and for Jo and me the five-hour train trip to London was an unbelievable adventure, with its chuffing steam engines, its rhythmically clattering wheels, its windows blacked out for night travel, and that unmistakeable acrid smell of coal smoke and steam in the damp air of London town.

Percy Bawtree was then in his late seventies. A mane of white hair combed smoothly back from a broad, high forehead; a white moustache turned orange in the middle by cigarette smoke; soft, pudgy, pink hands – this was all we ever saw of his physical self. The rest of him – and there was a lot of him, including a capacious paunch – was enclosed in pinstripe trousers, gleaming black shoes, a waistcoat with many buttons and draped across by a watch-chain, a wing-collar and grey tie and a black morning jacket. A Liberal since his youth, when Liberals had been a major force in the land, he still walked two miles every day to Wallington to pick up his Liberal newspaper, *The Star*. He liked to talk, slowly and with deliberation, and in his youth to debate. I can still remember following a grown-up conversation in his dining room after dinner, and in particular one phrase: "Not in my lifetime but perhaps in yours." Why this stuck in my mind I cannot tell: perhaps because of its whiff of mortality. A barometer hung on the wall in his study, with which he had been presented late in the previous century by 'The Wallington House of Commons', the local debating society of which he was for many years the Speaker. In those early days I am not sure I didn't believe it was more or less of similar standing to its namesake in Westminster.

Percy's Scottish wife Margaret (*née* Anderson) had been a beauty in her youth, and she still had clear smiling blue eyes, a lovely complexion and a helmet of tight-curled hair, now silver and sometimes kept in place by a velvet cap. Like her husband's, her clothes seemed frozen in time. The two of them had been married in 1900, when Victoria was still on the throne, and in the 'forties she was still wearing her stylish middle-class Edwardian finery: bombazine black dresses down to the ankle, lace collars and sleeves, button-up shoes and a long, rattling necklace of black gemstones.

Looking after this stately couple since around 1930 were 'Cook 'nd Alice'. Housemaid Alice was plain and petite, dressed always in statutory black, with starched frilly cap and white apron. She was birdlike in her movements and humbly submissive to her employers, though even more so to the crag-faced Cook, who appeared to rule the whole household. This was an illusion; she in her turn was kept firmly in line by our grandmother, whose sweetness of look and manner masked an iron will, as her husband occasionally found to his cost.

We were given many instructions on our way up to London about how well we must behave when we arrived at 22 Shirley Avenue, and for our grandparents, locked in their Edwardian ways, the invasion of our young family up from the country must have been trying. But this is to forget that for much of their married life, from 1901 to 1920 or so, there was a seemingly endless procession of sons born into the household, and both Percy and Margaret were well used to the rough and tumble of growing children. Cook and Alice, I suspect, were less forgiving.

Fragments of memory survive of life at 'Allendale'. We ate all main meals in the dining-room, a dark-panelled affair weighed down with a shining mahogany table, chairs and sideboard, and a palm in the window. At breakfast Granddad would fascinate me by slicing off the top of his boiled egg with a silver boiled-egg decapitator. He would also insert his knife into the cut side of his toast and spread the butter and marmalade into the slit before eating it: something I have never seen done by anyone else. And for his tea he used a moustache cup: an ordinary cup with a curved bridge of china straddling it, to keep his yellow moustache dry. We all had to sit up at the table, while Alice served the food from the left in the accepted style. In the evenings after the dinner things were cleared we would play the card-game of Lexicon, a forerunner of Scrabble. A green baize cloth was spread over the brightly-polished surface and each of us given a wooden rack to hold our letter cards. We took turns to build up interlocking words in crossword style over the table. Granddad would smoke a cigar, and no doubt Dad would be puffing away on his cigarettes. Words again: this was the family tradition, handed down through the generations.

On a visit a few years later, when I was eight, Granddad took me into his study and sat me down in front of him. "I am going to tell you something, Michelangelo," he began, "and I want you to remember it. Many, many years ago, when I was about the age you are now, my grandmother, who was very, very old, told me that when she was very young she had an old Scottish nurse who told her that when *she* had been a very young girl, Bonnie Prince Charlie had stayed in her house overnight, on the run from the English soldiers. That would have been in 1745. Now, when you are very old, as old as I am now, I want you to tell your grandson this story. Will you do that for me, Michelangelo?"

"Yes I will, Granddad," I replied. And though I sadly have no grandson to tell the story to, its leap back two hundred years into history fired my imagination. It stayed with me, and I have shared it with my nephew and with many other young people.

The year 1942 saw a new and final addition to our immediate

family. In my fifth year, I was beginning to develop coherent memories, and can recall a woman coming to stay in the last months of Mother's pregnancy, to help her in the house. Perhaps there was some concern about Mother's health, because at the end of May she was rushed off to a hospital in Plymouth, where on June 2nd she gave birth prematurely to our new sister, to be named Jennifer Margaret. When she was born, so we were told, Jennifer could 'fit in a shoebox.' (Mrs Worth took one look and said matter-of-factly "You'll never rear 'er", but she turned out the most strapping of us all.) I had been sent away to stay with a family in Brentor, but can well remember my first visit to the hospital and being distinctly unimpressed with this wrinkled, yelling, yellowish little fragment I was called on to admire and call sister. Mother gave Jo and me a toy each on that visit. I forget what Jo's gift was, but mine was a blue monkey, and I remember having no doubts about preferring it to the new Bawtree.

At least a week or two passed before Mother returned home, and I had been boarded out at my temporary home long enough to feel abandoned and badly homesick. It was not to be the only time this sadness and anger would run through me.

There came a time in that same year of 1942 when it was clear that the brave enterprise at Lyd Valley had run its course. Dad was beginning to sketch out a new plan. He established a business designed to assist the farmers of the area by contracting with them to take on some of their vital operations. The war had put serious pressure on farming. Farmhands had gone into the services, equipment was hard to come by and beyond the means of many small farmers, and diesel oil was severely rationed. Dad invested some of his dwindling capital in purchasing four or five second-hand tractors, along with ploughs, seed-drills, hoes, harrows and muck-spreaders, and began to hire out their services, supplying both machinery and experienced drivers, including two or three of his Lyd Valley men and at least one Italian ex-prisoner of war. He also took out a licence to cut peat on Dartmoor, selling it to an agent in Tavistock.

I think Farm Operations Limited first saw the light of day at Lyd Valley, but a move was already planned, and it must have been late in 1942 that I can remember, at the age of five, trailing behind my father and a huge stranger, as they walked through the woods discussing our turning over the lease of the farm to a new tenant. The stranger was Oswald Flecker, brother of the poet James Elroy Flecker and at that time Headmaster of the famous Christ's Hospital School in Surrey. Oswald had a young family, and had been looking for a place in the country to bring them to in the holidays. He chose Lyd Valley House. To look after the farm he enlisted his sister-in-law Wilma Hessey, who had been serving as a land-girl since the outbreak of the war and was both skilled in and passionate about animals and farming.

So early in 1943 the Bawtrees packed their sparse belongings into a rented moving van and drove with them up the road ten or fifteen miles to Bridestowe, another small village on the edge of the Moor. We spent a night in the Royal Oak hotel, and next day took possession of an attractive, roomy cottage called Poole, which faced directly on to the main Okehampton road. Father had leased it for a year. Though heavily thatched, with diamond-paned windows and white stucco walls, it was not an old house but had been built perhaps in the 'twenties by someone in love with the romance of country cottage living. It had in fact been designed to be convertible into two separate living spaces: a large front door opened into a thatched porch from which two oak doors with black latches led into two identical but mirror-image sitting rooms, with steps leading up to two end rooms, a kitchen at one end, a playroom at the other. From each sitting room two open staircases with looping ropes for handrails led symmetrically but in opposite directions to two bedrooms and one bathroom on each side, with a connecting door between the central bedrooms upstairs making it possible to live in the house as a single unit. I sometimes wonder what effect this reflecting-pool living had on my five-year-old mind: gave me a later taste for Borges' short stories, perhaps.

Wilma Hessey had already become a friend of our parents, and helped us with the move. On the first night at Poole she and I slept on mattresses on the floor in the second bedroom, and I can still remember lying there watching her strip off her clothes in front of me, and seeing her firm breasts. When the house was sorted out, Jo and I found ourselves each with our own small bedroom at opposite ends of the house. Wilma kept the second bedroom as her own when she stayed overnight with us, and my parents slept in the other central bedroom with Jenny in a cot against the wall.

I am not sure what Wilma's duties for the Fleckers might have been back at Lyd Valley House, but she soon seemed to be more or less a fixture with us, handling a lot of the secretarial business of Farm Operations, but also organizing the contract work and delivering tractors and drivers to their tasks on the nearby farms. Dad had a motor-cycle for a while at that time, and both he and Wilma would use it for getting around. He once put me on the pillion seat and drove me up the hill and back: highly illegal even in those days, and an excitement which stayed with me a long time.

Wilma was in her late twenties when she became part of our family, a fact which seemed entirely natural to us children at the time but which in later years led us to wonder at the dynamics of the arrangement. When she was a very old lady, Wilma was asked by a great-niece why she had never married, and she replied: "I was in love with a man who was married to my best friend." So perhaps this was what underlay the way her life intertwined with our family's for over twenty years. But we are reasonably convinced that our mother would not have put up with any sexual competition, and that our father was entirely virtuous in this respect. Wilma, we found later, was sadly prone to forming highly emotional but unrequited romantic attachments, usually with unavailable men.

It was while we were at Poole that I celebrated my sixth birthday. At my birthday tea-party with a few other little friends, I heard my mother speaking to another parent, and using an expression that was common with her to denote surprise or shock: "I nearly died!" I turned to my small neighbour and said casually and matter-of-factly, "Mummy tells lies sometimes." Unfortunately I was overheard, and my father, ever fierce to protect the reputation of his fayre ladie, sent me up to my room. I was outraged. Did Mummy really 'nearly die', or did she not?

One morning in the early spring of 1944 we were surprised to hear the sound of heavy traffic outside on the Okehampton road, usually a sleepy thoroughfare. Jo and I ran outside, followed by Mum, to discover that a convoy of American troops was driving by: Jeeps, trucks, tanks, personnel carriers, more Jeeps, more trucks – a never-ending khaki stream grinding up the hill from the village, carrying hundreds, no, thousands of G.I.s in their rakish caps and loose fitting, somehow swanky-looking uniforms. They continued to pass all day. Jo and I stood there in wonder on the bank outside the house, just above the road. We must have looked a little pathetic, because suddenly a roll of 'candy' was thrown our way from a Jeep; a minute or two later came another sugary missile fired from an open truck: then another, and then chewing gum, and then some gob-stoppers. Soon we had amassed quite a pile, and we scooped it up and ran inside with it, dropping the loot on the kitchen counter, to Mother's amazement and disapproval. But we immediately rushed out and started looking pathetic again, and were soon rewarded with more treats from the good ol' USA. Never in our strictly-rationed lives had we seen so many sweets in one place. Our mother's disapproval was rather lessened when we ran in shortly afterwards with a tinned ham.

Only years later did I realize that these troops had evidently just landed in Plymouth, and were heading east to prepare for the great D-Day invasion in June of that year. I've wondered since how many of those cheery soldiers we had seen that day were soon after to die on the Utah and Omaha beaches of Normandy.

Even before we moved to Poole, my own life had taken a new direction. I had reached the age of five while still at Lyd Valley, and my parents had been convinced that the grand education they had planned for me could no longer be delayed. They were not keen to send me off to the village school at Coryton – no doubt afraid I would lose my middle-class accent and start talking like a Devon boy. But where then? They had been lucky to find a girls' school for Jo, but there were no boys' schools around which would take a lad of five, and daily transport to and from the depths of the country in wartime was an impossible obstacle.

Finally, and in some desperation, they decided to approach the headmistresses of Jo's school in Launceston and ask whether they might be prepared to find a bed at Pendruccombe from Monday to Friday for a small boy, whose sister was already a weekly boarder. Their day-school kindergarten was full of boys as well as girls, but to admit a male, however tiny, to the sanctity of the girl's dormitory area was another thing entirely, and Miss Bell and Mrs Suttie must have debated the idea with some alarm. But when another little boy's parents made the same request for the same reason, the good ladies decided that in view of the special wartime situation they should do what they could. They set aside a small room at the top of the stairs for little Brian Lyle and little me.

So in late September of 1942, Jo and I, accompanied by our loving and anxious mother and our new sister Jenny in the 'wheely-chair', took the train to Launceston station, where a taxi picked us up with our luggage – including the obligatory gas-masks in their cardboard cases – and dropped us in front of the gaunt, redbrick Victorian pile which housed Pendruccombe School. Jo, of course, was very much at home and ran off to find her school-friends. I was introduced to the noisily effusive Miss Bell (she had a laugh so loud and insincere I can hear it now), and then taken in to meet the school's prime mover. Old Mrs Suttie was crippled, and was pushed from room to room on the ground floor in a white, wooden, upholstered armchair on wheels, rolled along usually by Miss Bell. Mrs Suttie's hair was white and straight and very, very short, with a parting; I remember looking at it with fascination, and thinking it looked like the hair of a man. Her sitting-room was also her bedroom, and I wondered whether she got out of the chair to get into the curtained bed in the bay window, or whether the chair somehow got in with her. Mr Suttie was nowhere in evidence.

I was shown round the school. Off the dark, white-and-black tiled hall of the main floor lay the dining-room, and another bay-windowed room big enough to hold the whole school of around thirty girls, together with an assortment of staff. I was introduced to the formidable Miss Caird, with her reddish grey hair pulled back into a bun and a nose like a Roman emperor's, who taught mathematics to the senior girls and stalked around the school in billowing black academic robes. I met Mrs Steele, who wore plaits tied up round her head, and was to teach me the piano. In the kindergarten room on the basement floor, with its French windows opening into the back garden, I met Miss Weekes, who was to be our classroom teacher. She had a fierce temper, and I have a vivid frozen picture of her in my mind, holding a raffia mat and needle in her hands, stamping her foot, and scarlet-faced with rage. But today, in front of my worried mother, like Miss Bell she was all smiles and simper.

We were led up into the little bedroom I was to share with Brian. To my surprise I found we were to share it with someone else. Beyond our two cots was a folding screen, and behind the screen was a third bed, where portly 16-year-old Jean Bailey from Lydford was to sleep – presumably to serve as a monitor or guard or maybe substitute parent for the two little boys.

The time came for my mother to leave for the station and catch the train back to Lyddaton Halt. I clutched tightly to her and sobbed. Miss Bell's pealing, forced laughter assured her that all would be well, and my sister Jo, calm and comfortable, promised Mother she would look after me. The front door finally closed – on my five years of early life, on my parents, my home, on everything that was familiar and loved. Miss Bell's grimly tinkling laugh and her rictus of a smile turned instantly into something else. "Run along now and unpack your things, children," she snapped. "And don't be late for supper."

Ahead of me was a new world. And I didn't much like the look of it.

CHAPTER TWO

UP OVER

I'm amazed by how little I remember of my infant life at Pendruccombe School, considering that I was there for five days a week over four twelve-week terms. What memories do shunt through come in separate chunks, as though a small mind cannot see an overall pattern – just odd events and objects looming out of the mist.

So I recall that at the school we each kept the weekly ration of butter and margarine (carefully weighed out) on our own separate dish, with the owner's name on a wooden label stuck into its small pat of butter or 'marge'. Mine was on a pink Bakelite saucer. Before meals we would each take our dish out of a meat-safe in the pantry, returning after the meal with whatever was left. I think this was our only personal contact with the world of food rationing, apart of course from our sweet ration, which fully occupied the minds of all children of the day: woe betide anyone coming between us and our full legal quota of gum drops, Mars Bars and boiled sweets. (The dentist played a big role in our young lives. I used to hide under a table in his waiting-room and be pulled out screaming.)

Our communal meals of course were limited not only by rationing but by the school's thrifty budget: I remember disliking bread-and-butter pudding, and relishing beetroot in cheese sauce. What else we ate has fallen off the cliff of time – except for the day that a gift parcel arrived at the school from the USA, containing not only gaily-coloured exercise books and pencils but also packets of 'candy', carefully raffled among us, and tasting like toothpaste.

The little orange-varnished desks in our classroom were laid out in a wide circle facing away from the French windows, with the five-year-olds on one side and the six-year-olds on the other. This I can see clearly, but little else. We must have been learning to read and write, and to dash off our multiplication tables. We made glass-mats of green raffia wound over cardboard. We drew pictures. We played games. I believe I was one of the brighter of the group, and was even nicknamed 'the Professor', but this may be more to do with my wearing spectacles (to cure a wandering eye) and sporting long hair than with native intelligence. This was my first encounter with a group of children, and I do know that I hated to be told off, hated to be teased, and hated not to get my own way. When things got to be too much for my pride or my will, I would lie on my back on the floor and kick and scream. I don't know how often I resorted to this display, but can remember the satisfying sensation. It created quite a stir, and I think Miss Weekes must have hauled me upstairs to have a talking-to from Mrs Suttie. No doubt there were discussions with my parents as to the reasons for my bad temper: I think now that it may have been my outlet for a deep sense of abandonment. It took me a year or two to grow myself out of it, trying it just once at my next school and receiving little sympathy.

Probably my happiest lessons at Pendruccombe were at the piano, alongside the oddly-braided Mrs Steele. I learnt scales and chords, and small pieces which I quickly memorised. But early on I decided I wanted to compose my own piece, which was about Giants (in the bass) and Fairies (in the high notes). I was given a little manuscript book, and taught how to write the notes down. At the end of that term I was taken along to Mrs Suttie's room to play my composition to her, enjoying the surprise and adulation.

For the concert at the end of one Christmas term, Brian and I were rehearsed in a playlet, involving a traveller and a highwayman. I was given a cloak and a burnt cork moustache, and hid behind a rock – two chairs on their sides with a black cloth thrown over them – to waylay the unsuspecting Brian as he came by. Perhaps I sprang out with too much abandon, because poor Brian forgot all his lines and I had to speak his as well as my own. The show was not a success.

In our school breaks we used to be sent out to play in the back garden, which boasted a tennis court where the older girls darted about on fine days. We little ones took to burrowing holes in a bank on the far side of the court, which we furnished like rooms inside dolls' houses, camouflaging them when we left to avoid them being demolished by teachers or gardeners.

Our sports days were held at the end of the summer term on a public sports ground a few minutes' walk from the school, and Mother came for the excitement, watching her son and daughter doing a little running and jumping, and then herself taking part with other mums in the egg and spoon race, which I think she once won – to our pride. It was in the midst of one of these events that we heard the approach of a plane. It turned out to be a German fighter, and we ran to hide behind the stands as he flew low over the field. Jo swears she could see the pilot quite plainly. He was quite capable of opening up with his machine gun and obliterating the entire student body of Pendruccombe, along with their parents and teachers. But he flew on; it's pleasant to think he was sentimental enough to spare a bunch of children.

On Fridays after lunch the junior girls had their Brownie meetings, kindergarten being over for the day. But I was still hanging around, since the bus for Tavistock didn't leave until mid-afternoon. So I was often corralled into the gentle rituals of the Brownies, skipping round a toadstool with the best of them, and sweetly unaware that I was the only male Brownie in the West Countree.

Of all my schoolmates, I can remember only Brian very vaguely – and rather scornfully because of our playlet's disaster – and George Metcalfe, who was a dayboy and who at that time stuttered: he was rumoured to have a fierce father who had brought it on. George was to come back into my life several times over the years, and we shall meet him again. The only other lingering memory is the plump Jean Bailey, who slept behind the screen in our room, setting up I don't know what complexity of thoughts and dreams in the two small boys the other side. I do know that I dreamed of her for some years afterwards: in fact I have to confess I dreamed of killing her with a knife, and seeing her naked body in the bath, awash with blood.

Nothing was happier than the moment on Friday afternoon when Jo ran out from her last class and she and I were accompanied across the road to the bus stop, where the little green bus picked us up for the thirteen-mile ride across the River Tamar to Tavistock. Now, at the end of the journey, I would join my big sister in jumping out of the bus and running to hug our beaming parents.

For children sent to boarding schools, memory divides into two utterly separate compartments. There is the life of the school, and then the life at home. There is no way of integrating their timetables: they run on parallel lines that never meet.

My father had leased Poole for just one year, and with my young memory having become gradually better able to retain experiences, I can recall more of our little home world. For example, the cottage had its own generator in a slate-roofed shed beside the house, introducing Jo and me for the first time to the heady world of electric light. I even remember the landlord – Mr Smith – showing my father (with me in tow) round its shiny machinery when we first arrived.

Mother continued adding to her collection of *obiter dicta*. Beside the generator hut was a patch of ground belonging to the house, thickly overgrown with gorse and brambles. Mother decided to have it cleared and – like so many housewives during the war – to grow vegetables. The venerable villager she engaged came up to have a look at it, and after contemplating for a few minutes, said to my mother: "Tell 'e what oi do: oi burn 'e, oi skim 'e, oi dig 'e, an' I knock 'e abroad." And he did.

Like all small children, I was fascinated by oddities in people. I remember a woman in the village who had a goitre, her distended neck flowing down over her chest like a monstrous double chin. And there was an old man there who had a growth on his cheek so like a raspberry that I remember reaching for it to pluck it off, to my mother's embarrassment.

It was around this time that I developed the usual childhood mania for collecting things. I had a notebook in which I collected hundreds of car licence plate numbers over the next year or two. But my oddest passion was to collect the names of different lavatory chinaware. When we visited a pub or a hotel, or even the house of one of my parents' friends or acquaintances, I would ask, the first chance I had, to go the lavatory – not to pee, but in order to check up on whether it was a Sankey or a Johnson, or even an authentic Crapper. It beats me now why this should have so engaged me, but

I was an early reader while still very small, and I suppose these proud manufacturers' names displayed so close were some of the first reading exercises I had. I guess this had to be mainly a little boy's interest, since little girls would be facing the other way, now wouldn't they...

Our stay at Bridestowe had one other outcome, a fateful one for me. My parents were beginning to look around for a boys' school for me to go to when I reached the magic age of seven, and Mother was invited by some friends to bring me to tea and meet the headmaster of a local boys' preparatory school. She used to recount how we were sitting in her friends' garden along the road just out of Bridestowe when she saw a shock of wavy white hair moving along the road above the hedge towards the garden gate. The gate opened, and in walked the owner of the hair: a tall, ample, forty-ish, high-browed, florid-faced, big-featured, big-handed man in a sage green tweed suit and orange tie. He advanced like a ship under sail, beaming and self-assured. This was Arthur Harrison.

Arthur's school was called Marlborough House. Originally founded in Hove as early as 1874, it had been bought by Arthur in 1930, and shortly afterwards he moved it to an estate outside Hawkhurst, in the Kentish countryside a few miles from Cranbrook. But, as with many schools in London and the south-east, the war forced evacuation westwards away from the bombs and the aerial dogfights. Arthur had searched the west country, and finally leased a rambling mediaeval manor-house called Bidlake, a few miles from Bridestowe and set among orchards. It was from here that he had walked out that day to meet a prospective parent and child. One way or another a deal was reached, and it was agreed I would enter Marlborough House in September of 1944, a month after my seventh birthday.

In June of my last term at Pendruccombe, unbeknownst to me,

the Allies finally invaded France, and the western front so long awaited by Stalin became a reality. A month later I left the school for the last time. So did my sister Jo, who was bound for another school, called Sydenham. I don't think either of us shed many tears as we kissed Mrs Suttie goodbye on her furry cheek and left her odd little establishment for ever.

That summer saw another change at home. Our time at Poole was over, and we had moved again (I remember nothing of the move and suppose it happened while Jo and I were in our last term at Pendruccombe). Once again it was not a major relocation: the family shifted itself this time along the road from Bridestowe back towards Brentor, to the ground floor of Langstone Manor, a stone pile with 16th century hall and nineteenth century additions, set in a large garden and approached by a long driveway lined with trees.

The Manor was the home and farm estate of Major and Mrs Gallup, who had divided the ground floor from their own apartments upstairs, and were leasing it out. Beyond the lawns of the house, complete with summerhouse and tennis court, was a walled vegetable garden (off-limits to the Bawtree children) and above the house the driveway opened into a large cobbled farmyard, with barn, cowshed and weather-vaned coach-house.

There was a pony trap sitting in the coach-house, and on the floor above lived Mr Robey, who had been coachman to the Gallups – and no doubt to previous owners – for most of his eighty or more years. The old retainer, red-faced and rheumy-eyed, was now living out his last days, unable to do much to earn his keep. But he fascinated us children with his hand-cranked Victorian knife-sharpener, which he was still able to operate: we would regularly bring our mother's kitchen knives to him simply to watch Robey inserting them into the ancient machine, adding some rust-coloured powder, and grinding them to a razor-edge.

During the couple of years that we lived at Langstone, Major Gallup died. He left my father his .22 rifle and his First World War binoculars. The rifle sat in Dad's office for years, and was occasionally pulled out to get rid of a grey squirrel preying on his birds. But the binoculars became without any doubt my father's most treasured possession, accompanying him on every walk, every drive, every holiday, for the rest of his life. Old Mrs Gallup continued to live upstairs, and kept a mistrustful eye on us adventurous children. Jo and I would climb out of our ground floor bedroom window, trying to avoid the flower bed just beneath: "Don't tread on the dahlias!" was her cry; like so many phrases it became an oft-repeated saying in the family. Nor was Mrs Gallup best pleased when her smalls became embedded with woody fragments: we had tried the experiment of crushing pine-cones in her clothes mangle, which she unwisely kept in the summer-house where on hot summer nights we children used to sleep.

Mother settled in to the new house, and was especially happy in the spacious old kitchen with its vast pine table in the centre. She was still buoyed up too by her sense of humour. As always, we kept a dog or two – the usual cast-offs from other homes – and had at this time a little dachshund bitch called Squiggly. When my mother walked the mile or two to Brentor village to do her shopping, she would often take young Jenny in the pram, and have Squiggly running along beside her. One time it happened that Squiggly was on heat, and her arrival in the village roused the lustful interest of every dog in the neighbourhood. Desperately anxious to avoid a litter of new puppies, Mum finally resorted to pulling Jenny out of the pram and installing the dog in her place. It was just her luck that as she walked along pushing the pram with the reluctant dog inside it, and an equally fractious Jenny dragging along holding her other hand, whom should she meet but the local vicar. The moment must have been memorable for both parties.

I doubt that my father's Farm Operations were going well during those years, but we children knew nothing of this, and after the restrictions of a small cottage on a main road found ourselves once again in a vast playground. Not only were the gardens and fields of Langstone huge and various, full of excitement and interest, but beyond the fields behind the house lay the oak woods through which the local railway wound to Lydford. A path through the woods led across the railway line and down to our old home, Lyd Valley House a mile or two away. We became good friends with the Fleckers and their family, and would often visit.

But it is the woods themselves that still inhabit precious space in my memory. My sister Jo was by that time reading the novels of Violet Needham, among them her tale *The Woods of Windri*, set in a fictional country based on mediaeval Italy. Jo shared with Miss Needham the capacity to spin magic worlds out of her imagination, and for both of us those wooded groves became peopled with knights and witches and heroic young children and monks and priests and villains. Deep in the woods there was also an old well, which of course became a magic wishing-well, and received our whispered requirements each time we walked by.

For our father, the woods were a sanctuary for his beloved birds, and he would often take us for walks through their winding paths, teaching us to walk softly so as not to frighten his friends away. Once he borrowed an old nag, loaded it up with food and camping gear, and took the whole family into a favourite glade – less than a mile from the house – where we pitched camp, lit a fire and watched Mum cooking us our smoky-tasting supper. Jo and I were finally bedded down in the open, where we could look up through the skein of branches to the stars above. That excitement made it hard to sleep; it is with me still.

One late summer Sunday Dad came into the summerhouse at

five o'clock in the morning to wake us up and get us dressed. The weather had been set fair for some days, and he had decided the night before, with his usual suddenness, that we should all drive across Dartmoor to catch the sunrise over the tors, and then cook breakfast on the beach at Slapton Sands. Jo and I always groaned when our parents stopped to admire a view at some hill-top, or to focus on a kestrel or a sparrowhawk hovering overhead. But the sight of that red flurry of fire coming up over the moor from the east still sits in my mind as the archetype of all the dawns of my life.

Our first enchanted summer at Langstone was over, and it was school-time again: this time a whole new school, a whole new world of people, and a whole twelve-week term ahead. I was just seven. No more weekly boarding; this was the thing itself. And I was being transported from a world of girls and old ladies to a much grubbier land of small boys. But whereas at Pendruccombe you could pass days without even seeing a member of the opposite sex, women were very much in evidence at Marlborough House, and sometimes seemed almost to be the backbone of the place. This was no doubt partly a result of the war, which had turned thousands of schoolmasters into more or less reluctant soldiers, sailors and airmen.

I remember arriving in the middle of the afternoon at Bidlake House on the first day of my first term, and being greeted by Arthur and his wife Muffet. I was clutching a new favourite, a toy giraffe, which had somehow got torn in transit; the spring inside its long neck was escaping through a hole. I don't remember crying but no doubt I did, either at the giraffe's injury or at the sadness of life in general. But I was soon whisked upstairs and introduced to Miss French, who was to be my first teacher. And in Hilda French's sitting-room, on that first day at Marlborough House, I was sat down and given a cup of cocoa to drink while she took my toy giraffe and patched him up – even painting new markings on the patch she had sewn on. Her kindness and her warmth made those wretched first moments of homesickness almost bearable. Miss French, as we knew her, was to play that role for myself and countless other wretched little tykes for years to come. She was soon to introduce me to Miss Gale (her name was Joan but we never heard it spoken) who was Matron of the school and a formidable sight in her starched matron's head gear. Miss Gale, we soon found out, played bad cop to Miss French's good cop – though we wouldn't have put it that way at the time. It was a sensible arrangement, I suppose.

Bidlake House had been a private home until the war, and was not handily set up to accommodate a school. So the Harrisons had to make the best of it and improvise. The classroom for us smallest boys was a kind of farm loft set above the house's ancient apple cider press. Along the floor at the back of the room was fastened a six or eight-foot section of a huge oaken tree-trunk. This served as the upper anchor of the cider press below, and, soon after that autumn term began, the farmhands – who were still around the place – started squeezing raw cider out of their wind-fallen apples. I can remember the delicious smells of 'scrumpy' rising up from below, but remember even more keenly our wonder as the huge threaded screw of the press came slowly riding up and down again through the great tree-trunk. Poor Miss French had a hard time keeping us focused on our Latin grammar.

The only space large enough to seat the whole school and staff comfortably was the great Tudor cattle-barn, and here we assembled for daily chapel – a fifteen-minute session conducted out of a book called 'New Every Morning' – and for a longer service on Sundays.

It was also our gym, our boxing ring and our theatre. Its huge beams, crumbling plaster and lofty roof were cheered up by a mural which Muffet Harrison (who taught us Art) must have organized early in the war, and which appropriately depicted Noah leading his animals two by two out of the ark and around the wall, with a splendid rainbow curving above them. This was something to look at during prayers.

Pendruccombe had taken its religion with lady-like seriousness, and since my parents were neither of them believers it must have been there that I first found myself expected to kneel and say my prayers before bedtime. No doubt it was there too that I first learned the Lord's Prayer by heart, and some of the more familiar hymns. At Marlborough House, Arthur Harrison's Christianity was of a more easy-going type, but his love of the English language assured his devotion to the Book of Common Prayer and the King James Bible. He delighted in quoting from Bible stories, particularly relishing quaintnesses like "and when they woke up in the morning, behold they were all dead men." Agag's "walking delicately" before being hewn in pieces before the Lord would be pressed into service to describe some guilty small boy expecting punishment. He would read to us from Henrik Van Loon's *Story of the Bible*, and it is to these sessions, over many years, that I owe a fairly thorough knowledge of both Old and New Testaments – though I can't read some sections of the Old Testament now without a shudder.

It was at my new school too that I was introduced to the mysteries of organized games. On the field behind the barn Arthur and his staff had erected goal-posts, and here I first learnt to play football – poorly – and to endure the wretched blue knees and freezing hands and feet that went with it. In the hard winter of that year it was here that we made snowmen and snow tunnels and threw snowballs.

One boarding school tradition which was very much in evidence at Bidlake was the School Walk. Two or three times a week we would set off under the watchful eye of Arthur Harrison and his bouncy Dalmatian dog, walking along the edges of the lanes two by two. But once into the open countryside the group would break into a gaggle and run and play. A mile or two away there was an open scrubland covered with bracken and called The Brake, which we joyously explored. And once we walked all the way beyond Bridestowe village to the quarries below our old house Poole, to visit an ancient timber water-mill, where we watched the mill-wheel turning and driving the saw, which was slowly and majestically carving great planks out of tree trunks. The sound of hissing, gushing, threshing water, the low wooden roof and the strange, mediaeval workmen at their tasks still occupy a corner of my memory.

Before the snow flew, the chief joy of playing outside at Bidlake was the Dell, a two or three-acre copse that lay beyond the farmyard. Through the Dell ran a number of small springs, and these had generated among the boys of Marlborough House an extraordinary culture of dam-building, which must have begun soon after the school settled into this old Devon farm. The local yellow clay was dug up and softened, and then fashioned together with sticks and stones into an amazing series of breastworks, spanning the streams and creating great pools, with sluices pouring water down and back into the stream-bed, where it flowed until it reached the next waterworks. The dam-builders worked in teams, and it wasn't long before I realized that the older boys had the best dams and the most elaborate water systems, with canals and even locks – some no doubt inherited from dam-builders of past years. The upper sections of the stream were of course controlled by these very senior and scarifying gentlemen, aged eleven or twelve or even thirteen, and we new bugs quickly learned that we were not welcome there. So we messed around in the lower reaches, and learnt the dam-building craft as best we could, hoping eventually to attract attention and even to graduate to one of the teams up-river.

What with football and walks and dam-building, I learned now for the first time in my life what it meant to be wretchedly, miserably cold. There were boys who were always warm, and seemed quite impervious to cold weather. But those of us with poorer circulation would be almost permanently numb, with blue nose, stinging red cheeks and watering eyes. Chilblains swelled up on our fingers and toes: red, shiny welts which itched madly at night, and would not go away until spring. One of the hardest trials was simply getting into bed, with one's feet cold as any stone – they had sometimes not been warm all day. The sheets too were cold and probably damp, and even under the bedclothes there was no relief. It was always a miracle to me that when I woke up in the morning I found my feet were warm! How had it happened? I was never sure.

It would be unfair to blame the school for such misery. This was wartime. Coal was difficult to come by. I cannot remember now whether Bidlake was centrally heated, but most English houses at this time boasted very little heating, and it was assumed that all you did was to put on another layer of clothes and keep as warm as you could. Being cold was one of those things that went along with winter, like getting up in the dark, and root vegetables, and lentil soup.

I can't remember any source of heat in our classroom above the cider press: perhaps there was a paraffin stove there. But nor can I remember much about the lessons. Miss French no doubt introduced us to the dip-pen for all our scrawled writing: a thin wooden shaft, which had a metal end to hold the nib, making our fingers sore. Our desks all held inkwells, and our index fingers and thumbs were stained daily with blue ink, which we had to scrape off at night with pumice-stone. Along the way I suppose we heard a little about history and geography, and I know that we began both Latin and French, and learned to improve our English skills. I do remember reading aloud from an Everyman edition of Thackeray's *The Rose and the Ring*, which at this distance seems a little advanced for seven-year-olds – I remember being laughed at for pronouncing 'determined' as 'détter-mind'. And, perhaps because we were sitting atop the cider, we were introduced to John Drinkwater's poem *Moonlit Apples*: "At the top of the house the apples are laid in rows... moon-washed apples of wonder."

But I recall little else from those two terms at Bidlake. The wrenching dislocation from home to school, and all the other boys, and the intimidating presence of Arthur Harrison and his staff, were perhaps all I could cope with, though I remember I got an early reputation for inventing stories to tell in the dark of our little dormitory, so perhaps I was gaining some sense of myself. It may be significant that I vividly remember coming home from school the first Sunday I was allowed to take off. Where the Langstone driveway reached the grounds of the house and turned sharply towards the farmyard, there was a gate leading directly into the front garden. As we reached it I saw Dad, binoculars as ever strung around his neck, walking on the lawn beyond the gate. Wilma stopped the car (she must have been driving, since my mother didn't drive), and I hurtled out, scrambled over the gate and ran full pelt into the arms of my dear father.

How much those homecomings meant over the many years of boarding school I can only guess, because they stayed so long in my memory.

By the time Jo and I returned home from our respective establishments for Christmas 1944, the Allies were moving steadily towards Germany, with the Russians closing in from the East. Our local newspaper the *Western Morning News* printed a daily map showing the advances on the western front. Dad had pinned up a map of Europe on the back of the sitting room door, and he would lift me up so that I could pull out the American and British and Canadian flags and pin them back in to show the new positions. This was as close as I got to following the fortunes of the war, though I well remember my father's shock and sadness at the news of Franklin Roosevelt's death in April 1945, only two or three weeks before Hitler shot himself and the Germans surrendered. I still remember asking my father, much to his amusement, whether the newspapers would all stop now because there was no more news to report.

Hitler, by the way, had been a convenient bogeyman for us children for years. One day Jo had said she 'hated' someone and our mother said, "Now then, dear, you must never say you hate anyone."

"Can we say we hate Hitler?" asked Jo.

There was a slight pause, and then the concession: "Yes, you can say you hate Hitler."

With victory imminent in Europe, Arthur Harrison decided that spring to leave Bidlake and move Marlborough House bag and baggage back to Kent. I suppose my parents thought about transferring me to a school closer to home, but by this time they were unswerving admirers of Arthur and all his works, and they would not even consider such a change. So, after the happy spring holidays, my tuckbox and large blue trunk were packed, and Mother and Father set out with me for the long train journey from the West Country to the Weald of Kent, initiating a tradition which we were to follow through the years. Either one or both parents would accompany me in the train to London, leaving around dawn and arriving at Paddington by noon. We would then take a taxi to Piccadilly Circus and have lunch, either at the Hong Kong, the Chinese restaurant on Shaftesbury Avenue, or Veeraswamy's, the Indian establishment off Regent Street, or at the Regent Palace Hotel. These were exotic places, and I still find myself occasionally pining for the Hong Kong's crispy noodles and sweet and sour pork: neither of them familiar dishes on the edge of Dartmoor.

I think our father genuinely enjoyed showing his children round on these trips to the capital: after all, he had spent three years of his young life there – in fact I realized much later that his office in Golden Square was just around the corner from the Regent Palace, which had opened in 1915 and was for a time the largest hotel in Europe. The art-deco Atlantic Bar must have been a favourite place for an after-work noggin with his fellow accountants, and Dad continued to gravitate to his old drinking-hole and its dining-rooms whenever he found himself in London. (He visited there most memorably when he was rearing a couple of baby redstarts whose mother had deserted their nest. Having to go to London on business, and needing to follow his charges' regular feeding times, he took them with him on the train, in his binocular case. The waiter at the Regent Palace Grill Room was apparently only mildly surprised when he brought a bowl of mock-turtle soup to his customer to find him serving his baby birds out of an eye-dropper.)

After lunch there was usually an hour or two to spend together, and we would visit the Royal Academy, Madame Tussaud's wax museum, or the London Zoo, or the Burlington Arcade (still partly closed off with bomb damage), or simply feed the pigeons in Trafalgar Square. But around four o'clock the fateful hour had come and I would be delivered to Charing Cross station, where the Marlborough House School Special awaited us, along with a

gaggle of boys – including many of my schoolmates from
Bridestowe – and, of course, Arthur Harrison. Another wrenching
goodbye, and I was off to a new world again, soon catching my first
sight of the hop fields and oast houses of Kent.

I don't often remember the state of the weather on any
particular day, but I do know that it was a cloudless, warm May
evening when we left the train at Etchingham and boarded the
waiting coach for the four-mile road trip to Hawkhurst. Turning
off the main road we entered the school grounds through a stately
gateway in a long brick wall, finally drawing up outside a large
redbrick Georgian mansion with pillared porch and high,
generous windows.

We were led through the front hall and up the elegant front
stairs to our dormitories. If there was any doubt about Marlborough
House being a 'feeder' school, it would be dispelled here: the
dormitories on the first floor were all named after the major English
public schools. Even now I believe I can recite them in order:
Stowe, Winchester, Haileybury, Bryanston, Radley, Wellington. On
the second floor was Rugby, and I think Eton and Harrow. Small
boys started in 'Stowe' and over the years graduated down and along
the hall to 'Wellington'. As a third-term boy I think I started out in
'Winchester'.

We were already homesick, but it was impossible not to feel
some excitement at seeing the place we had heard so much about.
And after a cup of tea, Arthur – who was clearly elated to be back
on his home ground – took a group of us who happened to be
standing around for a tour of the estate. We walked out to the
playing-fields, which after years of neglect were being mown and
rolled to make ready for the summer's cricket. Arthur pointed out
a lone poplar tree, its top sheared off – so he told us – by a
Doodlebug sent over erratically by the Germans in one of their

final flying bomb attacks on London. We were shown 'Sessele', a stylish red brick house at the far end of the sports ground, which Arthur and Muffet had built for themselves before the war, and whose top floor was soon to be turned into a dormitory to cope with the School's rising numbers. We walked over to Spectacle Pond – yes, in the shape of a pair of spectacles – and then to the larger and deeper Big Pond below the school. We inspected the swimming-pool, which was being cleaned and was soon to be repainted white with a bright sky-blue bottom. We looked into the Chapel, all light oak and cream panelled walls, which had been built just before the war by the staff carpenter Bubbles (with the help of the boys) and sat quietly among trees at the end of a gravel path. We saw the long, low, black-creosoted carpenter's shop, a lean-to shed just inside the school's gateway, where we were to spend many, many hours in the years to come. We explored a 'Wendy House' which I think had been sitting on the estate when Arthur purchased it originally. And – O joy! – we were led into the original Dell, a one or two-acre woodland alongside Big Pond and covering both steep sides of a small ravine. There were no streams there, and no dams. But there was something equally exciting: tree-houses! Many of them had rotted almost to nothing in the five years since they had been abandoned at the start of the war. But we knew it would not be long before they would be fixed up and pressed back into service.

Full of excitement, our group strolled back in the fading light to the main school building. Here we were introduced to some new teachers – the first youngish male teachers we had seen. Most immediately memorable was Dick Thompson, 'Tommer', who had been on the staff at Marlborough House at the outbreak of the war, and had actually assisted in the move down to Bidlake before he was called up. We were to get to know him well. Tall, long-faced, with a voice like a rasp and a sardonic manner, Tommer lacked charm and had a dismissive, unsentimental way with him which disconcerted and somewhat alarmed the boys. He was determined that we should not be pampered. But it didn't take us long to realize his commitment to the school – and even to us, scornful as he might sound. Tommer was to teach us mathematics and history, to look after the sports grounds, to coach football – and, most demanding of all, to organize the school timetable.

Then there was Geoff Martin, Muffet Harrison's brother and so Arthur's brother-in-law. Major Martin had taken part in the D-Day landings and stepped on a bomb in the early fighting, losing a leg and gaining a Military Cross. He arrived sporting a squeaky wooden leg, which of course fascinated the boys and soon took on mythic status: it was known as 'George'. Geoff, tall and good-looking, had all the charm that Tommer lacked, with a warm and friendly smile. We were to discover shortly that he also had a ferocious temper. He was to teach us French and Geography and coach swimming and rugger – and in later years took on a select group of three or four of us for Ancient Greek.

The third was Meyrick Browne, fresh out of a war in motor torpedo boats: brown eyes, sallow face, black hair slicked back, subtly perfumed and perfectly turned out, with every hair in place, every nail perfectly manicured. Mr Browne, we learned, had been appointed king of the carpentry shop, which he was to maintain with the same care and attention to detail that he lavished on his own person. From him we learned lessons which many of us took through life: not only how to cut dovetail and tenon joints, how to plane, how to use a chisel, but also how to care for one's tools, how to sharpen them, how to oil them, how to store them. He demanded perfection in the craft of woodworking.

There were others too – were they all assembled that first May day or did some of them arrive the following term? I don't remember. But now or eventually there was Alan McNeile, who shared the teaching of Latin with Arthur Harrison and Geoff Martin, and also taught geography; June Knight, who would teach crafts and art to the younger boys and Miss Sheaves, Olive Sheaves, who was to teach piano and group singing and to coach the chapel choir. And of course we were happy to see the familiar and friendly face of Miss French. We were somewhat less happy to catch sight of the fearsome Miss Gale, sailing past in her blue uniform and matron's head-dress.

So this was the place, and this the team. Here I was to spend eight months of every year of my life until the age of thirteen. It became as familiar a territory as home: known in all its details, from the grain on the wood of the pine desks to the white-painted wainscotting of the old passages, to the lime trees and the cricket pavilion and our ramshackle boat on Spectacle Pond; from the rough edges of the swimming pool to the spartan black iron bedsteads and the jerries beneath them; from shiny conkers under the chestnut trees in autumn to the huge spreading crimson-trumpeted rhododendrons in May.

And the team? They became as familiar too, so much so that half a century or more later I can recall precisely the reddish and long-nosed face of Tommer, see the red nape of his neck and his pendulous adam's apple, and hear the harsh melody of his sardonic phrase. I can summon up the trim, tiny, tweedy, rapid-moving figure of Miss French, with care and even love beaming from her slightly droopy eyes. I can remember the scrupulous, tiny, crunched handwriting of the austere Mr McNeile, as he corrected our messy papers. I can see the grey speckling in Mr Martin's hands, from the exploding bomb on which he trod in Normandy, and Miss Gale dispensing treacly spoonfuls of Haliborange and Radio Malt to us as we queued up in the bathroom after lunch. I remember the shock when we occasionally saw her without her billowing sail of a head-dress – she looked so short and so, well, human.

Familiar as home, yes. But loved like home? Surely not. Like most of my fellow schoolchildren, I had been brought up from the earliest age with the full knowledge that 'school' meant eventually leaving home and going to some other place. I was entirely ignorant as to how few children in Britain or anywhere else had been brought up in this expectation. And I am still not sure why my parents, who had both attended day schools all their young lives, were so insistent that their children should be sent away and put into the hands of strangers for their education.

In my mother's case, I have the strongest feeling that social aspiration – some might call it snobbery – played its part. A good friend of my parents in Newcastle, back in Australia, had been Dick Parry Okeden, who ran Lysaght's sheet metal rolling and galvanising works, recently established in the town and producing Australia's distinctive roofing material, corrugated iron (Australia has been described as 'the spiritual home of corrugated iron'). Dick was an Old Etonian, urbane, handsome and ebullient. He wore perfectly-tailored light grey suits, and was wealthy well beyond the modest means of the young Bawtrees, but Dick and his wife Pick had become the closest of friends, living as they did in a fine old lodge just up Barker Street from our modest clapboard house, and with a daughter, Belinda, of the same age as Jo.

Father and Mother remained in touch with 'Pick and Dick' after we had settled in England, and every so often they would come over to the old country, always invited to stay a while wherever the Bawtrees had perched themselves. And it seems likely to me now that my mother wanted her only son to grow up in the image of Dick Parry Okeden. Why else did she dream of sending me to Eton?

It's equally clear that my mother had no particular affinity for my father's father: formal, Dissenting, starchy and ungenerous – and unforgiving of my father's reckless adventuring and his inability to turn a profit at anything he tried. Dick Parry Okeden was a firmly establishment figure, a business success, a vivid personality; my father's family was genteel and not without means, but entirely unconnected and not at all urbane. Dick was a flamboyant *bon viveur*, my grandparents were puritans and sadsacks. Would my grandparents – even were they able to drive – be the owners of a Humber Super Snipe saloon car once owned by Raymond Chandler?

Not surprisingly, then, Mother developed a relentless determination that I should not follow in the footsteps of my father's family but should receive the very best, the very classiest education, preparing me for Eton College at the age of 13; after Eton, Oxford. And after that the world would be my oyster. Ambassador? Judge? Prime Minister? Black Rod? Whatever I chose to put my hand to.

Pendruccombe was not an auspicious start on this journey, but at least, in my mother's eyes, it was not a lowly country school. And Marlborough House, led by the flamboyant, Oxford-educated and indubitably well-bred Arthur Harrison – grandson of an Anglo-Irish judge, after all – put me fairly in the way of my glorious future. Both Dick and Arthur had a serene confidence in their social status: conservative, well-read, witty – and connected.

You might think that my father's continuing failure to make a decent living might have put these ambitions – however keen – firmly out of reach. But here Jo and I were in luck: our Great-Aunt May, who had died soon after we arrived in England, left a couple of thousand pounds to each of us, to be held in trust until our twenty-first birthdays – but to be used before that if necessary to pay for our education. Over the years these funds became slowly depleted, but in what my parents felt was clearly a good cause. Besides, the fees of private schools were on a very different scale in those early days during and after the war. We recently found an ancient bill for my sister's and my twelve weeks of schooling at Pendruccombe, for five days a week, in 1943: with tuition, food and board for us both, it came to just over £13!

My little prep school, then, was for my elders the first rung on the ladder to fame and fortune. That continuing sense of abandonment, that sickening ache in my tummy, was all part of the game. And after all, I was not alone: five or ten other little brats were also being pushed out of the nest for the first time, most weeping, and most of their mothers weeping too. But it was thought babyish to weep for long, and once the tie was cut we began gingerly to acknowledge our classmates, exploring almost for the first time how to construct our behaviour towards others, and what it is to make friends. And slowly, as classes began, and games began, and singing and piano and drama and swimming, and camping in the summer, and playing in the Dell; slowly home life and even parents faded from our consciousness, to be supplanted by the routine of school life, and the daily interchange with teachers.

Perhaps the test of a good school lies in how many special, non-routine events stand out from the daily, weekly, monthly grind of classes, games, meals and bed. In those junior years at Marlborough House we were too busy absorbing the routine, and only just beginning to carve out a place for ourselves in this odd society. But during that first summer in Kent world events cascaded around us and were forcing themselves into the school's daily round. On May 8th, a few weeks after term began, the Allies received the unconditional surrender of Adolf Hitler's pulverised armies. Like schools all over Britain I am sure we celebrated VE Day with a half-holiday – perhaps even a full day off; I don't recall it. (Back in Devon my sister Jo had more cause to remember: she was one of two young girls chosen to light the victory beacon on Brentor Hill.)

What does still flicker in my mind is a ragged memory of that summer's General Election campaign. The Labour Party had split from Churchill's wartime National Government as victory approached, and forced him to go to the country. Though voting took place at the beginning of July, it was another three weeks before the results were announced, since time had to be given to bring in the votes of the armed forces. There was no doubt at my smart school that Churchill and the Conservative party would win, and that so they should. Had not Churchill led the country to victory in the war?

We soon had more important things to think about. Home life may have receded into the back of our minds during that first summer term, but as it drew to an end 'the holidays' loomed larger. The weekly letters home we were required to write became less occupied with the cricket score in our last match against Boarzell or St. Ronan's and more full of excitement about what we might be doing for the summer holidays. There was just one final mountain to climb between us and home: the end of term exams, and the announcement of marks. Then, on the last day, we came together in chapel for our final service – always to the same pattern – where we sang the Vaughan Williams hymn *God Be With You Till We Meet Again*, and Arthur Harrison read the last chapter of the Book of Ecclesiastes: "Remember now thy Creator in the days of thy youth ..." I don't think we made much effort to follow this precept, but some of us certainly responded to the poetry of that miraculous piece, which is inside me now as I write: "In the day when the keepers of the house shall tremble, and the strong men shall bow themselves, and the grinders cease because they are few, and those that look out of the windows be darkened ..."

By train to London, an outing with the parents somewhere, and then by train again from London to Devon. I was back in the real world, and with the election still not announced I was there in time to see posters everywhere, with Churchill striding out confidently against a blue background. But Churchill did not win. On July 26th the results were announced, and the Labour party under Clement Attlee had won by a landslide.

Churchill was not the only one to be astounded. My parents were loyal enough to the war leader to feel hurt for him, indignant at his rejection. But while they were conservative they had no strong ties to the political party, and little enough property or investment to feel threatened by the 'spectre' of socialism. For Arthur Harrison, of course, it was another matter: for the next five years of school we were treated to a steady diet of light-hearted scorn for that brave Labour government, as it hacked into the class-ridden society of Britain and shaped a welfare state.

Though I was much too young to understand the political battle which had been won by Labour, I suppose I began around this time to learn for the first time that I was a member of a social class, and that the gardeners and the tradesmen, and the scruffy children from the local state school – or those from the local Barnardo boys' home, whom we would sometimes meet on our walks through and around Hawkhurst – were of another class; and that we were in some way superior, and had to ensure that things stayed that way. At home, too, the villagers and the farmhands and the milkman and the baker on his rounds were also of that other class. We were taught to be polite, but we also expected them to be respectful. I had no idea that envy and even hatred might lie behind the pleasantries we exchanged. We had, I suppose, what would now be called a sense of entitlement.

That August we had our last family holiday by the sea. We had 'gone to the seaside' in previous years, and learnt the joys of buckets and spades and sandcastles and shrimping in rock pools. But this summer Father had rented – for a whole two weeks! – a little bungalow called 'Furzy Close', on the hill behind the village of Polzeath on the north coast of Cornwall. There were picnics and walks, and expeditions to the fishing ports of the coast, including the ghostly Port Quin, which had been deserted centuries before when its entire fishing fleet sank in a ferocious storm and all its menfolk and boyfolk lost. We licked ice creams and ate candy floss. We had our first sight of cormorants and choughs. We played on the beach and paddled in the shallows. And one night, way past our bedtime, Father took us out along the cliffs beyond our cottage to glimpse the full moon riding over the sea, its silver pathway beckoning us toward the stars.

It was while we were at lunch at 'Furzy Close' on August 14th, 1945, that to our mother's surprise and initial resentment our next door neighbour came in unannounced through the kitchen and on into the front room. He apologised but thought we would like to know; he had just heard on the wireless that Japan had surrendered to the American forces in the Pacific, and that the Second World War was over.

A few days later – an event almost as significant for me – I celebrated my eighth birthday, receiving the present I had been hungering for: a handsome sheath-knife, its leather sheath to be threaded on at once to my stripey, snake-buckled belt. This was no doubt an important status symbol at my school. I had been looking enviously about and realized that it was what was needed to ensure I could hold my head high among my grubby little peers. It made me almost look forward to the next term. I made no connection between that wicked blade and the atom bombs which had smashed into Hiroshima and Nagasaki.

It was that summer too, I think, that Father gave Jo and me each an empty stamp album — second hand of course, and no doubt picked up for a shilling or two. But along with our albums he also gave us each half of his considerable stamp collection. He had been gathering these stamps since his boyhood in the First World War. He left them with his parents when he emigrated to Australia, and for years after the family's return they were missing and presumed lost. But one day when we were staying with the grandparents the big, fat album had been discovered with great jubilation in an airing cupboard, and was restored to its owner. There were some valuable items in it. Stamps of the British Empire and its Dominions were of course prominent, and the faces of Victoria, Edward VII and George V in blue, black, orange, red and purple covered page after page and etched themselves on my memory for ever. But it is also to those stamps that I owe a fairly comprehensive knowledge of the nations of the world. Soaking the stamps, attaching new and fiddly stamp hinges on to their backs and sticking them under the right country heading: all this was an education — at least in how the world used to be in the old colonial days. Perhaps it was then that Canada first became real to me. I also became interested in how much my stamps were worth, and acquired an old Stanley Gibbons catalogue to check the official estimate of their value. I dreamed of finding a Victoria 'penny-black', and for a while thought I had stumbled on an extremely rare triangular stamp from the Cape of Good Hope. It was perhaps the first time that I imagined the possibility of amassing wealth. How much this had to do with my parents' continuing poverty I cannot now be sure.

September and the return to school came soon enough, and like many other boys I proudly brought back my new stamp collection and began to embark on the business of 'swapping' — getting rid of duplicates and filling blanks in our stamp families.

But this was just one of the activities that occupied me. I was beginning to show some basic skill on the piano, and to be able to read music, and before the end of that year I was invited into the chapel choir as a budding soprano soloist. I was starting to shine somewhat in my classes, blessed with a good visual and aural memory. And I think I can say that I began to make some friends, although I am not sure quite what that means at so tender an age: perhaps no more than some boys of my age being specially nice to me, or laughing at the same things. It says something about my doziness that I can remember only one moment during the whole of the next year at Marlborough House – at least, only one event that I can pin to the time. For November 5th, Guy Fawkes Day 1945, Tommer had built a huge bonfire by the football field. Our enjoyment of its frightening size and warmth and glow against the night sky was very much enriched by our burning an effigy of Hitler, perched on top of the heap and clutching a crude swastika painted on a piece of card.

But it's hard to forget the end of that school year. By this time sister Jo had been transferred to Bedgebury Park School in Goudhurst, only four miles away from my own school, and I think we must have finished term the same day in late July, and shared the same train to Charing Cross. Here we were met as usual by our mother and father, this time with four-year-old Jenny in a pram. But we both at once blurted out one eager, excited question: "Where are we going?"

For earlier that summer the family had left Langstone, and said goodbye to Devon for ever. Father had finally disengaged himself from his various frail enterprises, and the family was about to set out on a new path. Neither Jo nor I knew what the path was, or where our home was to be. And the answer? We had no home. So that night, that very night, we were to go camping.

Our parents were by now in their late thirties. They had been married for fourteen years, and had three young children. My father had been a book-keeper, a failed pig farmer and the creator of a failed farm service operation. They had very little money. And now they had no home. They must have been worried that day about Jo and myself and how we would react to the uncertainty of that moment in our family life. So I like to think they were relieved and even buoyed up by our almost incredulous excitement at the idea of spending that very night in a tent – as though we were setting out right away on a camping holiday. "Where?" we asked. After all, we were just off Trafalgar Square, in the middle of London. "Wait and see," they said.

Was Dad driving his own car that day? Perhaps. During those last years of the war we had picked up one sickly old jalopy after another for a few pounds at a time, each of them cranked and coaxed into daily life for a few months before expiring. Perhaps we had already acquired the little maroon Lanchester (CXR259) which was to see us shakily through the next two or three years: I boasted to my schoolfriends that on the Guildford bypass it had reached the amazing speed of 63 m.p.h.

We drove south out of London and on into the Surrey countryside. My father had already reconnoitred a site, and late that warm, sunny afternoon we drew up beside an old farmhouse, in a small village called Holmbury St. Mary. By suppertime we had put up two tents in a low-lying field behind the farmyard, and built a fire out of deadwood from a neighbouring copse. Mother was cooking, while Dad sat on a camp stool smoking the curved Peterson pipe he favoured in those days and consulted a gazetteer. Jenny played with a ball. Jo and I explored. We ate. The sun set behind the woods, and Jo and I were sent off to our made-up beds in the small tent. I'm not sure about our parents, but I think both of us older children were at that moment entirely happy. A whole summer holiday like this!

Not quite. A few nights later the weather turned around, and we woke up to find ourselves under storm clouds, rain drumming on the canvas and both tents lying in several inches of water and mud and sagging from the collapse of the guy ropes. Mother, who had the only air mattress among us, was gently floating. We had camped in a depression – probably an old pond. To make matters worse, Dad had been away that night on his search for a job, and until he came back we would have to sit in the cold and wet, eating bread and cheese and apples, with Mother cheering us up and leading us in games with her usual dauntless good spirits.

By that evening Dad had arrived and moved us to higher ground a mile or two away, where we set up again, this time in a glade among great swathes of bracken. And here for the next two or three weeks we made our home. On fine days Jo and I tunnelled through the bracken until we had made a rabbit warren of the place, with Piccadilly Circus at the centre and branches stretching out in all directions. And while we were here we received a visit from grandmother, come to tea in her stately black Wolseley, driven by her usual driver in peaked cap and bowling incongruously through the fields. She looked with some concern at the primitive state her fifth son's family had been reduced to, and no doubt relayed her concerns to husband Percy when she got home.

Did Dad feel some shame at our apparent poverty and evident homelessness? Perhaps: we children would not have known it. I still marvel at our mother's bravery and ability to cope. What did she do about dirty clothes? Washed them out in a tin basin, of course, and set them out on the line, as in any gipsy encampment. And many days we set out to explore Dad's home county. We climbed Leith Hill and the Hog's Back at Dorking. We saw the famous clock at Abinger Hammer, spent a day at Chessington Zoo and visited 'the Aunts' at their home 'Brambleacres' in Banstead. And, after some four weeks of the outdoor life, we packed up and moved to our Uncle Stewart's house in Banstead to look after the place while they were away on holiday. There we remained through the rest of August. We were both given roller skates for my ninth birthday, and roller-skating along the road below the house with my sister is all that I now remember of our stay. Soon September came, and Jo and I were once again shipped off to Kent and our respective schools.

Though they would never have admitted it, this must have been one time that Mother and Father were relieved to have us off their hands. In rocky circumstances they had succeeded in giving us a happy summer, and could once again take up the struggle of inventing their future. And that future was in fact taking shape. Some time around now, in discussion with their closest friend Wilma Hessey, who had stayed in Devon managing Lyd Valley for her sister's family, they began to explore the idea of coming together to lease a large old house somewhere and open up a country hotel. This was 1946, and large old country houses for rent or sale were easy to come by: the world of upper class country house living had been dealt a final deathblow by the war, helped on its way by the Labour government's quite unfeeling attitude towards inherited wealth, which they attacked with high taxes and swingeing death duties.

We were let in on the plan by mid-autumn, and my regular letters from 'home' would recount the latest adventure, as they travelled through southern England hunting for the ideal place. I can imagine the romantic view all three of them took of this new enterprise as they contemplated it. They could live in and look after a lovely old house set among beautiful gardens – wonderful for the children. They would have 'nice' people coming to stay and to dine.

Wilma could keep a few cows and grow vegetables for the hotel, as well as handling secretarial chores – she was an expert typist among other things. Mother would look after the staff, and oversee the cooking of delicious meals, and arrange the flowers. Father would run the business and serve drinks in the bar and generally act as mine host. It was an agreeable dream, if a little vague on the business side of things.

By Christmas three months later the dream had still not become rooted. But we were in a kind of dubious luck. Our uncle Donald was lying ill in hospital with lung cancer. His marriage had been broken up for some while, so his house on the edge of Cobham was vacant, and he kindly offered it to his young brother Ray and his family for the holidays. It was here, then, that Jo and I were brought to at the end of our autumn terms.

I had no thought at the time that this nomadic existence might be having any effect on my nine-year-old state of mind. I had been continuing to do well in class at Marlborough House, and had even begun to show some kind of doggedness if not ability on the rugger field. I was making friends, some of them friends of mine still, like John Le Mare and Brian Knox-Peebles. I was even beginning to write poetry. But perhaps our unstable home life was not providing much of an anchor. I had frightening dreams around this time, from which I would wake with a scream.

The Cobham house where we spent that Christmas holiday did not do too much to settle me down. Several times I saw that hideous old man standing at the foot of my bed, and would cry out in terror, to be rescued and calmed, usually by Father. But other things were happening too. My parents, who were entirely sceptical about anything supernatural, several times heard footsteps on the stairs at night. They kept this from their children, but once we were all in the sitting-room – including Wilma Hessey who had joined us for a few days – when I heard a window opening upstairs. "What's that, Daddy?" I asked. He looked over at Mother and Wilma, and then said, something like, "I don't know. We sometimes do hear funny things in this house. But it's nothing to worry about."

When Father went to visit Donald in hospital after Christmas, he happened to say that we had been hearing strange things in the house: footsteps, windows opening by themselves. "Oh you mean George!" Donald said immediately. "Oh yes, everyone hears George. And sometimes they see him. He's been there for years." Apparently there was a history of death hanging around the place. A builder had fallen off the scaffolding when it was being built, and broken his neck. And in the thirties a cook who was working for the owners at the time had taken an evening off in the town, and been discovered in a back alley with her throat cut. Dad brought this cheerful news back to Mother, but didn't share it with us until we were well away from there. It seemed all of a piece with the house's star-crossed reputation that its present owner, our Uncle Donald, was mortally sick with cancer (he died that spring) and that somewhere in Sussex Wilma's brother-in-law fell off his horse in a hunting accident on Boxing Day, and died a few days later.

My next term back at school coincided with the horrific winter of 1947, the worst in Britain – and Europe – for hundreds of years, with one blizzard after another choking off roads and railways, desperately low temperatures freezing root vegetables in the ground, acute shortages of coal leading to daily blackouts, newspapers reduced to four pages, potatoes rationed, the army called out to clear snow and to distribute food to isolated villages, naval vessels providing electricity for coastal towns. It was a crisis for which the fledgling Labour government was blamed: even more so when, with a massive loss in industrial output, it was decided to devalue the pound by over 30%.

During these multiple national calamities my parents and Wilma did their best to continue their hunt for a country house. A possibility had turned up in Lewes, Sussex, but it had not materialized, and by the middle of January their search had taken them by slow and halting train to Oxfordshire. I still remember a long letter from Father, written in his copper-plate hand, describing the long journey from Surrey, and the beauty of Oxford's spires and colleges under snow.

I had this letter read to me in bed, because in the middle of January, like scores of my fellow schoolmates, I had succumbed to the epidemic of chicken-pox which had overtaken the place. One dormitory after the other was converted into a sickroom, and for three weeks or more we were looked after behind drawn curtains, forbidden to read, our temperatures taken, meals served on trays, watered-down orange juice administered at night, periodic doctor's visits to gauge our progress, and strict instructions not to itch the spots which flamed up on our faces and bodies: "You'll be scarred for life." Contrary to what you might think, boarding schools were always quite happy when one of these scourges swept through: once it was over, it meant that we were all immune to chicken-pox, and safe for a few years from another bout. The following winter we would move on to another delightful infection: measles, or mumps, or scarlet fever. We boys were also happy, once the first few days of high fever and low spirits were past. No classes of course, and a chance to be read to, and play silly games, and stay warm, and to become increasingly mischievous as good health returned. Tucked up in bed, we were also more or less insulated against that wretched winter, which we only heard about from our teachers and the occasional visitor, and from our regular parental letters.

Meanwhile things had been moving along on the home front. My intrepid parents and their friend Wilma had gone to Oxford to follow up an advertisement they had read in *Country Life*: a handsome Elizabethan manor house, Studley Priory, was available. Somehow they managed to cover the seven snow-banked miles out of the city to reach the hamlet of Horton-cum-Studley, on the edge of Otmoor. They found the entrance, drove up the long drive through laurel bushes, and there in front of them was a superb Elizabethan house in Cotswold stone. They no doubt gasped at the beauty of it. At the front door they were met by Captain John Henderson, owner of almost the entire village and also lord of the manor of Studley. They toured the huge, freezing, dilapidated house. They surveyed the ten acres of snow-draped lawns and walled vegetable garden, the six-acre paddock and the cowsheds, and they looked over to the edge of the 300-acre oak woods beyond the paddock, to which they would be offered access and shooting rights. They viewed the sensational view over Otmoor from the front lawn. They must have spent a little time matching the place with their dream, but not long. Some time in February they signed a fourteen-year lease, with the option to sever it after seven years. The rent for the entire estate was £500 per annum.

The trio took possession of this vast house on March 1st, 1947, as the accumulated ice and snow of the previous two months were just beginning to thaw all over Britain and turn into the worst floods in living memory. They settled, to begin with, into just one handsome oak-panelled room with a fireplace, and turned the big, gaunt bedroom above it into a family dormitory. The garden was still under snow, and letters had told of the fox that had wandered up to the window to see what was going on, and the owl that kept them awake at night, and something too of the beauty of the place.

Our school term was over towards the end of March, and once again I took the school train to Charing Cross, to be met by Father. After the statutory lunch at one of our favourite spots, we took a taxi, as so often, to Paddington station. But there, instead of embarking on the long ride to the West Country as we had for years, we caught the 4.45 to Oxford. We were met at the station by Wilma, and for the first of hundreds of times crossed Magdalen Bridge, climbed Headington Hill, reached the roundabout, and dived off into the countryside. Night had well fallen by the time we reached Horton-cum-Studley. We climbed the hill past the King's Arms and turned off down the driveway, our weak lights wavering through the dark.

My mother and sisters were there to greet us at the door, and tired from the long day I fell into my mother's arms. After a garrulous and excited supper I wanted to explore. But I was persuaded to wait until daylight. Mother and Father showed me up the winding back stairs to the family bedroom, and led me to my bed in one corner, with a few knick-knacks of my own put thoughtfully beside it. Fading into sleep didn't take long, and I heard nothing of the rest of the family when they came up to bed. But one happy thought was going round and round my head:

We had a home again!

CHAPTER THREE

LORDS OF A MANOR

Studley Priory may have become our home, but it was not to be long before the first guests wandered in for a meal, or even took up residence. If we now had a home, we soon learnt that we were obliged to share it with other people.

They came to a place which since the first of March, 1947, had been gradually furnished from war surplus, country auctions and junk shops. Many of the beds were of iron like those we had at school, the familiar thick curved piping at head and foot, with rails to hold on to in your dreams, and mattresses which had seen better nights. The bare boards of the corridors were lined with coconut matting, scratchy under bare feet. The tables in the dining room were big and small, mahogany and oak, round and square, fitted up with odd chairs culled from many cast-off dining sets. The armchairs and sofas in the lounge were of every floral design, rounded, creased and comfortable, worn from years of sitting and being sat on in other homes. The bedrooms were whitewashed, with the barest essentials of hanging rails and chests of drawers and bedside tables, and with the quintessential chamber pot under each bed. The lounge was changed from its light and dark Victorian green to a cheerful ivory, the ribs of its high Victorian-mediaeval ceiling picked out in black with gold rosettes where they crossed. The oak panel walls of the bar (formerly the library) and the dining-room were washed down and polished. Rugs in various stages of wear covered a few empty spaces.

And among all these changes and all this cheap utilitarian stuff, a few survivors from the world of the Hendersons still kept their place, too bulky to move: a full-size billiard table with its vast carved legs and set of ancient cues; glass book-cases full of Annual Registers of the nineteenth and even late eighteenth century, along with the Edwardian travel books which had no doubt adorned every country house in their day: *With Rod and Gun in Canada*, *Fox-hunting in Rawalpindi*, *Along Warwickshire's By-Lanes*. Oil-paintings were fitted back into their niches in the dining-room walls, for which they had been painted – or for which the niches had been let into the panelling, bought perhaps by the yard for the upwardly mobile Hendersons of the 1870s. *The Glorious Twelfth* stood above the mantel, a huge antlered stag nervously facing the artist among the banks and braes. Opposite, a little girl and her mother sat in an arbour beside a gently-rolling Victorian sea.

The house's wartime occupation as a convalescent home for wounded officers had also left its mark. Only two of the rooms on the first floor boasted their own bathrooms, so two front bedrooms further down the hall had been converted into communal bathroom facilities, with five baths, each tub in its own latchable stall, the eight-foot-high separating walls made of pasteboard, and brown linoleum on the floor. None of this was quite in the spirit of a great country house, but it was a time when queuing up in dressing-gowns outside shared facilities was the lot even of middle-class man and woman, even in the more expensive hotels. Guests housed in the former servants' wing, with its six bedrooms, had to make do with two bathrooms and WCs.

Our kitchen with its ancient coal-fired range – soon to be replaced by a newer version – had been fashioned by the first Hendersons out of what had been the family chapel, and retained its high windows and lofty ceiling. The chapel wing was still complete with belfry: the bell, we were told, used to be rung by the lords of the manor at midday to signal dinner-break for the labourers in the garden and the fields around.

The Hendersons had also bequeathed us their gardeners. Sidney and George and their boss Taylor (known only by his surname, in recognition of his senior standing) had worked the Priory gardens as young men before the First World War, in which they had all fought, and ever since. Now in their fifties, they were true men of Oxfordshire, with the soft burr of the country, the slow steady pace of the rustic labourer, the flat caps and aprons, and the deferential manners of the olden time: they were old enough to have watched from a distance the proud folk of the Priory and their friends playing croquet on the lawn or tennis in the back garden during the golden years. They were the first and last people who ever addressed me as 'Master Michael' and my sisters as 'Miss Josephine' and 'Miss Jennifer'. My father was inevitably 'Sir', with a touch of the forelock.

With these three stalwarts came all the venerable paraphernalia of the old garden: a green-painted and hump-backed lawn mower from the thirties, still lovingly nursed and shining with oil, trailing clouds of blue smoke and clattering as it criss-crossed the sward; two or three vast and sculpted wooden wheel-barrows, in faded blue and red, made perhaps by an estate carpenter before the beginning of the century; stately brass watering-cans; spades and forks and edgers and axes and sickles and billhooks and secateurs, their old Sheffield steel hard as diamonds, ash handles worn smooth from years of work; bamboo poles; binder twine; strawberry nets; scores of flower-pots; huge trugs for bringing in the vegetables and flowers; and vast tree-saws with their five or six feet of rippling toothed blade, an upright wooden handle at either end.

The garden they had to work on demanded every tool in their shed. In front of the house, circled by the main driveway, spread one large lawn, from which you looked west past a majestic single sycamore down over the fields and out towards Otmoor. On its south side stood an enormous clipped yew tree. Behind the house, which was long and thin, stretched another lawn, with fields beyond and Brill Hill in the far distance. At its north end, behind a slight rise, was the old tennis court, still to be reclaimed. South of it, hidden behind a tall thick curtain of more clipped yew trees, was the more formal 'lavender garden': crazy paving pathways separating irregular beds edged with box, and filled with lavender and shrub roses, fragrant in their season, and a tiled summer house in the corner. And beyond this again was the brick-and-stone wall surrounding the spacious vegetable garden: a two or three-acre expanse of fruit trees, strawberry plants, and gooseberry and raspberry and black-currant bushes, and a peony walk, and rows and rows of vegetable beds. A gate on the far, southern wall gave on to the paddock and the stables. At the south end of the house lay an attractive stone courtyard, with a rock garden to one side and in the centre an ageing pigeon-cote on a high post. Opening on to it was the old family brew-house, now Henderson storage, and a long, rambling array of outbuildings, all of stone, and roofed in the warm, lichen-covered red clay tiles of the big house.

At the house's north end, beyond the stables and the mounting block, beyond the handsome garages built in the 1920s beneath the servants' wing, a path led through the shrubbery to a gentle slope, dropping down into a half-overgrown pond. Here, we were told, the carriages and carts and gigs of the old household would be backed into the water to be washed down. The path continued to a small brick building, which housed the magnificent green and gold diesel engine used to generate the house's electricity. Twice a week Mr Beckley would come up from the village to set his beloved machine going, for the two or three hours it would take to recharge the rows and rows of batteries which sat in their own room at the end of the engine-house. I remember old Beckley showing me round, and being fascinated by the oiled beauty of the engine, its great steel piston thrashing back and forth. While it ran, he would often doze off by the door. It was a wonder to me as a boy that he was able to sleep in all that rhythmic clamour.

The Priory also had its own central heating system, fired by two mammoth coal-burning boilers, one at each end of the long house. It was the job of Taylor, the head gardener, to arrive in the dark of early morning during the cold months, clean out the built-up clinker, re-fill the fireboxes and set them blazing, then damp them down for their day's work. He would be back after nightfall to repeat the process. No doubt he had followed the same routine for twenty or thirty years. In the cold of winter these two massive boilers consumed a ton of coal a week.

My parents, in other words, had not simply leased a vast Elizabethan mansion. They had taken on the almost feudal trappings of a manor house, with its rigid routines, its old retainers and its high obligations.

And this, all this, was to be our home. The family had spent a year as little more than gipsies, camping in the bracken, lurching from suburban house to suburban house, depending on the kindness of relations. Sister Jo and I had shared this nomadic world in our holidays, leaving it every few weeks to return to the far greater stability of school. Our young sister Jenny, now in her fifth year, had been carried along with our parents through those dire winter months. And then, that March, suddenly, in one stroke, we had all stepped out of limbo and into this superabundance of stuff, of history, of beauty, all at once made kings of apparently infinite space. It was a world we children could never exhaust, never find the end of.

I remember little of that first Easter holiday at Studley. I certainly had no conception at the time of the gargantuan task which Wilma and my parents had taken on. Father told me many years later that their entire capital at the outset amounted to no more than £500. Which explains why they did so much of the cleaning and renovating themselves: I have a distinct memory of Mother and Wilma in overalls with scarves round their heads, up ladders here, there and everywhere, brushing away the cobwebs, dusting and whitewashing. If they had an overall plan – surely they had a plan! – I have no idea what it was. Where would you *start* on a job like that? Father, I think, kept out of the painting department, though he did undertake some crude and highly dodgy electrical wiring. He was no doubt busy preparing in other ways. There was advertising to devise, a brochure to put together, a cook to hire, a club licence to apply for, legal business in Oxford, and, I think, meetings set up with the hoteliers of the county, picking up tips of the trade. In addition to her refurbishing work, Wilma sat with Father typing letters and preparing an already burdensome payroll. She also began to take over responsibility for the gardens, working with our old retainers to decide on plantings and jobs for the day. With her somewhat brusque manner you might think she would have antagonised them, but they were and remained devoted to her. It's true she did not behave in the least like the lordly owners of the place in the days before the war. But they admired directness, hard work and high spirits, and Wilma was indefatigable in all these ways. Within a year or two she bought our first Jersey cow, and added milking to her other routines. The herd later grew to six.

Jo and I, reared on children's books in which middle-class boys and girls went off exploring a strange house and found themselves in the grip of an adventure, wasted little time before setting out to chart this new country called Studley Priory. We ventured up to the top floor with its quaint rooms under the eaves and its balcony looking over the back garden. We climbed out on to the leads of the massive old tiled roof. We crawled into the rocky space under the dining-room floor, accessed through 'The Tunnel' which in the old days enabled the staff to cross from the kitchen to the rest of the house without disturbing the master at his dinner. We found our way along the worn stone-paved corridors to the furthest reaches of the house's south end, thought to have been once a part of the original priory.

On fine days, we ranged through the garden, its long grass now bright with daffodils, and climbed inside the cavernous yew trees. We discovered an old icehouse built half below ground in a copse beside the fence which ran along the front field. And on our first walk to pick primroses and violets in the three hundred acres of woods which began at the bottom of the paddock, we came across a mysterious railed and overgrown enclosure in its own small glade: peering through the bars we were excited and a little nervous to see a granite tombstone. One of the earlier Hendersons of Studley, we later found out, had insisted on being buried among his trees. We heard from Taylor about the day of his burial, with farmhands struggling and slipping through the mud in a slashing rainstorm to consign him here.

Many years later, the back prospect of Studley was used as the home of Sir Thomas More in the film of *A Man For All Seasons*.

We saw Thomas arriving up the Thames from London in a wherry, and clambering over a wall into his garden. Later Henry VIII arrived in his barge, and the two friends had their fateful conversation on and around a bench, past which I could see the window of my own bedroom. In fact, of course, the Thames was many miles away: the producers of the film had had a wall built both here and also on a reach of the river, cutting from one scene to the other as the Tudor gentlefolk climbed over.

In that disastrous spring of 1947 we were lucky indeed to be high and dry above Otmoor, and away from all rivers. Otmoor itself was under water, visible from our front garden. The Thames and all its tributaries suffered their worst flooding since the 19th century, with water covering Port Meadow and Christchurch Meadow to the depth of several feet. The whole of Britain was affected. The Fens turned into an inland sea. River valleys became lakes. There were places where families had to retreat to their upper floors, with boys earning pennies converting zinc tubs into boats and delivering bread and groceries to the marooned. Canada – good old Canada! – sent food parcels.

Easter came and finally went. When Jo and I took reluctant leave of our magical new home and boarded our trains back to London and down to Kent, we could still see vast lakes along the rivers, trees and hedges and woods waterlogged, telegraph poles sagging and lines askew. But the floods had at last begun to recede. They left the country battered and heavily damaged, crops destroyed, countless roads and bridges washed away and the Labour government reeling once again from this second natural disaster.

This did not mean much to us. We were each quickly swallowed up into our respective schools in the Kentish countryside, comfortably protected once again from politics and the world outside for another twelve weeks, while spring slowly ripened into summer.

Cricket was not my game. I came to realize years later that as a boy I had unconsciously resisted any attempt to teach me physical skills. Whether bowling or batting, or swimming or diving, or playing the piano, or even drawing, I found myself quietly rejecting any idea of copying or imitating when a teacher or coach tried to show me how it was done. This was not rebellion, nor even an early show of originality. It was simply that I believed these things would come by instinct, and that if they didn't it meant that I couldn't do them at all. I had no patience with instruction, and tended to switch off until it was over. I think too that I was poor at constructive analysis, at dividing up an action into its component parts and working on each before putting them back together. I preferred to take a blind swipe at things. My slightly pigeon-toed stance didn't help: fancy footwork was not my speciality. If I scored at all in any physical activity, it came as a surprise; all luck and no judgement.

All this meant that many summer afternoons were spent as a fielder on the edge of some lowly cricket pitch at the far end of the sports ground, mooning about and thinking about other things while more gifted boys got on with it. If I went in to bat, my time at the wicket was mercifully short because I simply couldn't co-ordinate eye and hand fast enough. I was also dismayed that the cricket ball was so very hard, and my bat so very narrow.

But there were other things to do. In the classroom, without trying too hard, I was beginning to be quick to grasp anything put in front of me, and very retentive, whether I was learning history, or French, or Latin, or geography. Arthur Harrison's English lessons were perhaps the sessions I looked forward to most. He taught us enthusiastically that now almost forgotten subject, English grammar, painstakingly sorting out adjectives, adverbs, nouns, pronouns and prepositions, and the difference between a clause and a phrase, a simile and a metaphor. But he also brought us into the world of poetry, and required us to learn some of it by heart. Shelley's *Ozymandias* is one sonnet I have known since I was nine. Since then, too, I have known what a sonnet is, and by the time I was twelve had attempted two or three myself. Above all, whether he was conveying to us his own love of language, of the beauty of language, or parsing a sentence, or enjoying a short story, he had an abundant sense of humour, and a sharp, ridiculing wit. His own laugh was rich and irresistibly contagious. I wonder now whether he was as patient with slower learners as he should have been. He certainly responded happily, as all teachers do, to the brighter ones, and I was lucky enough to be one of those.

And then there was music: piano lessons with Miss Sheaves, group singing (*Dashing Away With the Smoothing Iron, The Ash Grove*) with Miss Sheaves, choir practice with Miss Sheaves. Marlborough House took its music seriously. For the chapel choir we were able to muster four-part harmony, joined by Arthur (bass) and his wife Muffet and June Knight (alto); by Mr McNeile (bass) and Geoff Martin (tenor); and no doubt other teaching staff were dragooned in from time to time. Miss Sheaves ran the practices, but there was no doubt who was in charge: Geoff Martin took his music very seriously indeed, and had a fine and discriminating taste, which he imposed with dyspeptic authority on his fellow staff and us boys alike. Through him we were introduced to Bach chorales, and Thomas Tallis, and Byrd, and Mozart's *Ave Verum*, and Mendelssohn's *Hear My Prayer*, and had a chance to show off our 'anthems' on festivals and Parents' Days.

Being a member of the choir involved quite a few extra hours in practice and even homework, and once a year the ten or so of us would be rewarded with a choir outing. That summer we were taken one sunny Sunday afternoon to the home of Anglo-Irishwoman Katherine Everett, who had designed several homes for herself and others, in England and Italy, and was shortly to publish her memoir *Bricks and Flowers*. She had built this last modern, round-cornered, flat-roofed house of hers in Sussex just before the war, setting it in a copse above a miniature valley, which she later made into a woodland garden, the marshy bottom transformed into an exquisite lily pond, complete with rowing-boat. Here we wandered and boated and swam and chased one another and ate jam sandwiches and sticky cake, revelling in the freedom from school. And towards the end of the afternoon Arthur persuaded old Miss Everett to take us on a tour of her house, superbly furnished with Sheraton pieces and paintings by Augustus John and others. I remember little of these. But I have never forgotten her telling us that as a girl of seventeen she had gone to a dinner party and sat next to Oscar Wilde.

I am not sure how it was that we found ourselves at Miss Everett's place. Did our headmaster's Irish upbringing bring them together? Perhaps. It was only much later that I unravelled this Anglo-Irish connection. Every Sunday evening Arthur would gather the whole school and read to them from a favourite book of his, needing to choose something which would not be over the heads of the smaller boys but not beneath the interest of the seniors. *Three Men In A Boat* was an obvious choice, and for me and many others it inaugurated a lifelong love affair with 'the funniest book ever written'. Chesterton's Father Brown stories were another standby, incidentally introducing us to the fact that there were people called Roman Catholics in the world. But many of his other choices were heavily weighted in the direction of comic or light Anglo-Irish literature. *Spanish Gold* by George A. Birmingham; short stories by Lord Dunsany (*Here's Something You Won't Put In A Book*) and Oscar Wilde (*The Canterville Ghost, The Happy Prince, The Selfish Giant, Lord Arthur Saville's Crime*).

In fact, it may be that Arthur, who was born in Dublin in 1900, the year of Oscar's death, was influenced by Wilde's views on art and life, and by the aestheticist movement. Perhaps his family even knew the Wildes; Oscar's father was a prominent surgeon in Dublin. Arthur certainly had an abiding passion for beautiful things. He once came into our English class with a large, shiny apple, just picked out of the orchard, and told us to look at it. "Who's going to eat it, sir?" one of us inevitably asked. He dismissed the question scornfully, and asked us simply to admire its beauty: its shape, the delicate shading of its colours, its sheer presence as a striking object. Sixty years later that lesson still stays with me.

Like Oscar much earlier, Arthur left Dublin as a young man to read classics (Mods and Greats) at Oxford. After coming down from Queen's College he stayed in England, being appointed as a young master to Haileybury College, where one of his colleagues was Wilfrid Blunt (brother of the spy Anthony Blunt), who went on to teach art at Eton, and whose aesthetic – and also homosexual – interests have since been well documented. Blunt used to pay visits to Marlborough House during the late forties because Muffet Harrison was working with him on his book *The Art of Botanical Illustration*. While with us, Blunt was often invited to give a concert, showing off his weighty baritone voice and accompanied by the tireless Miss Sheaves. I'm not sure what we made of it.

It seems likely, in other words, that during the twenties and thirties Arthur lived at the edge of the world of British artists. The brick house Sessele, which he built on the edge of the Marlborough House grounds just before the war, was very much in the spirit of the times with its parapet roof and rounded corners. The reproductions he (and probably Muffet) chose for the walls of the school dining room were from the work of contemporary artists like Paul Nash, and included 'Blue Horses' by Franz Marc ("Why blue?" we would ask.) The elegant blue-green chairs he chose for that dining room were designed by an old boy of the school, who worked for Heal's, the furniture company inspired by William Morris. Even his own baggy suits of green tweed and his bright ties suggested more Bloomsbury than the Carlton Club. And his wife Muffet, who taught us art and was an avid grower of roses, no doubt reinforced the general interest in Things Beautiful.

And then there was her brother, Geoff Martin. He was much less obviously of the arts fraternity, with a bluff manner and dress that was more in line with his military background. But in fact it was Geoff who not only directed the musical choices of the choir, but who brought the whole world of music and drama into the school, aided by his technical expertise. Within a year or so of arriving he had wired the Gallery, the school's main gathering place, with large speakers at one end, and connected the system to his own room upstairs, with its array of turntables. So on Saturday nights we would be treated to concerts of classical music on records: Bach and Beethoven and Brahms of course, but also Vaughan Williams, Shostakovich and Sibelius. He even introduced us to Britten: *A Young Person's Guide to the Orchestra* became a regular treat, helping us – as intended – to identify the sounds of the various orchestral instruments.

But 'Mr Martin's' creativity went a good deal further. He soon had the equipment to record the choir's singing on vinyl records, and by 1946 he had acquired a tape recorder – one of the first in Kent, he told us with pride. With two or three high-quality microphones he was soon able to turn his very small upstairs sitting-room into a fully-equipped recording and broadcasting studio.

The next step, naturally, was to introduce radio plays, and before long he had written an hour-long detective drama, which of course involved not only boys and staff playing parts but the whole excitement of creating sound effects. The high point of this buzzing activity took place one of these early years, when we needed to record the sound of a train arriving in a station, and then pulling out again. Geoff packed up his mikes and his bulky tape machine – the size and weight of a large portable sewing machine at least – and drove up to the station at Tunbridge Wells. He had already rung the station-master, who was intrigued enough to play along, and soon walked out on to the platform. "Bill," he called out. "Take No. 36 and bring it into the west siding, and then brake it to a stop. Hurry now!" Geoff quickly set up his gear, and within a few minutes No. 36, an ancient shunting steam engine, came puffing into the side platform and screeched to a halt. Sound levels needed adjusting, and Bill had to pull out and re-enter two or three times before Geoff got what he wanted. The sheer impossibility of such a thing happening on today's rail system says something about the lost world of post-war Britain. As I've noted already, trains were simpler things in those days.

But Geoff's activities on behalf of the school went far beyond these excitements. He was also the principal teacher of French, which he spoke with a fine Parisian accent. To help us with the basics of grammar he even put together a 40-page booklet, which

I still have. It is dated 1945. Its front page reads:

FRENCH GRAMMAR
WITHOUT GROANS
AND
SYNTAX WITH A SMILE

———

AN UNORTHODOX PRIMER
by
GEORGES JAMBE DE BOIS
(Ancien Professeur de l'Académie de la Plage,
Bernières-sur-Mer.)

———

To
The Boys of
MARLBOROUGH HOUSE SCHOOL
This Book
is
DEDICATED
(without their Permission)
by the
UNREPENTANT AUTHOR.

———

As the slightly arch humour of this suggests, the book was designed to amuse small boys while setting down some of the ground rules of the language. (I have always remembered that the author was named after Geoff Martin's wooden leg, but only now do I realize that 'Ancien Professeur de la Plage, Bernières-sur-Mer', must have been a private joke, referring to the beach in Normandy where Geoff landed with the Royal Berkshires on D-Day. I recently discovered that he survived that day intact, that he was transferred to the Suffolk Regiment some weeks later, and that he stepped on a mine in their attack on Overloon in Holland.)

Geoff Martin's dedication to the school didn't stop here. He also wrote and produced plays in the school gym, put together a school orchestra (in which the fearsome Miss Gale, *sans* head-dress, sawed away on a violin), wrote most of *The Marlborough House Times* newspaper which appeared on the notice board on Parents' Day, ran the swimming pool and coached our swimming and diving teams, coached the First Rugger XV, and taught Greek to a few senior boys (like myself later on) who were being pushed in the direction of a classical education.

It's hard to imagine how all this could be fitted into a school term — and term after term. Certainly we boys took it all very much for granted at the time, and only now do I look back and reflect on how extremely lucky we were to be in the hands of a team of teachers so gifted, so creative, and so hard-working — and with it all so generous and kind.

Since it might be thought that we passed the time on a perpetual wave of love and caring and studiousness and larking about, I have to make clear, though, that there were areas where a rigid discipline was enforced. The centrepiece of this, the *ne plus ultra*, was the absolute necessity for us all to achieve regular bowel movements. In pursuit of this noble aim, each day after breakfast we would be herded in staggered groups to a highly functional area beyond the changing-room. Six WCs stood in line here, each with its own numbered door, its inside walls black with creosote. Opposite the row of doors was a long, white-tiled footbath, where we would wash off the mud after coming in from football or rugger. At one end of the WCs was a double shower, with a boy-shoulder-high wall dividing the two halves. Here, inside the shower area, stood the Lady of the Feast, Miss Gale, complete with Head-dress, Book, Pencil, Torch and Stick; her Book lay open expectantly on the dividing wall. Along the low front edge of the footbath sat the herd in a gloomy line, waiting for the call. We were not allowed to talk.

The first six boys would disappear into the six stalls, and go about their business. When one emerged, he would have to report on his success. There were only three ways of doing this: 'Yes Miss Gale'; 'No Miss Gale', or – believe it or not – 'Not very well, Miss Gale.' Was this the end of the drama? By no means. 'No Miss Gale' would mean that a '0' was entered against your name. But if you reported 'Yes' or 'Not very well', Miss Gale would march to your stall with her Torch to verify your report, if necessary poking about in the toilet paper with her Stick. She would then flush the toilet and return to the showers, motioning the next victim into the empty stall. She would write against your name either a '1' or a '1/2', representing her confirmation of your 'Yes' or 'Not very well.' If you had achieved nothing, or had only been partially successful, that evening Miss French would sidle up to you during 'Prep', and very gently and quietly say, "You didn't go very well this morning, Bawtree: better go upstairs now and try again." If a day or two went past with no better luck, you would be treated with a dose of revolting senna tea. It seemed to do the trick.

Senior boys would eventually be made trusties: instead of having their results verified with Torch and Stick, they were free at last to invent their own achievements. You may be sure that from then on they would report themselves as much more regular, throwing in an occasional 'No' or 'Not very well' just for credibility's sake.

What did it all mean? Where did this obsessive concern come from? Being regular was certainly in the air, so to speak, in those times: every railways station had its advertisement for 'Carter's Little

Liver Pills'. But inspection of faeces as a guide to health was surely more Continental than English: I am told that the shape of German toilet bowls was specifically designed so that you or your parent or your nurse could view your daily excretions on a flat shelf of the ceramic before they were flushed down. Was this preoccupation something Miss Gale brought with her to the school, part of the lore of her own upbringing before the First World War? I can hardly believe that the free-wheeling Harrisons would have insisted on such a regimen. But then there was no doubt that one of the serious jobs of a boarding establishment was to shoulder a general responsibility to parents for the health of the children, and maybe this bizarre routine was a useful daily guide to our well-being – or to our not-very-well-being, as the case might be. And perhaps it encouraged us to be regular for life, which is no doubt a GOOD THING.

Much of what I have set down here goes well beyond the confines of that summer term of 1947, describing some of the life lived by us little boys and our masters and mistresses at Marlborough House all through the late 'forties. But I cannot leave that year without broaching one episode of that summer, which remained with me for years, and which still haunts me from time to time.

One morning a message went round the classrooms that every boy who owned a stamp album must bring it to the Headmaster's study at the next break, and that there would be a special assembly of the whole school after lunch in the Gallery. We duly assembled, each of the four 'teams' grouped along its corner of the room: mine was 'Dunbar', and our regular station was around the Blüthner grand piano at the far end. It was Mr Thompson – 'Tommer' – who had called the meeting (I believe Arthur Harrison was away) and it was he who addressed us. Tommer told us that someone had been stealing stamps from other boys' stamp albums. This was a very grave matter, and he invited whoever was the guilty one to confess to the crime. He said that if no one owned up, the whole school would lose a half holiday.

There was a long silence. Boys looked curiously, but not too curiously, at each other. Eventually Tommer spoke again. He said that he would like to see – one at a time – some of the boys who had brought their stamp albums in that morning, and read out a list of names. Mine was among them.

When my turn came I went into the study, where Tommer was standing, holding my album in his hands. He opened it and pointed to a handsome group of stamps from Togoland. "Where did you get these?" he asked.

"My uncle gave them to me for Christmas. They were part of a package."

He turned to another page. "And these?"

"I bought them last year in London, when I went to Stanley Gibbons with my Dad."

"And what about these?" he asked again.

I paused, and eventually said, "I don't remember. Daddy gave me a lot of stamps from his collection. They may be part of that lot."

He looked over a few more pages, and then said, "All right, you can go. Send in the next boy."

I returned to my place in the Gallery. As I stood in line in my team, our Team Leader, Patrick Knox-Peebles, came up to me, looked me in the eye, and said very quietly and intently, "It's you, isn't it? I know it's you." I protested angrily, and he moved away.

Eventually Tommer came back in to the meeting. He told us that he had not been able to identify the culprit, but that if it ever happened again and the thief was caught, he would be expelled immediately. The guilty boy had one more chance to own up. There was silence. Finally, we were told that the following Wednesday half-holiday was cancelled: we would have two extra lessons in the afternoon. The meeting was over. We were told to come and collect our stamp albums.

You will probably have guessed by now that the thief was myself. At some point on one quiet evening early that summer term I had found myself in our classroom in the Annexe, probably coming to collect something from my locker. Suddenly I realized that I was all alone; there was no one about. I still can't bring to mind the sequence of events, but somehow a little later I found myself looking through another boy's stamp album, and seeing some gorgeous stamps, and coveting them. From there it was a short step to removing them and putting them into my own collection. He had lots of stamps − surely he would never notice, and if he did there were many of us who had the same stamps in our albums. Ten minutes later the deed was done. It was so easy. So easy that a week or two later I found myself repeating the routine. And then again a few days after that.

A few days later, for a fourth time and feeling more and more relaxed, I stole up to our deserted classroom after supper. I sloped in, only to find to my horror that our crafts mistress, Miss Knight, was sitting at one of our small desks. She was knitting.

She turned and saw me. "Hello Bawtree, what are you doing here?"

"Oh I forgot my pen − I'm just coming to get it." I went to my locker, took out a couple of pens and a pencil, mumbled something, and left. The missing stamps had been noticed and reported, I realized at once: it was obvious that she had been deputed to watch for the thief. This heart-thumping encounter spelt the abrupt end of my marauding visits. I am still surprised that the surprise and shock of seeing her there did not show enough on my face to mark me down immediately as the pilferer. But nothing further happened until the school assembly I have just described.

Why did I do such a thing? With my later tenuous grasp of psychology, I began to wonder if the rootlessness of family life over the previous year had something to do with it. I had been brought up to be thoughtful for others, to speak the truth, and not to steal. I had stolen, and when I was suspected I lied with deceptive calm and ease. And when I saw those stamps in the album of Will Thompson – yes, I even remember his name – I had somehow been dazzled enough by the colourful beauty of the stamps to separate them from their owner in my mind: to see them simply as things I must have for myself.

There was also, I am sure, the excitement of danger in these piratical raids: an excitement which became something of a drug with each success. Everything else we did at school we did with others. This was a private moment, which I shared with no one. Perhaps I needed private moments.

Early stealing is put down to a need for love. I don't think I had any doubt that my parents loved me. But then after all they had for years been entrusting me to the care of people who may have been kind but who could not be said to love me or any other of their young charges. Perhaps the need for love, for reassurance, for security, for kisses and embraces, translates itself unconsciously into something that tries to be satisfied by acquisition. Having no home perhaps reinforced the sense of abandonment.

The whole frightening adventure became the first instalment of that secret story of my life which, as with all of us, slowly accumulates inside, never to be shared except perhaps with a rare loved one, and even then only in translation.

Thirty years later I visited Arthur and Muffet Harrison in

Aldeburgh, two or three years before he died. Over a cup of tea I confessed to the crime which had been nursed guiltily in my bosom for so long. They laughed. They couldn't even remember the incident. But I felt a little better.

As far as I remember I never stole again. But lying? Yes I had already learnt to lie, and having now faced this rigorous test and found myself able to deceive with casual ease, I embarked on a life of well-tempered invention, which stood me in good stead for years to come. I know now that I had even at this early age developed an urgent need to be well-thought-of, to be approved. I don't think I could have endured the shame of being found out as a common thief: even now, the thoughts of my parents' pain, the disgust of my schoolmasters and the contempt of my schoolmates, all give me a shudder of terror. Why did I not think of all this as I was tip-toeing into that classroom to steal from a friend? Some irrationality was afoot, no doubt.

I am sure I was more than ordinarily glad to see that summer term come to an end, and to be away from the scene of my crime. Slowly the horror of it shunted into the past. But the memory has always remained with me, a slowly fading but never entirely removable stain.

By the time we boarding Bawtree children returned to Studley Priory in late July 1947, the business was slowly moving forward. We had engaged our first cook (words like 'chef' were not used in those days), a tall and charming young woman called Meg, who turned out to be superb in the kitchen and became a lifelong friend of the family. We had also picked up some staff from the village and the country round. There was Martha, who bicycled five days a week from Islip to wash up and scrub and clean. There was the miniature Mrs Ward – 'Wardy' – from the village, another floor-scrubber and cleaner as well as bedmaker. There was seventeen-year-old red-haired Bill, who cleaned boots and shoes, peeled potatoes, brought in firewood, and polished floors. And there was Mary Anstess, who 'did' the guests' rooms.

The hotel had also taken in its first P.G.s: Paying Guests. They added up to what must have been a representative cluster of ageing middle-class waifs and strays, often survivors from one or both World Wars, and with enough money squirrelled away even after those devastating years to be able to afford the unbelievably cheap rates of Studley Priory Country House Hotel. They paid 6 guineas (£6.6s.) a week all found in those first seasons: a hearty breakfast, a three-course lunch, afternoon tea with scones and cake, and a four-course dinner. Perhaps because they were our first in a long line of characters wonderful and weird, they acquired something of a mythic status for us, initiating a fund of 'Studley stories', recounted for years afterwards by my father and mother and their partner and friend Wilma; especially by my mother, whose ear and memory for conversation and comments was as sharp as ever.

There was Judge Hildesley and his wife, who insisted on having their own private sitting-room downstairs as well as the best bedroom in the house with *en suite* bathroom. The Judge came across as a mean-spirited, crusty old curmudgeon, who played a lot of billiards – even with me, when desperate and with no other opponents available. He was short and bald, with a fringe of grey hair round his pate like a tonsured monk, and with a red parchment face behind his half-moon glasses that put one in mind of the notorious Judge Jeffries: we were sure he had put on his black cap with pleasure many times, sending off some benighted offender to be hanged by the neck until he was dead. I never remember him smiling.

There was the toothless, feckless Major Gray and his

domineering wife. Major Gray was suspicious of any plate put in front of him, and would pick up a knife and push the food around as though expecting maggots. To his querulous "What's this?", Mrs G. once replied in a voice booming across the dining-room, "Oh, something hashed up from yesterday's left-overs."

There was Colonel Stranach, who would take our delighted dogs into the woods with his shotgun day after day, returning often enough with a rabbit or two, or a pheasant in season, to be handed into the kitchen. He was a bachelor who had no time for women, and was known to jump to his feet and leave the dining-room muttering rather than endure feminine chatter. He took a particular dislike to Mrs Gray, referring to her once as "that great big Norfolk turkey".

There was Mrs Highet, who was intent on keeping up social appearances. Always immaculately coiffed and lipsticked, with black twin set and pearls and in the highest of heels, she would flit around our rustic establishment as though she was teetering through the Savoy. An inveterate gossip, she would keep us up to date with the latest goings on among her fellow guests, and like my mother had an ear for the quaint turn of phrase. She was delighted to tell us one morning that she had been writing letters in her bedroom when our Mary, doing her daily chores, had knocked at her door and asked: "Anything in your chamber today, Mrs 'ighet?" Not quite how they did things at the Savoy.

There was Major-General Davidson, a widower originally from New Zealand, who had led a brigade in Mesopotamia in WW1, but had the sweetest and most pacific disposition of all those early Studley residents. Born around 1865, he was indeed a remnant from the Victorian age. He spent a lot of time in his room hooking rugs, one bearing his regimental badge. He came into the dining-room one morning and spying a fruit bowl full of oranges on the centre table rubbed his hands, exclaiming: "Jaffas, bejabbers!" He was also rubbing his hands when he came back one day from a walk, and said with glee: "Lots of hips and haws in the woods!" to the blushing enjoyment of Mrs Highet. He once had an old army comrade to visit, and as my mother was crossing through the lounge at coffee-time after lunch she heard the General reminiscing: "So I said to the staff officer: 'If we don't throw the pontoons across the Dum-Dum River, how the hell are we going to get the horses across?'"

Among these and other treasures, we were able to watch what might now be called group dynamics. Many were competitive for the best table, and the best armchair in the lounge, and their preferred bedroom, and the quickest service. Like children the ladies would leave their knitting and bags on the chair by the lounge fire each night when they went in to dinner, and each night, while they ate, Father would carefully remove their chattels to a side table. Like children they would sometimes get drunk in the bar and Father more than once had to carry one up to bed – men and women both. Like children they would have spats over billiard cues, or their favourite cup. Like children they would vie for the attention of my parents and Wilma, in the bar or over coffee. And like parents they would take turns in knowing how we children should be treated: some liking children more than others. Chief among child-haters was the Judge.

The friendliest to children was Barney Downes, who worked as a sales manager for Nielsen Market Research. Barney was an eccentric and something of a mystery: Mrs Highet said of him snootily that if he had not had a slight Scottish burr when he spoke his accent would be a lot less classy. A big, Panama-hatted fellow with a large belly and loud ties, he was a hypochondriac, and on his dining-room table had an array of bottles and pill-boxes which he guarded carefully, calling them his 'nutritive additives'. After meals he would sit by himself in a corner of the lounge, looking broodily into space. When Mother asked once if he was all right, he said yes, that he was simply "digestin'". He drove smart company cars, and was kind and generous. He once took my sisters and me to Badminton Park for the Horse Trials, where we were thrilled to see the Princesses Elizabeth and Margaret in their headscarves driving about in a Land Rover and mingling easily with the horsey crowd.

When the 'above stairs' folk ceased to entertain my parents and became merely irritating – as they often did – there was always a smile or two to be had among the characters below stairs, and the ancient village of Horton-cum-Studley round about us, from which most of our casual labour came. The village still reflected the manorial culture which had spawned it in the middle ages. Apart from the acres looked after by the Hendersons themselves, there were two large farms, run by the Honors and the Greens. The rest of the village was made up of any number of cottages tied to the estate, many of them thatched. Up the road from the entrance to the Priory there was a blacksmith's forge, presided over by a wall-eyed old craftsman who lived in a pretty cottage opposite, and who made a sparser and sparser living on the mending of agricultural implements and the shoeing of fewer and fewer horses, and the mending of an occasional bicycle. The sound of hammering from his smithy resounded across the fields into our garden for the first few years, until he shut up shop, or died, or both. It was an attractive place for a boy to visit, and I can still recall the smell of red-hot metal, and the furnace with its hand-operated bellows, and watching through the steam as he shaped his horseshoes around the ancient anvil.

Our gardener Sidney Jones lived across the road from the Priory copse, with his permanently sickly wife Tilly, a gloomy creature to whom he was devoted. Closer to us on the same side lived the Warings with their children, and next door to them the Anstess family, with 'anything-in-your-chamber' Mary. There was not much education to be had in the small village school down the hill near the church, but what there was of it seemed to have escaped the grasp of Bill and Mary, who combined sweetness of temper with a light hold on the things of the mind. Bill, our seventeen-year-old boot-boy, had a sort of quiet insouciance which took our breath away. Scolded for peeling the potatoes so thickly that there was hardly any potato left after he was done, he plunged his hand into the dirty water of the bucket and pulled out one of his peelings." 'Ere's a thick bit," he said, with a charming smile. And once when he was polishing the floor, mother came through and said reprovingly, "Oh, I'm glad to see you doing this, Bill, you haven't done it for two days!", he replied with the same smile: "Oi 'aven't done it for a week!"

Bill was an army cadet, and once a year would go off to a two-week training camp. One year, Father started one of his slightly patronising but well-intentioned conversations with the hired help:

"Good to have you back, Bill. Where was your camp this year?"

"Oil o' Woit."

"Oh, the Isle of Wight! I used to go on holidays there with my family when I was a boy. Where were you based – Weymouth? Newport? Sandown?"

A puzzled pause. "They never told us where it was."

Mary was a year or two older than Bill, and getting to be of marriageable age. Mother used to inquire kindly whether she had a boyfriend yet. "Naow," she replied rather gormlessly. Then, at a village dance, the story got about that she had danced with a boy. Mother asked whether she liked him.

"Yayss", said Mary.

"Oh good," said Mother encouragingly. "Have you heard from him since?"

"Naow."

"Do you know where he lives?"

"Yayss."

"Why don't you write to him then, and tell him you would like to see him again?"

"Yayss, oi will."

A week or two went by, and Mother asked again:

"Have you written to that boyfriend of yours yet, Mary?"

"Naow."

"Oh dear, why not?"

"Mother's taken away me pen."

It was the same mother who had had all Mary's teeth taken out when she was sixteen, "so she wouldn't be bothered with them a'ter that." Poor Mary.

Martha, cycling in from her village on Otmoor, used to complain that her varicose veins were troubling her, and she showed my squeamish mother her swollen, purplish calves.

"Oh, poor Martha. That looks terrible," said Mother.

"Oh it's nothin' really," replied the stoic Martha: "You shoulda seen my mother's. They used to 'ang down 'er legs like bunches o' grapes."

Wardy, from the council houses down in the village, was a diminutive fireball, who unsurprisingly was not a native of the village but had washed up here during the war as an evacuee from the East End of London. Mother loved her for her Cockney wit. One Christmas her whole family came from London for the festivities, and Mother asked how she could put them all up in her very cramped little house. She described where everyone slept and doubled up, and finished up with "Oh, an' Uncle 'Enry, 'e lost both his legs in the war, so 'e fits on the sofa just lovely."

By that first Studley summer my parents and Wilma had finally managed to colonise the top floor of the house for the family's own use, and for the first time in our lives we children each took possession of our own rooms. Mine – like Jo's – sat at one corner of the high house under the eaves, and boasted two diamond-paned windows; one of them a dormer, where I set up my little table, with pens and pencils and exercise books containing the beginnings of short stories, the beginnings of diaries and the beginnings of poems. My bed lay under a steep slope of the ceiling, leading up to a broad hand-hewn oak beam. Asked to choose the colour I wanted, I had opted for pale green. There were shelves made out of boards on bricks for my small but growing book collection, and for the odd toy animals that had stuck around during all our moves. I had to pass through Jenny's larger but less desirable bedroom to reach my own eyrie, just as Jo reached hers on the other side of the house by crossing through Wilma's. My parents had two inter-connecting rooms end to end beneath a gable. The first did duty as my father's dressing-room. The second was their bedroom: two single beds, one on each side. At the far end a French window opened on to a leaded roof looking down to the back garden and bounded by a stone parapet – low enough to give our parents the heebie-jeebies whenever we children got near it.

In addition to this entire attic floor under the eaves, the family was reserved one large private living room on the first floor, with bay windows looking east over the remains of Studley's parkland – after which the room was named. 'Park' would have made a highly attractive guest-room, but as far as I remember they never once turned it over to a guest, even on those fairly rare occasions when the hotel was full. For meals, though, we joined the guests, eating at a large mahogany table just inside the main dining-room door, from which Dad could keep an eye on the needs of his customers.

But that table, too, was our own, and only given up for capacity lunches and dinners. Our best family time was after the hotel's breakfast, when Mother and Wilma could join us there; and at afternoon tea, which for the guests was served in the lounge or even, in summer, out on the lawn or in the lavender garden. These tea-time sessions were the quintessential family moment, when sandwiches and scones and cakes disappeared at speed, and endless cups of tea were drunk, and talk and quarrels and laughter went on until, with sighs and groans, Mother and cook Meg would get up to start preparing for the four-course evening meal, for which the gong would be rung at a quarter to eight. At the same time, once we had launched into our own herd, Wilma would stride briskly off to milk the cows.

Thus, with our parents' help, we managed even that first summer to start carving out our own private space within the stately home around us. And for me, having my own room marked almost the beginning of my privately-imagined life.

There was no family holiday for us in 1947. Mother and Father were far too busy to take even a weekend off. But having a home meant that I could invite a schoolfriend to stay, and return the favour. It was maybe that same hot summer that I went off for a few days with Bill Shand Kydd, boarding alone the double-decker bus to Aylesbury, where I was met by Bill and his mother and driven to their smartly-renovated farmhouse outside Leighton Buzzard. Bill was something of a pirate, and certainly not intellectually in the upper echelon of our class, but for some reason we became pals, and I had my first introduction to the home of a wealthy family. His father, owner-director of Shand Kydd Wallpapers, drove an expensive Jaguar, and was peppery and impatient – especially with his son Bill. But they were kind to me, and I especially remember being treated to a day in London, where we visited the Shand Kydd Wallpaper Factory – in Bethnal Green, was it? – where we watched rank upon rank of rollers being embossed and printed with countless elegant designs. I wonder now what war efforts these machines had been adapted for a few years earlier, when the market in wallpaper must have evaporated completely. It had certainly staged a comeback by 1947.

Bill's return stay started well; Studley was as much a marvel to other children as to ourselves. But on the second day, during a walk in the woods, we got thirsty, and lay down beside a tiny brook to take a drink. Within an hour or two I was very sick indeed, and remained in bed on a diet of cod liver oil for the rest of his visit.

Later that summer I celebrated my tenth birthday. Like most children I was beginning to mark off these anniversaries as mileposts along the way to being a grown-up. They were used by parents too to open new doors: "When you are ten you can have a watch." And sure enough, at our Studley breakfast table that August 25th I opened up a small, slim parcel to find an Everite wristwatch, fresh from H. Samuel's jewellery store in Oxford's covered market. I kept it for years after it wore itself out: somewhere I have it still.

Sooner than I wished, September had swung around, and it was time to return to school. The last night at home was always something of an occasion; we could choose our favourite dishes for supper – visited of course on the guests as well. And after the meal and the guests' coffee-time the family – including Father to my greatest delight – would head up to Park, where it became a last-night tradition to play a riotous game of 'Pit'.

Pit was an American invention based on the US Corn Exchange, and at the time was a popular family game in Britain. Each player was dealt eight cards, from a pack made up of cards picturing the Corn Exchange and carrying the name of a cereal.

The number of cereals – flax, wheat, barley, oats, corn, rye and hay was the full list if I remember – was matched to the number of players in the family circle, and each player's aim was to accumulate all eight of one cereal. Exchanges were made by calling out 'twotwotwotwo', or 'threethreethreethree' and swapping these two or three cards (of the same cereal) with whoever was selling two or three of another. The first person to have all eight in their hands would shout out 'Corner in rye!' or 'Corner in flax!', and the hand would end, with points to the winner.

I describe Pit only to explain that the game was immensely noisy, with each of us becoming more and more insistent as we approached a full hand. So boisterous was it that our parents worried about disturbing the guests, and we would then deal hands in which the exchanges would be made in a hectic whisper, or even in dumb show, with one or two or three fingers desperately flailing the air. Naturally the silence made the urgency that much more extreme, and we usually finished in roars of hysterical laughter. Just the thing for a last night at home.

Slowly, while Jo and I were off at school once more, Studley Priory made its way. When Oxford's Michaelmas Term began in October, my parents began to see Oxford dons and their families coming for lunch, or perhaps just for a drink and a snack in the bar. Even the wealthier undergraduates used to come, bringing their girlfriends to candle-lit dinners in the oak-panelled dining room, and walking awkwardly hand-in-hand out in the garden. The hotel started developing a reputation for good food, and within a year or two was listed in the new Good Food Guide. Even Oxford celebrities made their way out through the Oxfordshire lanes to enjoy the very unluxurious but honest warmth and good spirits of the place. Gilbert Murray, the great classical scholar and translator of Greek plays (and first president of the League of Nations), would be driven over from his home on Boar's Hill, and once even came to stay with us for a week. C.S. Lewis took to making the trip out to Studley a regular Sunday morning occasion for beer and conversation after church, with his brother Warren and his intimate Roman Catholic friend Dr Havard. (It was with that good doctor that my father, while drawing him his beer, was making polite conversation, and asked absent-mindedly, "Let me see, Dr Havard, was your father a Catholic priest?") Dean Lowe of Christchurch, soon to become Oxford's Vice Chancellor, was also a regular, as were Maurice Bowra and Iris Murdoch and Jacquetta Hawkes. These worthies all added to the tone of the hotel, and money slowly started coming in in a promising way. By the time December came round and we were back from another term at school, the bookings for Christmas were filled to capacity, and a New Year's Eve ball promised to sell out as well.

While preparing for this festive onslaught, Father and Mother were not able to shrug off entirely their sense of *noblesse oblige* as lords and ladies of the manor, and decided that they should offer their loyal staff a Christmas party. It was held in the 'games room' at the far end of the house, on a Sunday evening, after the guests had been dispatched with a light supper. The ping-pong table was taken down, and the room transformed into 'The Priory Arms', complete with bar and hung with home-made Christmas decorations – including chains made of coloured paper – and holly from the garden, and mistletoe hung suggestively on one of the lights. We children helped serving food and drinks, changing the 78 rpm records and winding up the gramophone. Everyone arrived with their wives and husbands in their Sunday suits and all were on their best behaviour. But the beer and the food slowly loosened them up, and soon George sang his song *My Love is an Apple*, and there was dancing. My father, who was a fine ballroom performer of the old school, chivalrously asked every female in the room to a dance, and squired them through fox-trots and quicksteps and waltzes with fine grace. He met his match though when he finally approached one of our stalwart cleaners and asked her for the pleasure. "Oh no thanks, Mr Bawtree," she replied amiably. "You see, when I dances, I sweats, and when I sweats I stink like 'ell."

Father also took his duties seriously when fifteen or twenty village carol-singers made their way up the long Priory driveway a night or two before Christmas – as they had no doubt done for centuries – to give us their somewhat droney *Hark The Herald* and *While Shepherds Watched*. After they had sung, he invited them all into the front hall, offered them drinks, and to the fury of Wilma and Mother casually tossed a £10 note into their collection. (Father had always had something of a penchant for extravagance: of all vices, he thought of meanness as the very worst, and behaved accordingly. As a young man he insisted, my uncle Ernest told me, on smoking highly-priced Churchills, when his own father was quite satisfied with Passing Clouds. He tipped barbers and waiters and garage attendants lavishly. So now, at Studley, his vicarious position as lord of the manor played into this long-time habit, and it came triumphantly into its own. Of course the business suffered as a result. No corners were to be cut, no trifling economies could even be considered. When he decided to buy Jenny a pony, and the sweet and portly little animal was led up to the Priory door by a local farmhand, Dad asked him what he wanted for it. "Foive poun' " said the villager. "Oh, that's not nearly enough!" responded my father: "I'll give you ten." This was a charming and generous trait, but no way to run a railroad, let alone a hotel.)

Father certainly knew how to give his guests a good time, especially in the early years when energy and optimism were high and there was room even to be playful. As that first Studley

Christmas approached he casually mentioned to the slowly-assembling guests how there was an old superstition that at midnight on Christmas Eve the ghost of one of the nuns of the old Priory used to walk abroad in the garden: there was some story of her having died in the grounds, in mysterious circumstances. After a superb Christmas Eve dinner, followed by games and carols, and presents for each guest under the ten-foot high tree in the drawing-room, Dad looked at his watch and announced that midnight was approaching: "It's probably all nonsense, but why don't we just have a look and see if there's anything out there?" A frisson of nervous excitement ran through the more credulous guests as he drew the curtains, pulled back the tall shutters, opened the window, and looked out. He drew in his breath and stepped back. "Goodness gracious! — She's there! Come and look — quick." The guests crowded to the window. There, walking slowly across the lawn, heavily veiled and in a long white habit, was the nun. A ghostly glow lit up her chalk-white face, and a strange blue light shone around her. Slowly and sadly she walked past, and on into the darkness. The guests were immediately buzzing with chatter. Many of them were doubtful, but some were genuinely moved, and even weeping a little for the poor creature they had just seen.

We children of course were in on the trick. Mother and Wilma had dressed up our tall cook Meg in a veil and habit, and Meg it was who walked forlornly over the lawn, holding a bicycle torch in the folds of her sleeves so that it shone up on her face, which was deathly white from a lavish application of flour. Wilma crouched below the open window following Meg's figure with another torch, a piece of thin blue paper taped across it to give the final supernatural touch.

Dad confessed the next day. The gullible ones were no doubt genuinely disappointed, and perhaps even annoyed at being made fools of. Mrs Highet was tempted not to believe him. The Judge was not amused. But for all of them it was part of a Christmas to remember.

For us children the high point of that Christmas Day came not with emptying our stockings or unwrapping our presents, exciting as those moments were; but after tea, when darkness had fallen. The double doors into the drawing-room were closed behind my father and mother and Wilma for half an hour or so, while we, guests and family, waited outside in the lounge. Finally the doors opened again and we were invited in to the long, darkened room.

No one brought up on electric Christmas tree lighting will ever quite be able to appreciate the magic of a huge tree lit entirely by candles. The minutely-shifting points of flame, the little worlds of decoration lit by each, the smell of burning wax, and the miraculous glow of all the candles together basking the whole high room in a glimmering light, took the breath away. There was more magic too in the briefness of the moment. As Dad stood by with fire bucket and extinguisher at the ready, we watched for perhaps three or four minutes, as the candles in their holders burned down too swiftly to their sockets. Then with a sigh the step ladder was brought out, and the candles doused one by one. The lights were switched back on. And the spell was broken.

Another few days, and it was New Year's Eve. Thirty or forty couples came to celebrate at the Studley ball. A band had been engaged, and played many of the same dance tunes we had cranked out of the gramophone during the staff party the previous week: *Smoke Gets In Your Eyes*, *The Way You Look Tonight*, *Some Day I'll Find You* – along with the new hit from *South Pacific*, *Some Enchanted Evening*. My diminutive Titian-haired Mother was gorgeous in green velvet, and Father had the air of a Ruritanian count in his white tie and tails. We danced an eightsome or two, I struggling along with the help of sister Jo. And at midnight we joined hands for *Auld Lang Syne*. It was a boisterous end to a happy holiday season.

1947 was over. It had been a tumultuous year, setting us down, after so long in the wilderness, in a new and splendid home. The three proprietors of Studley Priory Country House Hotel – they called themselves 'the Props' – had shown that they had all the charm, the energy and the imagination they needed to create a happy atmosphere for their customers and guests. They had somehow managed to make the place a home for everyone who fell under their spell, to the point that lapses were overlooked, and imperfections forgiven. It was a place where the Duke of Grafton was able to wander down to the scullery to ask where he could clean his boots; where Oxford professors would bring their tea-things out to the pantry; where service was sometimes erratic but always cheerful.

Somehow, in spite of the load of work, Father was also able to pursue his love of birds and of natural history in general. He went on countless 'birdie walks', often taking a reluctant son or elder daughter with him, but usually accompanied eagerly by his youngest, Jenny, whose knowledge of birds was so great that at the age of five she was able to recognise every picture from *British Birds*. "That's a Dartford Warbler," she would say airily, to the astonishment of the guests. And some of the guests too became wrapped up in his passion, going with him through the woods and learning the song of the blackbird, the call of the yellowhammer. Only a year or two ago I heard from the daughter of Arthur Harrison that she owed her lifelong interest in birds to a walk at Studley with my father when she was ten.

He spent many hours carefully mapping out the exact boundaries of robin territories in the Studley gardens. One time he acquired a baby barn owl from a deserted nest, bringing him up in a large cage in the outbuildings: he often walked through the garden – and sometimes even through the house – with Henry perched on his shoulder. He even installed on the floor of the cage a pit lined with zinc sheeting, in which he would deliver mice – caught live – for the owl to learn to hunt before he was released back into the wild. Once he brought up two fox cubs (later released), and for a year or two he bred up and more or less tamed a pet badger, which would walk behind him through the lounge on a leash.

For my mother too, those early days at Studley gave her opportunities to display her extraordinary creative gifts. She shared many of the duties of cooking for the hotel. But she had time too for other things. Her treadle Singer sewing machine, bought back in Australia soon after she was married (and paid for in instalments, she told us: she would sometimes hide when she saw the man coming for his weekly one and sixpence and she had no money to give him), was set to work – in 'Park' – making clothes for my sisters and herself, and chair-covers and curtains for the hotel rooms, and turning sheets and pillow-cases. She learned how to make lampshades for all those bedside tables. She iced magnificent wedding cakes. She knitted fast and furiously when the guests were gone to bed. And every day in season, from the vast trugful of flowers which Sidney brought in from the garden, she would make the most striking and beautiful flower arrangements to decorate hall and dining-room and lounge. Every guest found a vase – or a jam-jar – full of flowers in their room on arrival.

And Wilma? Her demonic and generous energy was utterly taken up with the endless demands of this seigneurial but also business establishment: bringing up 'EMT' (early morning tea) to every guest who ordered it; working in the garden, milking the cows, typing business letters, managing payroll; often waiting at table, and always sharing in the endless chore of washing up the huge piles of dishes left after serving meals, sometimes to twenty or thirty customers.

I think it's fair to say that in that first year of their great life venture, 'the Props' were happy, optimistic and fulfilled, and always buoyed up by their sense of humour, taking enormous delight in the strange things said and done by staff and guests alike. Out of these sayings and doings there emerged over the years their inexhaustible fund of anecdotes, a kind of family mythology, sustaining them for the rest of their lives and passed on to their children.

For those children the arrival of Studley in our lives was a somewhat different story. We were learning that we had to amuse ourselves for many long hours without the help and support of our parents: our home was no longer just a family matter.

But there were many compensations. Life in the hotel was rich and varied. We learned to deal well with people, often having to greet guests at the door when no one else was about, to help with their luggage, to make conversation, or to answer their sometimes impatient questions. There were frequent visits to Oxford. There was swimming and punting on the Cherwell. There were bicycle rides around the ancient villages of Otmoor. There were occasional picnics. And there were our own rooms to come back to always.

In these private spaces, we could be alone. We could write our secret thoughts. We could cry at imagined hurts, at flashes of loneliness and fear. We could look at ourselves in the mirror, asking ourselves what this mysterious being in front of us was and would be. And we would begin to fashion, slowly and often painfully, our own ever more complicated lives.

CHAPTER FOUR

RIPER YEARS

Imagine, on one of the first sunny days of June 1949, two coaches full of small and chattering middle-class boys in grey shorts, V-necked jerseys and maroon caps and ties, trundling out of Kent, across Sussex and into Surrey, arriving mid-morning on Epsom Downs. It is Derby Day, and Arthur has decided, with God knows what in his mind, that the whole school should be there. As we clamber out of the coach we are handed a packed lunch, and told to be back without fail by four. We are on our own, but told to stick together in small bunches.

We look around. The racecourse and its surrounds are filled with people from all walks of British life, from gents in their toppers and ladies in their summer hats to touts, hawkers and gipsies, and everyone in between. Bookies shout the odds from their booths, including Prince Monolulu in head-dress and warpaint with his cry of 'I Gotta Horse!' Stalls are lined up under their huge black umbrellas with the words WHELKS and JELLIED EELS in big white letters, attracting a Cockney crowd but failing to entice us. Families are setting up their picnics, from fish and chips at one end of the culinary scale to cold pheasant, plovers' eggs and champagne at the other. Magnificent thoroughbreds, and jockeys in satin: green blue, scarlet. Horse-boxes by the score. Cars in the car park: everything from Rolls-Royces, Daimlers, Alvises and Bentleys to MGs, Rovers, Humbers, Sunbeam Talbots, Morgans and Austins (most of us boys could identify every one of these makes and models on sight). The TOTE advertises its betting with a green sign on the far side, hoisted high on a frame of scaffolding. A huge crowd is gathered along the race-course, and we little fish paddle our way through them to reach the fence. We watch some of the early races, before squeezing back out again to eat our corned beef sandwiches – still giving the whelks and jellied eels a wide berth. I stick with my friend John Le Mare, who knows his way around a race-course – his father is a betting man. Under his guidance we run to the Tote and he puts a shilling on a horse. Then we dart back through again and suck in the excitement as the big race draws near, and the noise of the crowd swells. Across, in the royal box, we are able to make out King George the Sixth, with Queen Elizabeth beside him, and, just behind them, the unmistakeable grey-blue toque of old Queen Mary.

It is the first time most of us have been in a huge mass of adults, to experience the noise, the bursting cries, the smells, the madness of hope and fear, the jumping and elbowing and cheers and groans.

Who won? I have no idea. But we had shared in a small piece of history. And – think of it! – we boys had been left among this crowd of many thousands to fend entirely for ourselves. It is astonishing to realize how deeply trusting this old society was, and the swashbuckling courage of our headmaster.

After so many comings and goings by my family, 1948 and the years following had brought this young ship at last into calm waters. I ferried more or less happily between the two ports of home and school, as winter turned through spring to summer and summer through autumn to winter. The changes were marked at school by shifting from football to rugby to cricket; by moving from the chill world of mud and snow and strange cleated boots and sitting on radiators to the soft winds and blue skies and rose gardens and swimming of our delicious summer terms: the vast old lime trees along the walk to the Dell were so brimming with leaves and scent and the murmuring of innumerable bees that Arthur Harrison sent us down there in the middle of an English class specifically to see and hear them and to breathe them in. On a recent visit I walked that way again. They were gone.

But along with the cycle of the seasons came also the forward movement of growing up, as my contemporaries and I edged term by term from classroom to classroom, from the lowly Sixth and then Fifth and then Fourth forms out in the annexe, to the stately rooms in the old Georgian building: the Third – with its French windows looking out beyond the roses to the playing fields; the Second, which housed the school library and also displayed the school scholarship boards, recording the academic honours won by boys of the school over the years. There was also – ambling around two of its walls – a two-foot high, ten-foot long, illustrated timeline of English history, heavily emphasising kings and queens and battles long ago, varnished to look like parchment and put together no doubt by masters and schoolboys before the war. And so finally to the First Form in the Gallery, with its long central tables and its bay window with bookshelves and window seat. Here sat the elect, the senior boys. It was not only their classroom but the meeting-place of the school – as I have already described. It was also the setting for live concerts. It was here that we listened to Geoff Martin's music on Saturday nights, piped in from his room above the kitchens. It was here in the last week of each term we were treated to documentary films (I remember seeing the rolling wheatfields of the prairies in one National Film Board of Canada short) and also comedies of the day: Alastair Sim and Margaret Rutherford in *The Happiest Days of Your Life*, Will Hay in *Oh Mr Porter*, Bud Flanagan in *Alf's Button Afloat*. On Sunday evenings after supper in the winter, it was here that the whole school sat, younger boys cross-legged on the floor, to be read to by Arthur from his table at the top end. And it was outside its French windows that the brass school bell hung on its bracket – a gift from a naval old boy, salvaged I think from a first world war Royal Navy vessel, and rung to signal the beginnings and ends of school periods. We enjoyed the job of ringing it.

In one nook of the Gallery, there were even some easy chairs, where as older boys we could sit and read our books. The many adventures of Biggles and his pals Ginger and Algy were high on my list. So were the books beginning to come out of the war just lately over and giving us the excitements of escape from German prison camps; *The Wooden Horse,* and later *Stolen Journey*. I also remember battling with an old, small-print edition of *The Count of Monte Cristo*. Then there were, God help us, our comics: *The Champion* with its tales of Rockfist Rogan; *The Beano* and *The Dandy* (starring Desperate Dan) and *Comic Cuts*, with later on the much glossier and bigger and more sophisticated 'Christian' new addition, *The Eagle*. Many boys had these sent to them, and shared them around, and I suspect that Arthur viewed them with a certain amount of contempt. I cannot remember now if the senior boys grew out of them or not. I think not.

We were getting bigger and stronger too: moving from the Midget teams into the third and second cricket or football elevens or the rugger twelves, and eventually if talented enough becoming one of the school's top representatives, playing in the first team against the familiar roster of local prep schools. Cricket and football found me moseying along in the rear. But in rugby I was discovered to have a talent for bringing big people down in spectacular tackles. This, coupled with my lack of speediness, put me squarely at full back in every rugger team I graced. My clearing kicks – a necessary skill in that position – were, I'm afraid, no more than passable.

Boxing we had to learn something of too in the winter, coached by the rasping and mock-scornful Tommer. I disliked it a lot, and did as little of it as possible. Cross-country running was also led by Tommer, who ran with us: I once found him on my heels in the last stretch into the school, and gave my every remaining ounce to keep him behind me over those final few yards. I still remember being oddly happy to overhear his comment to another master in the changing-room: "That Bawtree's an atrocious runner, but he's got guts." But guts or no guts, I was not for running either. I preferred PT, run by ex-marine Meyrick Browne, who led us through all the statutory stretching and bending, as well as vaulting the horse, shinning up parallel bars and learning to climb a rope. For all these delights we wore strange bright pink and flimsy shorts. Why pink?

Mr Browne's carpentry lessons, though, were a high point of the week, when we were able to crowd our class into the long, thin creosoted shed which served as a shop, with its long thin bench and its lines and lines of woodworking tools, all perfectly sharpened and oiled and calibrated. We made boxes to begin with, learning to chisel out dovetail joints for the corners, learning how to work along and across the grain. We learned the properties of the different fine woods. We learned the traditional methods of French polishing, with endless sandpapering and buffing, applying Condy's crystals to stain the wood a brilliant reddish brown, and then shellacking over and over till we could see our faces in the box-tops. We then graduated to more ambitious projects. I completed a half-decent table lamp, which still does service for my sister in France over half a century later.

The shop was something of a refuge from the rest of the school, and only much later did I realize that this was because of the entirely different skills we had to call on: hand-eye co-ordination, the feel and touch of both wood and tool, the precision of measurement, the multiple fine judgements, the smell of machine oil. Perhaps because of this I had a recurring dream of making the perfect box. It was work but it was play; and the discipline was demanded by the work and the material – not imposed on our behaviour by a hectoring authority. The 'carp shop' was in fact a kind of liberty hall: we could go there in our free time and continue working on our projects. And it was perhaps in this spirit that when we were not under the sharp eye of Meyrick Browne we would creep over to the lathe, and out of dowelling and a chunk of hardwood we would fashion pipes, which we would then stuff with wood shavings and smoke, sitting on stools and crates in the undergrowth outside the far doors of the shop, chatting away, and looking for all the world like a set of old gaffers outside a pub. We were never caught.

Once or twice in the summer term, a group of boys would be taken off to camp for a weekend at a Sussex farm, under the supervision of Meyrick Browne, or later of John Laing (who joined the staff in the late forties, and brought a piratical spirit to everything he did). With their guidance we learned how to pitch tents, how to dig a latrine, how to set a camp fire and even how to fry eggs over it. We took a .22 rifle with us, and were taught basic safety precautions before setting off to bag a rabbit or two – which we learned how to gut and skin before dropping them into the stew-pot. Sitting round the fire and singing songs as the summer sun went down was another of those happy Marlborough House memories. We arrived back on Sunday evenings, weather-burnt and all our clothes smelling honourably of smoke.

Perhaps, though, and strangely enough, I was happiest of all in the classroom, where my lucky quick and easy skills continued to serve me well, and brought me the approval I still seemed to crave. At some point it was recognised that I was 'one of the brainy ones'. I was competent in maths, algebra and geometry, and could write reasonable English — for brief essays in geography and history as well. I wrote predictable but correct poems, rhyme schemes and all. And French and Latin grammar both came easily to me, though I was often found guilty of the unpardonable sin of 'carelessness'. For all these 'subjects' — as we called them in those days — the sheer good fortune of having a retentive memory was what made everything so much easier for me; easier than for those equally bright lads who simply couldn't hold on to any nugget of information from one day to the next without having it repeatedly dinned into them.

A small group of us began to stand out a little from the others: John Le Mare from Essex, nicknamed Llama, who was by far the raciest of us all, expert in card games (especially pontoon) and never without his form book, which he used for placing imaginary bets on each day's races — checking the results eagerly in the *Evening Standard*; Gary Williams, stubborn and wry, and a hefty member of our rugger scrum, who lived up the road in Cranbrook — his father was something in the Sudan; and Brian Knox-Peebles, who had joined the school late in 1946 with his elder brother Patrick, straight from war years spent with their mother in South Africa: their father was by then a senior army officer in BAOR — the British Army of the Rhine. These two brothers arrived with strong colonial accents, which we had never heard before and were intrigued by. In their first months they talked disparagingly, I remember, about 'the kaffirs'. They were nut brown, having lived a wild and carefree life in shorts and bare feet for years, and they took time to adjust to the rigid ways of an English boarding school. We admired their lack of respect for rules, and wished we were like them. But we were not. And in the end they in fact became more and more like us. They were also brainy. Brian was a year older than I, but his late arrival put us in the same class, and term after term he and I found ourselves competing in the exam class lists, which combined the marks for all subjects. Sometimes he came first, and sometimes I did; and in his last term, with a certain amount of diplomatic juggling by Arthur I suspect, we were pronounced equal first with 715 marks apiece.

I was also growing into music, becoming a better and better pianist, as well as being eventually main soloist of the choir and able to sing most music at sight. I remember Miss Sheaves telling me after one of my piano lessons of her surprise that I knew how to 'produce' my good soprano voice, and that she had not taught it to me. Something about native talent… When Mr Martin's ragged little orchestra decided to get up the first movement of the Toy Symphony, neither my piano nor my voice was of any use. But rather than being relegated to playing the cuckoo, I was hauled into the gym, handed a baton, stood on a podium with the music in front of me, and told to conduct. I was no budding Beecham. But the feeling of those moments has stayed with me. Power? Maybe. The sense of being in the middle of a piece of music – surrounded by it? Maybe. Pleasure in their trust in me, however misplaced? Certainly.

From popular music, by the way, we were almost totally insulated, encouraged to treat even our parents' favourite songs of the 'twenties, 'thirties and 'forties with little less than scorn. I can remember Geoff Martin telling us how sad it was that with his really beautiful voice Bing Crosby had chosen to debase himself by becoming a crooner. It was a time, remember, when 'popular music' meant above all music for adults to dance to, and recordings were designed for our elders to flaunt their waltz steps, their slow foxtrots, their quicksteps, their valetas, with the occasional Latin tangos and rumbas and sambas. It was also music to romance to, which was not something of interest to us boys at all. Songs from the new American musicals – *Oklahoma!, Annie Get Your Gun* – were also catching on with our elders, but again, for the most part, translated into dance music. Folk songs for us meant not Pete Seeger but *On Ilkley Moor Baht 'At* or *Old MacDonald Had A Farm*. Jazz for us was an entirely foreign taste, unknown both to us and I think to most of our teachers. And the whole world of commercial music which arrived on the scene with skiffle groups in the 'fifties, and which blew the world apart with the Beatles in the 'sixties, was far in the future. Not one of us played a guitar or ukulele. Gilbert and Sullivan was for Marlborough House the outside edge of light musical taste.

All this school activity – music, classes, woodworking, games, camping – might seem to be going on for ever, except that there was ahead of us all the Big Test: whether, when the time came – somewhere between the ages of twelve and thirteen and a half – we were going to be able to pass Common Entrance, and so be accepted into the public schools of our first choice – or close to it. For us 'brainy ones', an even more arduous course was being planned: we were expected to set our sights on winning a scholarship. In my case, certainly, a scholarship was going to be a prerequisite: there was no way that my parents could afford to send me to any fee-demanding school unless I was more or less totally subsidised.

I can't pinpoint the moment that this course was starting to be laid out for me, but the charting of it was evidently taken on as part of the job by our headmaster and his colleagues. My parents had established their wish that I be an Etonian, which would be something of a rarity among the boys of our school. Arthur would probably have preferred a socially less pretentious goal – like his own *alma mater* Wellington; but he went along with my parents' – my mother's – whimsy. I even faintly recall him, one evening in the dormitory, musing about universities to follow – a huge leap into our futures. We must have been no more than ten or eleven when he suggested, not only to me but also to my friends John Le Mare and Gary Williams (who both went on to Wellington!) that Oxford should be our university, and that Worcester might well be a suitable college. So early did we find ourselves being nudged along the highroad of our adult lives.

We also happened to be one of the last generations for whom the usual educational study programme for 'the brainy ones' was the Classics, with a classical scholarship the immediate goal and 'Mods and Greats', the classical degree programme at Oxford, on the further horizon. This meant, first, a much more intense study of Latin, in which we must learn not only to build our vocabulary and dash off the principal parts of irregular verbs, but to translate 'unseens' from Caesar and Virgil and Ovid. It also involved learning not just to read but to compose Latin verses. So we were introduced to the mysteries of constructing Latin poetry: a poetry of 'quantity' rather than stress, in which every syllable was 'long' or 'short', and every line made up of a precise number of feet or syllables. In this apparently pointless exercise, which we approached somewhat in the spirit of a crossword puzzle, we were expected to consult our bulky green-bound *Gradus ad Parnassum* ('Steps to Parnassus') and to keep it with us even in exams. The *Gradus* gave us the precise quantities of most Latin words we would come across, as well as their synonyms and antonyms; and it listed adjectives grouped according to metre and declension. With its help we were eventually able to turn simple lines of English verse into stumbling Latin hexameters and pentameters, or occasionally even into Horace's more subtle verse forms: sapphics, or alcaics. Our brains buzzed with the various metrical shapes: iams and spondees and troches and dactyls.

Training for the classics also meant that we would need to have at least some familiarity with ancient Greek. This was not a subject generally taught at Marlborough House, but one summer Le Mare, Williams and I (not Knox-Peebles mi., who was considered too much of a late arrival to be included) were told that the following year Mr Martin would be giving us special coaching in Greek. From then on until the end of our time at the school, we would repair two or three times a week to Geoff Martin's cramped rooms, sit at his small round table by the window looking out on to Big Pond and the Dell, and launch ourselves under his mostly genial direction into a new alphabet, a new vocabulary, a new grammar, a new sensibility. I don't remember any of us ever questioning the classical direction we were being expected to follow.

Since all scholarship exams covered the normal range of subjects, we continued polishing our skills in French, history, geography and maths, and Arthur's English classes took on a new intensity, with essays to write, a précis or two to practise, and poems to compose. Early on, too, he had introduced us to Shakespeare, with recitations in class, and sessions in his drawing-room listening to BBC drama productions. (In case our cultural education seems unrelieved, it should also be remembered that we were allowed to sit in our pyjamas and listen once a week to the radio comedy programme *ITMA*, and later to *Much Binding In The Marsh*.) A group of us were once taken to Cranbrook, five or six miles away, where I saw my first live Shakespeare play: it was *Twelfth Night,* performed no doubt amateurishly by a group of local players in a back garden, but full enough of poetry and costumes and lights to entrance our young minds.

Having taken us scholarship boys under his wing, Arthur also drove us – twice – in his open green Rover all the way to Haileybury in Hertfordshire – the school where he had taught as a young man – for their annual Shakespeare production. The first time we were bedded down in a school dormitory because their term was over. But on our return visit the following year we were put up in a small hotel in the village, where we were served haddock for breakfast by an aged waiter in black tie and tails. I seem to remember this more clearly than the productions, but I think these were *The Merchant of Venice* one year and *Hamlet* the next. With this mixture of classwork, learning how to make rhythmic sense of Shakespeare's five-beat line and reading scenes from his plays, as well as exposure to live performances, I began to develop some confidence in my own speaking voice, and I suppose some facility with acting. There were no prizes given out at Marlborough House, but occasionally we would be rewarded for good work, and I still have and treasure a now heavily-worn copy of the Odham Press edition of Shakespeare's collected works, presented to me by Arthur and inscribed in his characteristic rounded hand:

Michael Bawtree
Marlborough House
18. xii. 1949.

Our own theatrical efforts didn't take us as far as Shakespeare, but we did put on some one-act plays in the gym, from which I only remember playing the ghost in W.W. Jacobs' *The Ghost of Jerry Bundler.*

Meanwhile, the work in class for us scholarship candidates was taking on a new urgency. The schools scheduled their scholarship exams at different times in the year. Eton held theirs in June, and it was decided that though young I should travel to Windsor to sit the exam in 1950 as a try-out, with the chance to sit it again in 1951.

It was natural that Arthur would approach his friend Wilfrid Blunt to put me up during the Eton exam period. I think my mother must have met me off the London train and accompanied me to Windsor, because I remember arriving with her at Baldwin's Shore, a fine old house shared by two or three bachelor Eton masters, including Blunt. To our delight, one of these, with the exotic name of Anthony Caesar, was an acquaintance: his father (a canon at St. George's Chapel in Windsor) and mother had stayed at Studley Priory as guests in the first years. Anthony gave us tea in the kitchen before Mother left for the station, and stayed comfortingly with me, lonely and nervous as I was, until I went early to bed. Neither of us knew then that our paths would before long cross again.

I remember almost nothing of the examinations themselves, other than catching sight of Eton boys dressed rather like our Haileybury waiter as I walked through the town to the ancient hall where the other candidates and I sat at our desks and agonised for a couple of days. I suspect that my rather shaky hold on Greek, and perhaps my 'carelessness' in Latin, didn't advance my cause in suing for a classical scholarship. Even if I wasn't entirely hopeless, I expect they felt that another year of study might set me up. In any case, I was awarded entrance to the school, nothing more, and returned to Marlborough House battle-scarred but not entirely without honour.

During these last years in our little Kentish world, my parents continued to battle away at their brave enterprise in distant Oxfordshire. And at the end of each term – '*God Be With You Till We Meet Again*', 'Remember now thy Creator in the days of thy youth... ' – I would take the now familiar train up to London (through Orpington I remember, because I was always on the look-out for Red Orpington hens as we chuffed by) and so back to Studley Priory: four weeks at Christmas and Easter, and eight weeks in the summer.

These were still early years for the hotel, and the optimism of 'the Props' helped them to survive one obstacle after the other: the prime difficulty being the obstinate refusal of enough money to come their way. The Priory, after all, was seven miles out in the countryside, at a time when petrol was only just being freed from rationing, and when cars were only beginning to appear on the roads. A bus went to and from Oxford to Studley only twice a week, on Wednesdays and Saturdays. Another clear sign of our rural seclusion was our archaic telephone number: Stanton St. John 3. When we wished to make a call we would lift the receiver and wait for the operator, Lily, whose voice we all knew well. (My mother once asked for the number she wanted: "Stanton St. John 6, please," – to have Lily respond at once: "If you want the Vicar, I've just seen him driving past on the London Road.")

In spite of the difficulties, we had to have a cook, and early in 1949, on Meg's departure, we advertised (in *The Lady*) for a replacement. A young woman, not much older than nineteen, with blonde, bobbed hair and a slim figure, answered the call, taking the train down from her home in smoky Sheffield to be interviewed. Studley was an astonishing new world for her, but she was immediately hired, and Joyce Belk soon showed her skills in the kitchen, her pleasure in hard and unremitting work, and her dry

Yorkshire wit. Somehow she acquired the nickname of Chookie. She was with us for five or six years, maybe more, and to all of us, like her predecessor, became a lifelong friend.

Summers were busy and generally thriving at Studley, with many families coming to spend a week or two in the country – before the Costa Brava was any kind of alternative. Winters on the other hand – when costs of heating the huge pile were continuous whether guests filled the place or not, and the payroll stayed stubbornly high – could be desperate, especially in bitter weather.

A high point of the summer's busyness was reached in late June towards the end of the Oxford summer term, during the season of Oxford's 'Commemoration Balls'. These extravaganzas were mounted by three or four colleges a year, and it was the custom for groups of six or eight couples to go out for dinner beforehand. Studley, with its generous meals, attractive prices and beautiful setting, became a favourite venue for these undergraduate forays, and its popularity eventually led to the advertising and selling out of two sittings, at 6.30 and 8.30, during 'Commem Week'. It was during one of these frantic evenings, with dishes being re-laid hot as fast as they could be washed and dried – all by hand of course – that my father famously came out to the kitchen to be greeted by Mother and Wilma complaining that it was all too much and that they must never do this again, and my father saying "Heavens, what are you talking about? We're just getting into our stride!" From then on, it was always known as 'Stride Week.'

One year, towards the end of the second sitting, my mother realised that they were running short of strawberries, and since the cooking was over, and Wilma and everyone else were at their last gasp serving the braying crowd in the dining-room, she thought she would 'nip out' to the vegetable garden in the failing light to grab a few more berries. The strawberry beds were protected from the birds by swathes of black netting, and Mother had to pull this up at the edge to get under it and at the crop. While she was crawling on her hands and knees with a bowl and hurriedly groping for the berries, her blouse rode up almost to her neck, and somehow the netting got tangled in the catch of her bra. The more she tried to free herself the more she became enmeshed. She was becoming desperate when by chance Sidney the gardener came plodding by on his evening watering schedule. She cried out to him for help, and soon the dear man – with considerable embarrassment – was crawling in under the net alongside her. After some fruitless attempts to disengage her, she had to suggest that the only way was for Sidney to undo her bra. Scarlet-faced and fumbling in the twilight, he began to do just that; and it was at that same moment that Wilma dashed into the garden calling out 'Tess! Tess! Where the hell are you? They're all waiting for their sweet?' – only to discover her half-naked among the strawberries with Sid. It took her – and Sid – a long time to live that down.

It was late July before our summer terms ended, so that my sister Jo and I arrived home well after Stride Week was past. But August was still a busy month, and 'Teas in the Garden' were a popular draw, with home-made scones and jam, sandwiches and cakes, for the trifling sum of four shillings and sixpence. The operation was heavily – crazily – labour intensive. My father would set up deck-chairs and coffee-tables around the lawns or in the lavender garden, and Mother or Wilma or Chookie would bring out the tea-things – cakes and scones and sandwiches all prepared in the kitchen. When bills had been paid and the guests had gone there would be the trays to be gathered back in, and the tables and chairs to be re-stowed. Then there was the washing-up. And when that was over it was time for Mother and Joyce to start preparing the dinner.

Somehow in between all this to-do there was a chance for the family to collect at our round table in the dining-room, to eat our cakes and scones together, and to *be* a family. It was a chance too for the three of us children to spend time with one another. By now Jenny had started attending Headington School as a day-girl, my father taking her in every day in the fine-looking but unreliable old second-hand Daimler we had acquired after our Lanchester bit the dust. Since Jo and I were already at school long before Jenny could walk and talk, we barely knew her. For our father, she as the youngest of us could do little wrong.

Jen had in fact been brought up almost as an only child, and with our parents' endless labour around the hotel she had long ago learnt to be self-sufficient, sitting in the guests' lounge oblivious of the activity around her, reading, or writing stories. In her struggle to be heard and cared about, she had become bad-tempered and selfish in the view of her siblings, and it was hard for us at that stage to build much of a friendship with her. Our love came later, but she was – as she has remained – very direct, a little remote, a loner, and almost totally unironic. Meanwhile, Jo and I, in spite of frequent tiffs and even fights, were much more of a team. It was through Jo that I began to read some very different books from the war yarns popular at school. We had long ago grown out of Enid Blyton, leaving her rather scornfully to our young sister. But the books of Violet Needham became more and more of a delight for me, especially *The Black Riders*: its young hero Dick, 'The Stormy Petrel', served as a model, with his intelligence in taking on adult responsibilities, his courage and fortitude, and the respect and admiration he drew from his elders. Dick's adventures continued in a whole series of books, including *The Emerald Crown, The House of the Paladin* and *The Stormy Petrel*. I gobbled them up greedily, one after the other.

Both our parents recognised that it was difficult for us to sustain a family life, and were insistent that somehow, in spite of financial pressures and hard labour at Studley, we simply must take off together, however briefly, for a family holiday. During our first summer in the hotel this was quite impossible. But late August of 1948 found Wilma driving all five of us down to Folly Bridge in Oxford, to take possession of a diminutive Salter Brothers motor cruiser, *The Pathfinder*. We were to spend a week on the Thames!

Father enjoyed his role as skipper, in white cricketing trousers and open white shirt, and he navigated the ropey little craft expertly through lock after lock as we made our way downstream. At dusk we would tie up along the towpath for the night, and Mother — poor Mother! — would be back in her role as cook and bottlewasher, slaving over a Calor gas stove in the diminutive galley, and serving us much more delicious meals than we had a right to expect. The *Pathfinder*'s engine was a sickly affair even when we started, and she broke down completely in a day or two. The men that came from Oxford to repair it told us she had been one of the fleet of small craft which had crossed over to Dunkirk in 1940, bringing back a few soldiers from the British Expeditionary Force. So perhaps her fatigue was not surprising.

Along the river we passed and admired all kinds of more elegant craft, and it was clear that my father, who never liked the feeling of being at the lower end of the social scale, decided that *Pathfinder* was not the superior vessel that his sense of style entitled him to. He was amused — but perhaps not entirely amused — to be using a public lavatory at a park outside Reading, and to be approached by a small boy asking for change for the penny-in-the-slot toilets: the boy thought he was the lavatory attendant. So the next August we would move up a big notch when once again we went down river.

Our home this time was to be the much pricier *Grayfinch* out of Virginia Water, a newly-built motor launch painted sky blue, with a swept-back windshield, chrome fittings, and the most graceful lines you could imagine. Her far greater speed enabled us to cover much longer distances. We visited friends – well, not exactly friends but former Studley guests – as far away as Windsor and Richmond. And the next day we had passed through Teddington Lock and were bowling towards the Pool of London, my father's greying hair streaming in the wind as he manned the wheel, heading – who knows? – towards a quick lunch at the Regent Palace and then maybe on towards the Channel, when suddenly a Thames Conservancy launch darted out terrier-like from the shore towards us, and told us fiercely that our boat's permit did not allow us to go further than Teddington. We were accompanied back to the lock, tail between our legs, and headed firmly upriver again.

By the following August the family felt we had 'done' the softly-running Thames, and we changed our conveyance, renting a caravan and touring the coasts of Devon and Cornwall. At Marazion, by St. Michael's Mount, Dad persuaded a fisherman to take him with Jenny and me out into the bay for an hour, to spin for mackerel. By chance more than skill, I think, our skipper led us into a huge shoal, and in the one hour for which we had paid we caught forty-two mackerel. We gave away sixteen of them and took the rest back to the caravan, where Mother gamely turned a few of them into supper. They appeared again for lunch the next day. But even Father's enthusiasm for fried mackerel eventually palled, and we finished up burying the rest in a field of cabbages.

My father served as the one skipper and chauffeur on all these family expeditions, since he had long ago in Devon decided that my mother was not capable of driving a car, let alone a boat. He thought her perfectly able to cook though, and I'm sure it never even occurred to Father that an ideal holiday for her would be a holiday from the kitchen. As I think now about this woman's tirelessly good spirits and humour and love and loyalty, I realize how immensely lucky we all were to have her in our lives – both as a wife and a mother.

There were other people too who had reason to be grateful to Tessa Bawtree. Soon after we arrived at Horton-cum-Studley, she was invited to join the local Women's Institute, whose hall lay across the road just outside the entrance to the Priory's drive. Somehow, along with the ceaseless labour of Studley, she found time to attend the WI meetings, to take part in their dramas, to participate in their classes – in jam-making, flower arrangement, wedding cake decoration and all the other crafts which were made available to the women of the village. She also entered their competitions, which – being exceptionally competent – she very often won.

An awkward moment took place at the 'Baked Apple' competition, an annual affair, judged by a visiting expert from Oxford, and won from time immemorial by Mrs Green, a doughty farmer's wife from down Church Lane. This year, though, Mother's offering was pronounced the winner. During the tea and sandwiches which followed, Mother was powerfully ignored by Mrs G., but was close enough to see her pinning the visiting expert against the table and asking her icily: "And exactly *how* do you judge a baked apple?" The question entered our family mythology.

It was not long before another nose was put out of joint. The position of president of the WI had been held almost as a matter of right by Mrs Henderson, as wife of the village's squirearch. But Mother was persuaded to put her name in at the next elections, and had already sufficiently impressed her energy, imagination and sheer kindness on the membership to win handily. Charlotte Henderson was not amused, but there was no doubt that the ladies of Horton-cum-Studley had made the right decision. Mother threw herself into the affairs of the branch, ran membership drives, organized outings, gave cooking lessons, arranged talks (Father gave them a talk on the behaviour of robins in the gardens of the Priory, and once came as a bogus lady lecturer in women's clothes), put together and acted in short plays and sketches, sewed curtains, re-painted the kitchens, and so on, and so on. One of our favourite pictures of Tessa was taken outside Studley's porch, with her modelling a dress as her entry for a sack dress competition. She wears a huge broad-brimmed picture hat, flourishes a long cigarette holder – and shows off an elegant dress made of jute potato sacks from the gardeners' shed. No doubt she won that one too.

The good women of Horton-cum-Studley can still be seen in some of the group shots in our family albums: all wearing hats jammed firmly down, and shapeless dresses, and splaying shoes, my mother the only hatless one among them. The village, after all, was still overwhelmingly rural. But there were already signs of change. Many of the menfolk had found work at Morris Motors as it swung into civilian production after the war, and if you were on the road towards Oxford in the early morning you would pass two or three dozen of them on bikes, pedalling along the straight mile, up Waterperry Hill, through Headington and into Cowley for a day on the production line, which they willingly exchanged for their fathers' and grand-fathers' and great-grandfathers' toil in the fields. Their womenfolk stayed at home and continued their rustic ways, looking after their houses and families. They were innocent and uneducated, but wonderfully open to my mother's enthusiasm – and also, strangely enough, to her total lack of 'side' when it came to working with them: full of kindness, warmth and assurance. Through her they learnt confidence in their own abilities, and took up arts and crafts they would never have contemplated without 'The Institute.'

What had become clear in fact was that Tessa was a born leader, a superb organizer of people and a tireless worker, who had had to wait too long, as an albeit willing adjunct of our father's schemes, before at last finding an outlet for her own gifts – if only as a big fish in a small pond. She went on, in fact, to be part of the Oxfordshire WI's Executive, and once even spoke at the Albert Hall, at the Annual General Meeting of the National Federation of Women's Institutes.

One other member of the family needs to be accounted for. By 1950 Jo was coming up to her sixteenth birthday. She had not been part of our family holidays since the year of the *Grayfinch*, spending her summer in exchanges with a family in Brittany, improving her French and in general introducing herself to the wider world – from which she was never really to draw back. During one of her last summers at Bedgebury Park School, I was able to borrow a bicycle from Arthur Harrison's son and ride over to Goudhurst for her speech day, where the speaker and giver-out of prizes was Victoria Sackville-West. I still remember arriving in time to hear this dumpy figure in black straw hat offering some moral guidance to the girls of Bedgebury (I have often wondered how Miss Bickersteth would have coped with the later revelations of her guest's sexual adventures). One of the prizes was to be given for the best essay on a subject of Miss Sackville-West's choosing: 'The Importance of Education'. First prize was a pair of nylon stockings, duly handed out to the winner amidst applause – and a great deal of envy among both elder girls and the mistresses, for nylon stockings in those days were a highly expensive and immensely desirable accessory. But Miss S-W went on to say that there was one essay by a younger girl which she highly commended, and for this writer she had brought a special award: a signed copy of her novel *The Edwardians*. The winner of this award was... Josephine

Bawtree. It is hard to believe that Jo was apparently pitied by her schoolfriends for not gaining the top prize and being fobbed off with a mere book.

Jo Bawtree was now a rebellious teenager, at a time when rebellion was the exception, not the rule. Her saving graces at her school were her high intelligence and superb performance in her classes, but even these graces barely saved her when early the next summer she master-minded a little piece of theatre. As exam time approached, many of the more conscientious girls had been getting up well before breakfast and going down to their classrooms to put in some extra study. This became known to the headmistress Miss Bickersteth ('the Beak'), who gave out the order that no girl was to get up until the bell rang at exactly 7.20 am, that they must take twenty minutes to wash and dress and that no girl could come down to breakfast before 7.40. So, at 7.40 sharp the next morning, all the girls in the school simultaneously left their dormitories at the top of the old mansion and clattered down the big, wide staircase in a single rush, making a tremendous din. Terrified mistresses in dressing-gowns and curlers popped out of their rooms on the lower floors, thinking the place was on fire, and saw this well-organized phalanx of their young charges sweeping past them down to the hall. Miss Bickersteth was out in the garden walking her pet corgi, but she too heard the commotion, and rushed in to find out what was happening. She insisted on calling an immediate general assembly, and asked whoever was responsible for this shocking display to come to her study.

It had been Jo's idea, and without too much concern she reported to the Beak, who at once accused her of leading a revolution. Jo assured her that it was just a practical joke in response to the new edict, but the Beak was adamant: Jo was no better than a communist agitator. She would have been expelled at once were it not for the fact that the General Certificate exams were only two or three weeks away, and that Jo, young as she was, was expected to score highly and so bring credit to the school. In the event she performed so well that she was awarded Matriculation (the requirement for university entrance) on her results, and left the school for ever, with no regrets. She would say afterwards that her biggest mistake was not giving any thought to what they would do when they arrived at the bottom of the stairs and reached their goal. In this, at least, their adventure was like many another revolution.

Jo went on almost immediately to the secretarial school in Oxford run by the redoubtable Miss Sprules. It was still a time when many bright young private schoolgirls – and their middle-class parents, including ours – assumed that university education was not really appropriate for women, and that they should become secretaries and take cooking classes, in preparation for marriage to Mr Right, who should have a trout stream in the garden, a stable of horses and a handsome private income. In the careful, hackneyed words of one of Jo's school friends: "I don't want to marry for money, but I want to love where money is" – which she promptly did. Jo, though by now very much romantically inclined, continued to be a thorn in her teachers' side: she was sent home from Miss Sprules for a week because when she made a mistake in her typing she had said "Hell!" to herself – but loud enough to be heard by the primmest of her instructors. Such was the extent of unruly behaviour by young adults in 1950.

It was in that same year that I went downstairs for breakfast one morning and came upon my father shining his shoes outside the pantry, and with a most doleful expression on his face, such as I had never seen. "Granny died last night," he said with tears in his eyes. She was younger and much healthier than Granddad, but had succumbed very suddenly and unexpectedly to an acute attack of gastro-enteritis. Mother and Father went down to Surrey for the funeral, and I heard later that in her will she had given instructions that her wrists be cut before she was put into her coffin: such was her morbid fear of being buried alive. I can't help feeling that Dad would have been less unhappy if his father had gone first. The old boy was to outlive his wife by five years, dying in 1955 at the age of 89.

September of that same year saw me trundling back to Kent for my final year at Marlborough House. I was to be working towards my second try at an Eton scholarship the following June. But Arthur Harrison had the idea that I should perhaps sit for another scholarship in the winter term, so that if I were successful I would have it to fall back on should I once again not make the grade at Eton.

There were several schools that held their scholarship exams in the early months of the year. One of them was Radley College, near Abingdon, and only four miles from Oxford. I knew of it primarily from its name on one of our dormitories. But the fact that it was so close to home made it a sensible alternative, and Arthur had no difficulty persuading my parents to approve the plan. So in late January of 1951 I made the journey back home for a night, and next day my parents drove me over to the school. For the first time I entered its rather nondescript gates, up the long drive lined with great trees, now bare of leaves, and into a sprawling cluster of redbrick Georgian, Victorian and Edwardian buildings. We eventually found that I was to be housed in Radley's one Tudor relict: 'The Cottage', home at that time of one of the masters, Cyril Lane.

Once again I remember little or nothing of the examinations, except that they took place in a room with a long, wide table next to the library, with some fifteen or twenty of us candidates scrawling away with pen and ink for a couple of days. I can recall only one moment in the whole affair. One of the questions in the English paper gave us the choice of writing an essay or composing a sonnet. I had chosen to write a sonnet, and next day a master came into the exam room and asked for me by name. He introduced himself as Mr Wrinch, took me aside, and proceeded to tell me how much he had enjoyed my poem: "*Very* remarkable in*deed*." I'm sure it was not, but during that whole stay at the school this was the only hint of any positive response to the pages and pages I had covered, along with the other tense and anxious candidates, shifting precipitately from Latin to Greek to French to History to Maths to English.

At some point during the visit we were taken for a tour of the school. As someone bound for the ancient school of Eton, I snobbishly found the whole look of Radley a little *parvenu*, with its ubiquitous redbrick and its Victorian Gothic chapel and dining-hall. This was still a time when Victorian architecture was thought of as distressingly fake, and I had no doubt picked up the prevailing taste. But the grounds were sumptuous, and there was something informal and friendly about the masters and boys we met, which I had not been expecting from a public school. My host too had been generous and kind. So I went back to Marlborough House having had on the whole a happy time.

Not as joyous though as a week or two later, on the day that Arthur Harrison with a beaming smile called me out of class and into his front office, to show me the telegram he had just received: Radley was pleased to inform us that they had awarded me a 'major scholarship' for 'all-round excellence'. Arthur gave me his telephone, and I was able to ring my parents and tell them the news. More joy and pride. Now I would be able to prepare for the Eton scholarships with the assurance that I had Radley to fall back on.

That, at least, was the plan. But over the next day or two, the more I thought about it, the more I wondered whether I really wanted to go through the same pressure and anxiety all over again. I had liked the look of Radley. I had spent over six years of my life at Marlborough House, and would have to come back for yet another term, and slave away until June, when I would have to journey up to Windsor and risk a second failure. I talked about this with Arthur, who had never much cared for the Eton option anyway, and rather to my surprise he readily agreed.

We then had a discussion with my parents over the telephone. Mother was no doubt reluctant to give up the idea of having an Etonian for a son. But the more we all looked at the situation, the more it seemed sensible to take up the generous Radley scholarship, and to forget about Eton for ever. Radley was only forty minutes' drive from Studley. After being schooled miles from home for so many years, I would now be more or less on the doorstep. For my mother, perhaps this was the deciding factor. But another trip with my parents to Radley confirmed our first impressions. Radley was a kindly, unpretentious place, where people smiled.

So it was that towards the end of April, 1951, my parents drove down to Hawkhurst, to pick me up and carry me away one final time. They were of course enormously grateful to Arthur for the personal interest he had taken in bringing me to this point, and had brought him a gift of two charming ceramic bookends, decorated with a hand-painted Oxford crest. As he turned them over he noticed that the Latin of Oxford's motto, *Deus Illuminatio Mea*, was wrongly written *Meo*. "No matter," said Arthur, "Every time I look at it I shall think of you, Micky."

There was one hitch. Reading Radley's literature we discovered that admission to the school was confined to "baptised members of the Church of England". Like my sister Jo, I had never been christened: our parents had never felt the need for it. But suddenly there was a very practical need: not indeed to save me from hell-fire, but to enable me to take up my award. Radley advised me to go about getting christened right away, and referred us to the baptism service in the Book of Common Prayer "for those of riper years". Consultation with the Vicar of Horton-cum-Studley followed, and he agreed to do the honours. But it was not to be a question of 'trotting round about five', as Jack proposes in *The Importance of Being Earnest*. I would have to study my catechism, and undergo a series of classes with the Vicar before the rite could take place. So my Easter holiday was much taken up with visits to the vicarage and the memorising of the Ten Commandments and the Creed, as I prepared to renounce the devil and all his works.

This would have been more enjoyable if Mr Bolus the Vicar had been other than he was. A tall, grey, grim man in his sixties, he had spent much of his life as a military padre in India, and was now eking out his modest pension by ministering to a country parish, which afforded him a spacious if draughty Victorian vicarage and a very sparse flock. Though well-intentioned, he was without charm or personality, and he had not the least knack for getting on with the ordinary folk of our more or less feudal village. His sermons tended to be re-runs of the homilies from his time in the Raj, with no allowance for cultural differences. One Christmas service he stood in the pulpit and intoned in his lifeless way, his face stuck in his notebook, his lips scarcely moving: "We all know the magnificent sight of the Himalayas at sunset, with the snowy peaks rosy red in the dying light..." "'Im an' 'is 'imalayas," scoffed Wardy afterwards, "Some of us 'ave never been up Brill 'ill, let alone the 'imalayas."

Dad's continuing and vicarious sense of *noblesse oblige* led him early on to issue a regular invitation for Mr Bolus to come over to the Priory for lunch every Sunday, a custom which once started could not easily be done away with. So once a week for several years the family had to endure his kindly but mumbled conversation. After one of his totally unarticulated effusions young Jenny looked at him and said "I don't understand a word of all that silly nonsense," for which she was sent away from the table by Father, stifling his amusement.

My memory held me in good stead, and I was able to satisfy my earnest but stodgy instructor that I had learned all I needed to know. So one afternoon around Easter our family assembled in the little village church of St. Barnabas, which we universally agreed to be as ugly as Oxford's Keble College, but which is now acknowledged as one of the Victorian architect Butterfield's finest achievements. I had had to choose my own godfathers, and unsurprisingly approached Arthur Harrison to be one of them, to which he agreed. Dick Parry Okeden was the other, suggested by my parents. Only Arthur was able to be present that day: Dick was represented by a proxy. I believe Wilma was my godmother. I seem to have performed satisfactorily, not only renouncing the devil, but also the vain pomp and glory of the world, with all covetous desires of the same. 'The old Adam in this person was buried, that the new man may be raised up in him.' It was done; and I was ready for Radley.

And so ended nearly seven years in the care of a small private boys' preparatory school in the English countryside. Looking back at that time from over sixty years on, I try to weigh it all in some kind of balance, some judgement of profit and loss. Did I love my parents more, or less, for being deprived of them for two thirds of every year? How happy was I – and what did that mean? What did I learn there that was to be useful to me in the life ahead? How did the character of Arthur Harrison and his fellow schoolmasters influence my character, my interests, my sense of myself? How useful or otherwise was it to be closeted for so long with children of my own sex, for whom girls were some other country, some alien tribe? What habits of thought did I pick up about my fellow Englishmen, the ordinary people from which we were so entirely insulated? Did snobbery enter the picture? Had I been shunted into a blind alley of classicism and snobbish middle class taste, unfitting me for the society of the world beyond? Had I and my school friends been led to believe we were more important than we actually were? Had we been taught by pitting our wits and strengths against one another: was competition the spur to all our efforts? Or had we at least begun to bury the old Adam, the self-centred world of our infancy, and to gain some notion of caring about others? Was I a spoilt child of privilege?

This welter of questions comes at me insistently, and is hard to find answers for. My egalitarian instincts became developed many years later, and have sometimes led me to feel uncomfortable at the very special treatment I received in those early years. But then I ask myself if it's right that no one should have something unless everybody has it too. My parents were certainly not in a position to buy me this education: they had almost no money themselves. I was blessed in fact by their ambition for me; their determination that whatever else they did they would ensure that my sisters and I received the very best education available, and would sacrifice their own creature comforts, exotic holidays, good clothes, new cars and so on, to make that happen.

And then: was this in fact the best education for me, to be sent away from home into a 'boys only' school, and to be entrusted to an unknown group of teachers for my safety, my health, my values and my learning? At the time they had absolutely no doubt that it was indeed the best: that no educational programme in the world for a child of my age could compare with that of a good English preparatory school.

And was this a good school? Through the chance of Marlborough House being evacuated to within a few miles of our home in Devon, my parents had been able to meet Arthur Harrison, and soon to be impressed enough by his charm, his humour, his self-assurance, his obvious love of what he was doing and his wisdom as a headmaster. It was into his hands that I was placed, and it was his judgement that they trusted in every other matter: choice of teaching staff, educational approach, range of subjects taught, disciplinary methods, inculcation of values and advice for the future. It is amazing just how much the strength, indeed the whole character, of a private school of this kind flows from its head. At the time I was a pupil, Arthur was sole owner of the school and of the land on which it stood. There was no Council or Board of Governors – though this came later. I shudder to think how much responsibility was invested in him, and how free he was to make a total mess of it.

One test of such a school is its success in attracting and holding on to its pupils and its teachers. Marlborough House's pupil numbers grew steadily through the time I was there and beyond, and the core of its teaching staff – Tommer, Hilda French, Geoff Martin – stayed with it for anything from twenty to forty years.

My schoolmate John Le Mare recently shared with me a document which has been precious to him since those early days. When he was made Head of the School in 1949, he received a hand-written letter from Arthur, who had apparently just been visiting John's home in Essex:

Dear Llama,

This is just a very hurried line, which needs no answer, to wish you every success in your year of office as Head of the School. We are quite sure you can, and will, do the job very well – otherwise we should not have appointed you – and you can always be sure that we shall give you our fullest support; and judging from the way the rest of the school received the news of your appointment I think you can count on their support too.

I was very glad to have seen you in your native surroundings but I must apologise for having been such a very dull guest. As a matter of fact I was suffering the major agonies of acute tooth-ache, and yesterday I had the face the size of any balloon. However I adjourned to the dentist today who removed the offender, so I hope I will have regained my pristine beauty when you see me on Friday.

I must now go and polish up your throne for you, all ready for the royal rump.

Wishing you all the very best,
Yours ever,
Arthur Harrison

Reading it now I recognise and recall the combination of warmth and wit which was Arthur Harrison's identifying stamp. The letter in fact gives an accurate sense of this unusual man's relationship with his pupils: the use of Le Mare's nickname, the combination of sincere good wishes and promise of support, the self-deprecation of his own dental woes, and the good fun of his last sentence – just in case 'Llama' should take his elevation too seriously. Arthur at this time was nearing fifty years of age: John Le Mare was twelve. Yet there is a total lack of condescension: no suggestion of talking down to a child. Arthur's readiness to laugh and to make others laugh is one of his legacies to those of us lucky enough to have had the wit to enjoy it.

John also once showed me another letter from Arthur to his parents, when they were considering sending their son to Marlborough House in 1946. His advice to them when picking a school was not to look at its academic prowess or its success in games, but to look at the faces of the boys and their teachers, to make sure that it was a happy school, free both of fear and of too much deference. If everybody is happy most of the time, he wrote, everything else – good marks, good sports, good habits – will fall into place. I am sure that so many of the memorable delights of Arthur's own school came out of his determination that we should have fun: the camping weekends, the trip to the Derby, the choir outings, the Guy Fawkes bonfires, playing in the Dell, the films, the easiness about religious observance, the jokes, the nicknames. Homesick boys, he said on another occasion, were not nearly as common as son-sick mothers. Apart from those wrenching moments when we kissed our parents goodbye at the start of another term, I think that few of us spent much time wishing we were back home. We were for the most part gaining self-confidence, making our own friends, learning to work and to play, and having fun.

Was this true of every boy at the school? Probably not. Some maybe could not resign themselves to life away from their mothers and fathers and siblings – especially their mothers. On the other hand, even though single parents and broken homes were much less a part of family life in those days, marital strife and domestic violence and wretchedness at home were no doubt the lot of many children, some of whom were only too happy to be at school and out of the line of fire. For all of us, our coping with this 'boys only' boarding school life was made easier simply by the fact that we were all in it together, and that it was unthinkingly accepted as a necessary stage in our growing up to be men.

One of Arthur's last sessions with us 'leavers' was to call us together for a mutually awkward session, in which we were advised among other evasive things to make friends at our new schools only among boys of our own age. I forget now how much he made of the dangers of our being courted by older boys. Not much I think; I seem to remember he told us that we would be receiving some kind of lecture about 'the facts of life' at the start of our public school career. He was surely happy in this way to be passing on the hot potato of sex to another administration.

In fact we received no instruction at all at Marlborough House about how to make babies, about the facts of copulation. But nor were we entirely ignorant. Among the dictionaries and reference books on hand in the Gallery bookcase was a slim volume on sex education, giving a series of simple lessons on puberty, on emotional development, and on the processes of insemination, gestation and childbirth. The book was well-worn, passed hand to hand by us older boys and sniggered over, but still found fascinating and informative. I believe it was left there on purpose, as a useful way of educating us without mutual embarrassment.

Very few of us had started on the road to puberty by the time we left school, but we were beginning to understand that something would happen before very long, which would bring us deeper voices and pubic hair. And one among us, I remember, had made an early start, and surreptitiously treated a small group of us one evening in the changing-room to a demonstration of his sexual maturity. We were intrigued, and asked whether it hurt. It didn't, he said. It certainly didn't.

But for the most part our life at this school, which brought together boys from the age of seven to thirteen, was pre-sexual. Our private dirty jokes and our furtive graffiti revolved more around the lavatory than the bedroom. Few of us if any had girlfriends at home, and, for most of us, girls were as I have said an alien tribe. In all these things we were innocent, entirely inexperienced. Sex would be one of the many areas of knowledge which we would have to fill out in the years to come – along with social and political awareness, the high seriousness of play, the pangs of love and heartbreak, the cares of office, and acquaintance with grief and even death.

To help me engage with these new interests, new delights and new anguishes, I was finally thrust out from my long home in the garden of England and into the new and still strange world of Radley College, on the banks of the sweet and still softly-running Thames.

CHAPTER FIVE

DOVES AND SERPENTS

It is May of 1951, and I am 13 years and 8 months old, fresh-faced and nervous, as my parents drive me through Oxford and out along the Thames Valley, to start my new life at Radley College. I had spent much of the last six years of my life in a small school dominated by the personality, the exuberant self-assurance of one man. With the help of my 'major scholarship' I was about to enter a complete and much larger new world, with its own language, customs, history and ethos.

St Peter's College, Radley, was founded in 1847 as an off-shoot of the Oxford Movement, which was dedicated to the revival of the moribund Anglican church. Its motto was "*Sicut Serpentes, Sicut Columbae*" ('as cunning as serpents, as gentle as doves'): a mystifying precept to live up to. The School's founder, William Sewell, saw the reform of Christian education as the over-riding imperative, if the Church were to recover its strength. During his career at Oxford, first as an undergraduate and then while a fellow of Exeter College and popular preacher and lecturer, Sewell expanded his views, and before long began to put them into action. In 1843 he founded a school in Ireland with the purpose of rescuing the Anglican Irish Church. Four years later he brought his initiative home, settling on Radley Hall as the site of his school for young Christian gentlemen. If my status as a gentleman might be disputed, there was no doubt I was a right and proper – indeed newly-minted – Christian.

The School had gone through many vicissitudes and some near-death experiences since those early days, but through it all it had retained its original High Church Christian bent. Sewell also believed that his charges should be surrounded by beautiful things, and he scoured not only England but the continent of Europe for fine pieces: Persian carpets, doubtful old masters, silver candlesticks and salvers, and – the prize – a handsome 15th-century Flemish reredos, which was installed behind the altar of his first chapel. These extravagances had helped to bring the young school close to bankruptcy, and no doubt some of them were carried off again more or less discreetly by bailiffs. But the original Radley Hall, now known as 'The Mansion' and the anchor of a sprawling brickwork fleet of buildings, was still graced by a handful of Sewell's early finds: chests, chairs and the odd massive armoire. My first of hundreds of Chapel services also found me staring at that distant Sewellian reredos, trying and failing to make sense of its mass of gilded human figures in deep relief against a shadowy ground.

Making sense of a mass of human figures, gilt or no gilt, was in fact very much the job of a new boy in 1951, as it no doubt still is. Radley's boys were divided among eight houses, each sheltering some 60 of us. Following an early Sewell precept these houses were known, oddly, as 'socials'. Three of the socials occupied three floors of the main college complex. The rest were housed in separate buildings around the grounds. They were each named after the master who was in charge of them. Mine was 'Morgan's' (though within little more than a year Mr Morgan left, to be replaced by the tall, kindly and lumbering Raymond King, and we became 'King's'). We were accommodated in a somewhat forbidding 1920s structure to the south-east of the Chapel. The pipe-smoking Clem Morgan, our 'social tutor', was also sub-Warden. Yes, our headmaster was known as the Warden, another Oxfordian import of Sewell's. And our masters were referred to as 'dons'.

New boys began their active life in a 'social hall', in our case a room on the ground floor of Morgan's, with windows on three sides. There were work spaces around its walls, accommodating the year's intake of boys. The room was also large enough to accommodate the whole social for occasional assemblies and even prayers. After three or four terms in this more and more uncongenial hothouse, we would be graduating to studies along the passage, shared with one or two others, and furnished with bits and pieces, which changed hands as boys left them behind and sold them to their successors: 10 shillings for a bureau, I remember, referred to as a 'burry'.

Our sleeping arrangements were more spacious: from the very start of his time at the school each boy had his own cubicle in the social's dormitories. Our cubicles, in the junior dormitory on the first floor, were divided from one another by pale green wooden walls some six or seven feet high, and were closed off from the corridor by a sliding door. Each had an opening window. They gave us just enough room for a bed, a chest of drawers and a chair, but as you can imagine, this one little patch of private territory was immensely precious to us.

It did not take long for us new boys to realize that it was not the 'dons' but the senior boys of the school who were in charge of us. Each social had a Head, who was a school prefect. Ours was a remote and fearsome figure, J. N. Stenhouse by name: tall, dark and handsome, and in fact very friendly. We would see him only rarely, and speak to him only if spoken to.

Then there were five or six house prefects, who did the basic disciplinary work, which in our case meant getting us up to bed at bedtime, overseeing our washing and tooth-brushing in the communal bathroom, keeping order during 'prep' and after lights-out, and in the mornings (since this was summertime) ensuring that we took our compulsory and unhygienic dip in the communal cold bath-tub. They also organized our initiation into the life of the school. We were each given a pamphlet containing basic information about the school's history and geography, as well as the names of all the dons, together with their initials, which we had to learn. We also learned what junior boys could and could not do: there were certain privileges reserved for school prefects (who were known as 'pups'), like walking across lawns. There was even a veto against crossing the gravel between Radley's Clock Tower and a nearby shrubbery; the tall, square, Germanic-looking Tower had long ago had buttresses added at each corner to make ball-courts, and the court on this particular side had in years past been reserved for school prefects. All this information we had to memorize in our first fortnight, when we would be tested on our knowledge. This is why over sixty years later I can still recall the initials of many dons long deceased, like C.P.T. Wrinch and C.J.M. Rickards and T.E.E. Cocks. We also had to con the names of School Prefects by heart, which that year included not only our own Head J.N. Stenhouse, but the great cricketing phenomena E.R. (Ted) Dexter and A.C. Walton.

Most boys started their time at Radley with the autumn term, so that those few of us who arrived in May found ourselves having to jump on to a train that was already steaming along. Friendships and groups had formed by now, and we felt amazingly green alongside these little know-it-alls with their full six months of head start. I was helped, I think, by arriving as an entrance scholar. At most schools this would be unnoticeable. But at Radley, as part of the Oxfordian overlay, every boy had to acquire a gown, which he wore to classes and to meals. The scholar's gown was some twelve inches longer than the ordinary 'shortie', giving us a way of distinguishing ourselves immediately from the general ruck.

The social was our home, and what friends we began to make in those first weeks came from among our schoolfellows in 'social hall'. (Friendship, though, was a fairly tentative affair, and we very formally continued, as at our prep schools, to call each other by our surnames.) We were encouraged early on to develop some pride in our social, which even had its own tie. This pride was heightened by various in-school contests. And it was from the social that we ventured out each day for the three major activities of the school: classroom work, sports and eating.

Along with new scholars from other socials, I was put into a form called I think the 'Classical 4th', which I seem to remember was a holding tank for our entrance into the classical stream that was mapped out for many of us for the years to come. We met in the furthest away of a set of classrooms referred to as 'the slums', which let off a large old barn-like building known as School. The form's presiding master was the Reverend Charles (C.E.B.) Neate, who had fairly recently joined Radley as the school chaplain, after a spell at the Anglican church in Paris. Tall and shiningly bald, he had been nicknamed 'chrome-dome' by one of our American exchange students. Warm and friendly, and somewhat arch, even womanish, in his capacious academic gown, he no doubt saw all these meek young scholars as potential recruits for his Chapel activities, with Confirmation being his chance to capture us for the faith in a year or two. Meanwhile he made it his business to get to know us all personally, and had a way of inserting himself into our confidence so smoothly that we felt able to share personal secrets with him. He was thought of by older boys as a gossip, and his much used and highly discreet phrase "strictly between you and me" was parodied as "strictly between you and me and the rest of College". As we later discovered, he fervently believed in the sacrament of confession to a priest, namely himself; thus providing more potential grist to his mill of confidential information. A good man though: kindly and jokey. Our initial nervousness as new boys in this new and strange academic environment was soon calmed by his cosy manner.

In summer terms at Radley the first class took place before breakfast, at 7.30, and was generally a sleepy affair for both masters and boys, to be followed by a very welcome breakfast at 8.15. It was served up in Hall, an early 1900s mediaeval-style refectory with high, beamed roof, large enough to accommodate almost the whole student population. Portraits of past Wardens and other Radley notables looked down from Hall's panelled walls, along with family crests of former noble or aspiring Radleians, and at the west end, high above the entrance doors, a vast royal coat of arms painted in bright colours reminded us of our duty to King and Country. This was the first place where we new boys, fresh from family-sized preparatory schools, had a chance to see the vast scale of the college, with almost all the boys assembled in one place.

Breakfast was the least formal of our meals. Eggs, fried and rubbery or chunkily scrambled, were served to each table in big, rectangular aluminium pans, with porridge or corn flakes, limp toast and milky tea in canisters. Coffee was not on the menu. The boys came and went for this meal, as I recall, more or less as they wished, for not much time was to elapse before the bell rang for Chapel at 9 am, and once again the whole school came together under one roof. A prayer or two, a psalm, a hymn (I remember being startled by the power of over four hundred voices belting it out), a few announcements, a blessing, and we were processing out and heading to our next class at 9.30.

It was at our first morning session with Charles Neate that we were introduced to the Radley custom at that time of starting the first class of each day with the reading of a short designated passage from the Bible, followed by discussion short or long according to the enthusiasm of the don in charge. I think many dons resented this exercise, but Charles as you might expect was generally expansive, being on his own territory.

Our other lessons took us all over College. The bulk of classrooms was in the attractive 1930s New Wing, with its elegant archway through to the playing fields. But there were other classrooms dotted around the place – our 'slums' off School, as well as one or two in the old Victorian buildings near the Octagon, and even one in the Mansion called the Singleton Library, next to the Wilson Library – which stretched the whole length of the building on the northern side. It was a familiar sight several times a day to see hundreds of black-gowned boys trudging – or cantering – along the passages or out on the gravel paths from class to class, carrying their 'college blocks' (notebooks) and their piles of books for the day's forty-minute classes. – For some reason we generally carried them in piles: I remember no use of knapsacks or satchels. Dons often moved between classrooms too, their gowns billowing in the breeze: among them Theo Cocks stately and flat-footed in his suede shoes as he stalked across the lawn from his rooms in the Mansion, Jim Rickards darting along like a ferret, and Charles Wrinch – the high-browed head at a curious angle, and in fact the whole body on a slant as he walked along carrying an enormous load of books, his raggedy gown flapping behind him.

At this distance it is hard to recall what it was that we were taught that first term, but Latin, Greek, French, English, History, Mathematics and Physics were certainly on my agenda. In fact it was not long before we were being steered in the direction of the academic goals that lay ahead of us during our time at the school. In two years' time we would be taking our 'O' (Ordinary) Level exams in as many subjects as it was thought we could pass. We would then concentrate on the subjects we had chosen for our specialisation: in my case, it appeared even at this early stage that I would be a classicist, and would move on to 'A' (Advanced) Level in Latin, Greek and Ancient History. All this however was in the future.

The justification for our wretchedly early start during summer terms was that the morning's classes would finish by 1 pm, enabling us, after lunch back in Hall and a half-hour compulsory rest on our beds, to change for the sports field or the river. On Tuesdays, Thursdays and of course Saturdays there were no more classes, thus giving us time for four or five hours of cricket, or lengthy rowing practices up and down the Thames, as the shadows slowly lengthened on those long, golden double-summertime afternoons and evenings. Return to the school grounds after rowing usually included a visit to the College Shop, where we were happy to eat egg-and-onion sandwiches and Smith's Crisps, washed down with something new and exotic for me called Coca-Cola. On Mondays, Wednesdays and Fridays we assembled for lessons again, from 4.30 to 6.

One afternoon a week, though, was reserved for training in the Combined Cadet Force. Service in this fearsome arm of Britain's military might was compulsory, and I can remember my first drill outside the armoury below the Music School, out beside the playing fields. We new boys were still dressed in our jackets and ties and school caps, as we were inducted into the mysteries of standing at ease and attention, of saluting, turning right about, of marching in time, the arms straight, thumb on top, fingers lightly curled. It was here, for the first but by no means the last time in my life, that I heard the strident music of a sergeant-major blasting away on a parade-ground: in our case the despairing voice of RSM Howe as he coped with our ineptitude. It was Howe who was later to issue us with uniforms, boots, green berets and bugle badges, and with old .303 rifles: surely from the First World War or earlier, and astonishingly heavy and awkward for young boys. Clasping these 9-pound monsters we were taught to shoulder and present arms, and march around with rifles at the slope. Later we even learnt to fire the things, at target practice on the shooting range behind the armoury. I found that I was a good shot, but it was not long before I realised that this was not my most loved activity of the week.

Every boy at the start of his school career had to elect to be a 'dry bob' or a 'wet bob': either a cricketer or an oarsman. My undistinguished performance – and deep disinterest – on the cricket field at my previous school made the decision an easy one. So my first afternoon of term found me joining hundreds of other boys on bicycles, riding down the drive in our school caps and shorts, turning left by Radley church, through the village, over the railway bridge and along a final narrow causeway to the boathouses. There we neophytes were introduced to the mysteries of pulling a vessel along, beginning with heavy, fixed-seat clinker-built foursome tubs decades old, but, later on, to the joys of solo sculling. I began to enjoy my time on the river, and the hours went by pleasantly enough, before cycling back up to the College for snacks, supper and eventually bed, which for us young 'uns was at 8.30.

In every direction at Radley, then, there was a lot to learn; not only in the classroom but throughout our daily lives in this strangely isolated but complete world, and with very much its own sense of itself as a world. It was amazingly addictive, it seemed. There were masters there who had started out as Radley schoolboys, had left for wartime service and a university degree, and had then come back as teachers – staying there for twenty or thirty years, until their retirement. For them especially, but almost as much for dons imported from other schools, Radley was something to be lived in and lived for. They would work their way up from assistant masters to sub-tutors to social tutors, often gathering up a wife as they went and sweeping her along with them as they cared for and nurtured the boys of their socials. They would head up teaching departments, spend their afternoons coaching teams and crews at every level, preside over clubs and societies, sit in their deckchairs watching the First XI on every fixture against another school, or drive down the Thames Valley to attend some regatta in which a Radley VIII was performing. Of course we were not aware of the tensions that may have been occupying them in their Common Room, and their salaries were surely very modest; but there seemed little doubt that for the majority of them life was satisfying, because they passed their devotion on to us all.

To some extent their apparent satisfaction must have emanated from the man who was in charge: the Warden. His name was J.C. Vaughan Wilkes. John Wilkes had been a scholar at Eton, and returned there after Oxford to become, eventually, Eton's Master in College. He had left Eton to become Warden of Radley in 1937, and seen the school through the difficult war years, when it had shared its premises with the boys and masters of Eastbourne College, who had been evacuated to Radley from the Channel coast. He had taken holy orders just after the war, and brought his devout Anglican probity to all his work at the school. A tallish man, usually sporting black suit and clerical collar, with greying wavy hair receding from his high brow, he had big brown eyes, which often seemed even bigger seen through his highly magnifying spectacles. He tended to hold his head at an angle, and when he took off his glasses to look at you seemed to be staring at a point somewhere above your right eyebrow. This was disconcerting, but we became used to it.

Warden Wilkes gave the air of being absent-minded, his thoughts perpetually somewhere else. This might have caused some frustration among his colleagues. But in fact he had an impressive reputation as an organiser, and his goodness, kindness and intelligence were plain to see, as well as his commitment to the school: he and his gracious if floppily dressed wife Joan were seen at almost every school event. My own acquaintance with him began early, because he taught us classical scholars Latin in my second term – whenever he remembered or had the time to turn up. I still remember him setting us a W.S. Gilbert lyric to turn into Latin verses: "The sun whose rays are all ablaze with ever-living glory..." from *The Mikado*. Our efforts are mercifully lost to history.

Radley's hold on its citizens, like that of many institutions, was to some extent bound up with the rules and rituals which it had established for the daily conduct of its affairs. Ritual of course found its chief expression in our High Anglican chapel services, with their processions and liturgy, not to mention their bowing, standing, turning, kneeling and letuspraying. We wore surplices over our jackets on Sundays and saints' days, which gave the whole school the slightly spurious look of a heavenly host. And Christian feast days were celebrated with special solemnity: red altar cloths for church martyrs, cross-bearing prefects, candles, acolytes and eucharists. The line which separated our practice from outright popery was drawn firmly this side of Latin and of 'bells and smells' – and the use of the word 'Mass'; though a few committed souls (including Charles Neate if I remember) did engage in the Roman Catholic practice of bowing or even bending a knee to the altar on entering and leaving the precincts, which in boys always seemed to me more attention-drawing than pious.

These rites carried over to the dining hall's more formal gatherings. Here, in a tradition no doubt inherited via Oxford from the mediaeval monastery, Latin was allowed place: for evening meals a grace was pronounced by the Head of School, a simple "*Benedictus benedicat per Jesum Christum Dominum Nostrum*". But at lunchtime we would all stand in our gowns as the Warden processed up the aisle with his school prefects and guests to the high table, which was raised in the Oxford manner on a dais above the common herd. Sunday lunches required a specially elaborate grace from the Warden :"*Tibi laus, tibi honor, tibi gloria, O beata et gloriosa Trinitas: tu das eis estam in tempore opportuno…*" I forget the rest but it went on for a full minute. The high table then sat down, to be waited on by Mr Boylett in his grey tie and morning coat. The rest of us lower beings sat on benches at long tables, social by social, with prefects at one end and we new boys at the other – well below the salt. But even there the tables were waited on, by 'servitors', who brought out the pans of food from the kitchen – to be doled out by the prefect at the head of each table – and then cleared away the empty plates we had piled at the end of each course.

Rituals also extended to our daily life, with its regular routines of bedtimes, meal-times, class-times and playtimes, and to our dress. Beneath our gowns we wore shirt and tie with the regulation tweed jacket (it could be green or brown) and grey trousers to all our classes, and on Sunday we donned our regulation dark blue suits, and a white shirt with separate, starched collar, involving us new boys in the mysteries of collar studs and cuff links – and a sore neck from the starch, I remember. We sported stiff straw hats –'boaters' – with our Sunday suits and for special occasions. Otherwise we wore school caps to our sports; special caps – as well as ties and hatbands – could be earned by being a member of a school team or crew.

We were told that good manners were part of what it means to be a Radleian, and that if we were wearing our caps we must always – even, sometimes dangerously, when riding our bikes – doff them to dons and their wives, or to visitors. The simple gesture impressed my own parents and no doubt everybody else, giving a sense to the outside world that Radley boys were kindly and polite. This was to some extent self-confirming: what began as an injunction became an automatic piece of *politesse*, and Radleians were known then, as maybe still, for their social charm and graces. Some of us have even felt this as a burden.

I was not a rebellious child, and took on Radley's baggage of custom, strictures, and *modi operandi* with calm, and even with pleasure. After all, most of us new boys at the very bottom of the social scale wanted to be accepted, wanted to be approved by those further up the ladder, which meant fitting in with the institution's ways. And then there were of course penalties for breaking the rules. The supreme punishment was expulsion. Next came a beating with the cane, wielded in extreme cases – lying, impertinence, plagiarism, drinking, smoking – by the Warden or Social Tutors. Minor infringements like being late for bedtime, not wearing a gown when it was required, being found out of bounds or missing a practice earned us what was called a 'check', which was marked up by our prefects against our record: five checks within one term could lead to a beating by the head boy of one's social. This whole carefully-structured framework of rules and penalties was viewed as the necessary underpinning of the school's social fabric, without which things would fall apart, the centre unable to hold. I was certainly one boy who was fearful of the cane, and worked hard to avoid breaking rules – or at least to invent winningly plausible excuses. But I did sneakingly respect those one or two among my contemporaries who seemed to be always getting into trouble, who rebelled against the rules and just hovered on the edge of insolence when talking to senior boys in authority. Obedience, after all, though drilled into us as a moral obligation, is not an entirely admirable virtue.

The public school practice of 'fagging', by which very junior boys served the needs of the prefects, was still in force in 1951. I think I was appointed a fag to J.N. Stenhouse, who as the Head of Social could employ two of us. As fags we ran errands, went to the College Shop to buy food for our faggees, and spent time in the social's kitchen with its four gas-rings, grilling toast and crumpets or boiling up baked beans for their snacks. I can't remember that we did much else; perhaps we swept their studies. It was not an arduous business, and we were too young and green to find it humiliating. But I remember being relieved when the year or so of servitude was over.

Outside the intricate framework of our compulsory activities, which began with that wretched dip in the cold bath-tub around 7 in the morning and ended with lights out around 9 pm, there were a few precious spaces of time which we could call our own. On Sundays, once morning Chapel was over, we could change out of our blue suits and starched collars and were free for the rest of the day, though Sunday evenings were set aside for 'socialising' with our social tutors or sub-tutors; a group of us each week would be invited beyond the inner door of our tutor's study into his living quarters, to talk or play games or listen to music. I suspect that this was a survival from Sewell's desire that boys be encouraged to develop their powers of conversation and their good manners in polite society. It was certainly a chance to spend an hour or two out of the charmless world of the institution and in a real home, with comfortable armchairs, teacups and saucers, homemade sandwiches and cake, and the kindness of a motherly hostess. We were after all only thirteen or fourteen years old, we new boys; home and parents were still much missed.

We were also free to take part in evening activities on weekdays between supper and bedtime. The school was rich with clubs and societies of every sort, and it was not long that first summer before most of us found ourselves drawn into one circle or another.

I was delighted to discover there was a Photographic Club, and that in the attic of the Music School there was a well-equipped darkroom. I had already grown to enjoy taking, developing and enlarging photos at home and had commandeered an old pantry at Studley, even making my own enlarger from a condensed milk tin with a lens from my father's old plate camera. Now I was able to work with more professional equipment, and to put my Voigtlander camera (a recent birthday present from the parents) to good use. And the darkroom was a blessed haven away from the clatter of social hall.

It was not long too before I met with the beaky old Precentor, Mr Dussek, to audition for the choir. With my choral experience from Marlborough House and a still unbroken treble voice I was snapped up, and from then on until the very end of my time at Radley the choir remained a central part of my life, as I graduated in due time from treble to alto to bass. It was not long, in fact, before I became aware just how active Radley's musical life was. My parents were insistent that I continue to take piano lessons, and I began that first term with a fine musician who was assistant to the

Precentor (Succentor, they called him), an Old Radleian who revelled in the amazing name of Mr Hammond-Chambers-Borgnis. It soon became a high point of my week to drop into his attractive little house above College Pond, to sit at his handsome Blüthner parlour grand and be wafted into the world of Beethoven and Bach and Mozart.

I soon discovered that in Morgan's social we had two Music Scholars, Paul Mizen and Richard Latham – or they discovered me. Both were pianists and also string players – Mizen on violin/viola, and Latham on 'cello. Before long I was roped in to accompany a Beethoven string trio for a social contest. Mizen was a senior boy, untidy and eccentric, and Radley's finest pianist of his day: later that first summer's Gaudy Day concert he was to perform the first movement of Grieg's Piano Concerto with the Radley College Orchestra. Latham was just a year ahead of me, and we were to become good friends through music, playing chamber works, singing in the choir – and also listening to records: the Gramophone Society kept a gramophone and speakers in the Singleton Library, and Latham generously took it on himself to educate me in symphonic and choral literature. He introduced me to William Walton's *Belshazzar's Feast*. And I still associate the last agonised movement of Tchaikovsky's *Pathétique* Symphony with the elegiac view of College Pond seen on an autumn afternoon through the tall windows of the Library.

I was also invited, though perhaps not in that first term, to join the Pantechnicon Society, which brought younger scholars together in the Warden's Lodgings a few evenings to read Shakespeare plays – dividing up the parts – or to listen to talks, including one by Joan Wilkes' father Cyril Alington, who had been headmaster of Eton, chaplain to King George V and later for many years Dean of Durham. I remember nothing of the occasion except his long pale face and his very long, startlingly white hair.

One other member of Morgan's administrative team needs to be noted. Every Social had its Social Matron, who had care for the health of their boys, and acted as a maternal presence for them all. Morgan's Social Matron was Gladys Wheater, known universally as 'The Wheater.' A little, sparsely-educated fiftyish lady in big horn-rimmed glasses, she had been born and brought up in the north of England, and used that lovely circular inversion which comes from Yorkshire: "It's a busy day for me is Tuesday." As we got to know her better, she would tell us how she had been engaged to a sailor in the First World War, and how one night she dreamed that something terrible had happened to him. Two days later she had a telegram telling her that her beloved Jack had died. After that, she said, she never looked at another man. She loved her boys, though, and would mother us when we were sick, be a shoulder to cry on, and occasionally invite us to tea in her little sitting-room with its gas fire. In fact it was there, in February of the following year, that a group of us crowded in to hear Winston Churchill − by now Prime Minister again − giving his famed eulogy of King George VI, who had died the previous day: *"During these last months the King walked with death as if death were a companion, an acquaintance whom he recognized and did not fear"*. Every evening the Wheater would make a large jug of Ovaltine and walk through the halls of the Social with her familiar cry, "Anyone for Overs?" She was an enthusiastic supporter of our social in all its sporting activities. It was two years later, when Morgan's − now King's − looked likely to bump its way to Head of the River, that the Wheater promised, if we won, to throw her hat into the water. We did, and she did.

So this was the hive into which I had flown in May 1951, this miniature city on a hill, this private realm. Augustine's City of God? − A theocracy, with John Wilkes as High Priest? Not quite. A *polis*?

Yes, that was more like it. But what kind of a *polis*? It was by no means an Athenian democracy – though, like the Greek *polis*, it was supported and made possible by a large crew of servants, of *helots*, who did not have the same privileges as the teachers and boys, but without whom it could not run, since they provided the material and labour infrastructure which kept the institution going. Boatman Reg Talboys, cricket staff like Bert Robinson, and anyone who had direct dealings with the boys, like the Longs who ran College Shop, had high status. But most were almost unregarded: gardeners, boilermen, cleaners, kitchen staff, painters, mechanics and carpenters, drivers – and servitors in the dining hall. One of these, a woman in her twenties, had a pronounced limp and was unkindly nicknamed Hopalong Chastity. I doubt we knew her real name. Most of the time we accepted their occasional presence beside us without thought.

Were we polite to these good people when we crossed paths with them? I know I was – not only polite but friendly. I was used to working cheek by jowl with staff at Studley, and though my father was always a little lordly in the presence of his working people (in fact of *all* people, including lords), both parents cared about them and looked after them. But both at Studley and now in my new world of Radley was also an acceptance – by both parties I think – that there was a difference between us. Was it about class? Was it about education? Was it about the way we spoke? Was it about the way each of us lived – the pattern of our lives, the very different amenities we took for granted? (I once stumbled into the gardeners' earth privy at Studley, and saw a seed catalogue hanging on a string for toilet-paper. I don't think it had ever occurred to me before that they must have needed a place to go during the day. And 'of course' they could not come inside and use the flush toilets there, now could they?) Was it about money? I've made clear by now that my parents were without financial reserves of any sort. But then again they probably spent far more in a month than our gardeners spent in six: these things are relative.

What seems to be clear is that after the Second World War, and in spite of the war's equalising influence, Disraeli's two nations – 'the privileged and the people' – were still very much in evidence in Britain, and that this was accepted *on both sides* as the way things were. For 'the people' it was simply a condition of life that a small group of men (and women) were living in another world and had access to power and wealth; the situation was as much ordained as death and taxes. It was not necessarily liked: from the early nineteenth century there had been repeated assaults against the *status quo*, both by a growing middle class against the power of the aristocrats who still ran the country, and gradually through that century by the working people, in revolt against the ruthlessness of industrial barons, wretched working conditions, acquisitive landowners, and privilege in general. But in the twentieth century the rise of the Labour movement was checked by two world wars in succession, each calling upon the 'two nations' to sink their differences in defence of the realm. The Labour Party's convincing success in 1945 was surprising to some, but it was as though finally – and through the universal suffrage which had been fought over for more than a century, and was now including women – the determination to make Britain a single and just nation had gathered enough momentum to elect a potentially reforming government.

Among the reforms considered by Clement Attlee's new post-war administration, and urged on by some of his MPs, was the abolition of the public schools in Britain. It was discussed and debated. But in the end – partly because many of Labour's leaders, like Attlee himself, and also his successor Hugh Gaitskell, were public school products – the idea was dropped. The decision not to take this particular bull by the horns between 1945 and 1951 has been described as one of the major failures in Labour's democratising mission, which achieved so much in other areas. Indeed I have seen English public schools recently and illiterately described as 'the bedrock of the inequality that cripples the country still'.

It was, after all, the public schools which since the early nineteenth century had been providing new recruits for the ranks of the privileged, from generation to generation. It was the public schools that set out goals, established a code of conduct, and perpetuated *esprit de corps* among the children of the well-born and the well-to-do, linking them in a close association of shared views, shared experiences, shared sports, a shared dress code, and even a shared way of speaking English — which enabled its members to detect in an instant anyone who was not one of their own.

I had arrived at Radley in the dying months of Labour's short and fragile second term, when the spectre of abolition no longer haunted the world of private, fee-paying schools, and when it seemed likely that the resurgence of the Conservatives, still under Churchill, would soon lead to victory at the polls. The cynicism I had witnessed at my preparatory school towards the Labour government and all its works was in full display at my new school, but there was a certain triumphalist air now, among those young Tory boys who were confident that Britain would soon be governed once again by gentlemen like their fathers, by men who were born and brought up to be leaders. Their mothers were not yet considered as part of the equation.

I think it's mistaken though to view a place like Radley as a hotbed of the kind of jingoistic conservatism sometimes associated with such places. In the first place, there was very little political activity among the boys at that time. There were no Young

Conservatives that I remember; certainly no Young Socialists. And none of the dons do I recall playing any active public part in the political life of our constituency, which of course was a firmly Conservative seat. Yes, they would vote for the Tories, and most of them – though not all – were tired of Labour Britain, which by that time had tired even of itself, with so much of its agenda accomplished. But the more egalitarian among them would have welcomed many of Labour's reforms. It was hard for any parent to deny the benefits of the new National Health Service; I can still remember my father's delight at having to pay only one pound (*one pound!*) for a complete series of my visits to the dentist, however protracted. Improved universal pensions and welfare payments, higher pay and the regulation of working conditions for miners; these changes were difficult to reject unless you were unusually, brutally reactionary. Besides, many of the major reforms affected primarily the industrial heartlands and the coalpits of Wales and Scotland, far away from the lush and pastoral Thames Valley. The North, where so much industry and so much misery and poverty were centred, was for most of us, boys and masters alike, almost unknown country.

What was more evident at Radley than any active class hostility or partisan political view was a genial and almost unthinking sense of entitlement among us. No one at the institution felt that our privileged life was undeserved, or that we were depriving anyone else by enjoying its good things. And that was simply because there was no one around to contest our ownership: no active resentment, no mobs at the gate. All this meant that we were able to practise our unbridled High Anglicanism, with its guides to strength of character and to an earnestly moral and well-intentioned life, without seeing any social disconnection.

But was I personally *really* entitled? Was I a part of this world or simply an impostor? My parents, after all, were 'in trade' – innkeepers, no less. This was the 1950s, and the world of aristocratic disdain for trade was well past; besides, Radley did not have more than a sprinkling of aristocratic scions when I was there. But I still remember having some nervous thoughts about my station as I consorted with the sons of landowners, lawyers, service officers and business people. My mother after all was Australian, and my father had no public school pedigree for me to boast about, nor even a war record. My saving grace, of course, was the great old manor house we occupied and called home – and the fact that our guests and visitors were very much of the same stamp as the parents and grandparents of my schoolmates. Like my parents, I knew how to behave amongst these people and had developed some self-assurance in dealings with them. I had also been brought up to speak what was still known with casual snobbery as 'the King's English', trained up by my own father's rounded tones, and with a little help from my preparatory school headmaster. There was also the fact (though I did not know it at the time) that I had grown up to be a reasonably attractive lad, with a nice smile and a ready laugh: "Like a ray of sunshine on a Monday mornin'," as one of our washers-up described me to my mother. And I was good at my lessons, which elicited some maybe grudging respect. It was not long in any case before I stopped worrying about any social inferiority – for the moment at least.

So my first term passed with no serious upsets, and, as with all lives of repeated routine, what I remember from that summer are the events which still stand out from the daily round, the common task.

There was the sunny Sunday when one of our teachers, Maurice Balme, took three or four of us new boys out in his open Morris Bullnose, a car which even in those days was a rare and wonderful antique, with a boot that opened up into a dickey seat. He drove us in this splendid, spluttering machine down the Thames Valley to Wittenham Clumps, a famous pair of hills topped by groves of ancient beeches, and visible as a landmark for many miles around. We parked in a lane, and climbed up through the fields to the great 18th century trees, where Mr Balme produced a splendid picnic.

As a young – and smallish – wet bob in Morgan's I was invited to cox the 1st Social IV which took part in the bumping races at the end of that term. We were bumped once, and so dropped into fourth position (from which, by bumping four times the following year with a different cox, we made our way to the Head of the River). This was my introduction to coxing, and it also led the following year to my coxing of Radley's 3rd Eight, which participated in a regatta at Pangbourne. We certainly didn't win the event, but as far as I remember we put in a creditable performance, and at least I didn't steer them into the bank. From this involvement I also picked up an early rowing cap, which I wore proudly down the river from then on.

It was towards the end of that first term that one of our House Prefects was expelled. There was a certain mystery about it, but the story was that he was let go for seducing, or attempting to seduce, another boy, who reported him. We were sorry to see him leave; he was one of the kindest and most gentle of our prefects, and also highly intelligent. Before he left, he offered his books to anyone who would like them, and I still have his copy of *Brave New World*, and of Burke's *Reflections on the French Revolution*. I have often wondered how his life unfolded after his Radley career was cut short. He was a good person.

There was a Radley custom that all the boys of the school had a whole holiday for the first day of the Henley Royal Regatta, which ran in the first week of July from Wednesday to Saturday. A special train was put on, and boys of all ages in boaters, blue suit jackets and white trousers swarmed on board, 'bagging' compartments, ganging up with their friends, and trying to exclude any wretched undesirables. It was not Radley at its friendly best, and of course got noisier and more larky as we progressed down the valley. We passed through Reading to Twyford, and there we were shunted on to the small branch line which led through the fields to the charming Victorian station of Henley-on-Thames, where the shouting, over-excited crowd of teenagers fanned out into the little town.

The Regatta boasted something of the voguish atmosphere of Ascot in those days; perhaps it still does. It was a chance for absurdly fashionable women to display their absurdly fashionable dresses and their outlandish picture hats, and for men to strut in their blazers with sporting caps and ties: pink for the Leander club, and every rowing school tie you can imagine – the Old Radleian (black with thin red and white stripe) prominent among them. I had never seen so many old men with schoolboy caps perched absurdly above wrinkled faces and swelling paunches.

Many boys arranged to meet up with their families at Henley, and would rent a punt, or take a picnic hamper and eat out of the backs of their smart cars in the expensive parking areas. Great efforts were made to get admission to one of the Enclosures on the far side of the river; the General Enclosure or – even more prized and less accessible – the Stewards' Enclosure. It was my first exposure to the tightly-controlled exclusivity of British sporting life.

Unsurprisingly my mother got it early into her head that she would like to join me at Henley for that first Regatta day. Unsurprisingly too, she decided she would like to cut a dash, and spent many evenings through June making her dress, picking out her shoes and handbag and gloves, and decorating her hat for the occasion. I believe she travelled down from Oxford by bus. In any case she was there to meet me at the station in her finery, and not unhappily I said goodbye to my mates, to spend the day with my dear mother. Lunch was at the Angel, beside Henley Bridge.

From that year onward throughout my time at Radley, the outing to Henley was one of the high moments of my mother's pathetically sparse social calendar, and every year, even when she was Studley's only cook and in the full flight of their summer season, arrangements were somehow made to ensure that she could make the trip – sometimes one of our former cooks even coming back to stand in for the day. Her outfit was always a major concern. One year she decided she should sport a parasol. Unable to buy one, she purchased a cheap white umbrella and spent the evening stitching a strip of white lace around its edges and decorating the handle with a pretty bow. Sadly the gods ordained that that particular Henley day would turn to heavy rain in the afternoon, and I can still remember dear Mama grimly tearing the carefully-sewn lace off her fake sunshade to restore it to its original purpose.

In those years Radley was competing in the Princess Elizabeth Cup, and on that first day in 1951 they won their heat, a success which the crew repeated on the second and third days of the Regatta. It was the tradition that if the College VIII reached the final the whole school would return to Henley to cheer the crew on. So there we were once again that Saturday, yelling our hearts out from punt and bridge and towpath and Enclosure, as the Radley men battled down the course against their fellow finalists. I forget the name of the winner, but it was not Radley, and we returned with the wind taken out of our red and white sails, consoled in some cases with a certain amount of beer smuggled on board the train by older boys, and even with a whiff of cigarette smoke in the air. Punishments were usually meted out after these occasions.

Radley, with classical studies still at the prestigious top end of the school's academic programme, had a tradition of mounting a Greek play – in Greek – every three years. My first summer coincided with the production of *The Trachiniae* of Sophocles. Produced ('directed', as we should say now) by Charles Wrinch, it was set on the lawn on the north side of Mansion. I remember little of it, save the procession towards the end of the play when night had fallen and Heracles, in horrendous pain from the poisoned cloak which his wife had unwittingly inflicted on him, was carried in procession on to the stage under the stars, accompanied by flaming torches. The production was flatteringly reviewed in *The Times*.

It was also that summer of 1951 which saw the extraordinary feats of Radley's First Cricket XI, which won or drew all their matches, propelled to victory by the superb batting of A.C. Walton, E.R. Dexter and others. A page of *Country Life* devoted to public school cricket was accompanied by a picture of Radley with the caption HOME OF THE GREAT. Cricketers or not, we were all proud of the accomplishment, and I think that any lingering doubts I may have had about choosing Radley over Eton were finally put to rest.

I returned home having survived my first term. The prospect of entering a big new school had overhung my life for a year or two: now at last I had launched into that strange and alarming world, and by the end of July had managed to whittle away at the massive ignorance with which I began, and at the fear which attends the not knowing. I had also managed to hold my own in class and among my peers, learning some self-assurance but also the value of discretion. I had not been bullied, and I don't remember any other boy being bullied either, although there were always those timorous waifs who attracted scornful words and unkind jokes from other boys unable to resist the ease of domination. For all the sense of being a very small sprat in this new ocean, there was also some feeling of club membership, both of Morgan's Social and of the school as a whole. Henley had been the first time I had seen a mass of cheering Radleians as an entity in which I had my small part to play. There is an attractiveness about being in a miniature world, knowing your place and your task in it. I had begun to be proud of the school, proud of the school colours, proud and even boastful of the prowess of our senior sportsmen. Coming back to Studley, too, I found myself telling guests that I was at Radley, and noting their recognition of the school's name and even fame.

Once again 'the Props' were at their widest stretch handling the busy summer season, and having returned from school I found I was not able to see too much of them. If I wanted to spend time with my father, I would have to go to the bar, where he held court, drawing pints of Mitchell and Butler's bitter and mixing gin and tonics. If I wanted to talk with my mother, I would sit in the kitchen while she darted about roasting chickens, baking scones and cakes, preparing fruit salads, making soups. Sometimes I would be asked to shell peas or stir the pastry dough or whip the cream. But I was usually spared these tasks, and simply chatted, watching the poor soul grinding more or less cheerfully along under the ceaseless pressure of time.

Mother, as we have seen, was adept at naming things and people, and her cooking gave this talent of hers a creative outlet on the menu. 'Dame Honor Soup' was named after Mrs Honor Steele, who had run the Brentor Arms way back in our Devon days, and who always said she put "everything into her soup that 'appened to be 'andy". 'Dame Nellie Melba Soup' commemorated the great Australian singer, who towards the end of her career toured the world several times, each time under the banner "Positively The Last Appearance." A soup that had already appeared on the menu more than once, as 'Mixed Vegetable' or 'Mulligatawny', each time with some new flavour added to disguise its origins, finished up as 'Nellie Melba' – positively its last appearance.

It was around this hectic time that I happened to be in the kitchen when one day Mother made a 'Cream of Chicken' soup, which headed up a Sunday lunch menu. The soup would come into the dining-room in a large tureen which sat on the sideboard, and as the guests entered Wilma, who usually did the waiting at table with Our Mary assisting and taking away plates, would serve them a bowl of soup from the tureen. Mother's cooking was highly appreciated, and there were murmurs of approval as the creamy elixir was slurped down.

As more guests entered and were served, Wilma noticed that the soup had taken on a slightly pink colour. She didn't think too much about this, especially since the guests continued to remark how very fine it tasted, with almost an exotic, eastern flavour. Someone even asked for the recipe, and was firmly told that our recipes were house secrets. Wilma came out to the kitchen and told my mother about the change in colour, more as a matter of interest than anything else. But as she continued to ladle out the soup it became rosier and rosier, until she ran back down the passage to the kitchen with it to show Mother. "We can't keep calling this Cream of Chicken, Tess," she said: "just look at it!" Mother, busy basting the roast beef, took a quick, amazed glance at the tureen. "Tell them we've run out of Cream of Chicken, and we're serving this instead. "But what on earth shall I call it?" asked Wilma. "Coral Island Soup," said Mother without a trace of hesitation. And 'Coral Island Soup' it became, continuing to earn high praise for its unique aroma and wonderful oriental tastes.

It was only after the soup course was over and the dishes brought out to the pantry for washing that the mystery was solved. At the bottom of the tureen lay a half-melted crimson lipstick. Our Mary used to keep it on a little shelf above the sideboard, and at some point it must have dropped in. 'Coral Island Soup' was never again to appear on the menu.

On my own, I would wander round the grounds or through the woods, sometimes taking my father's .22 rifle and taking pot shots at rabbits, which I sometimes killed. I was also given a licence by Father to kill grey squirrels, because they were stealing eggs from his precious birds, or killing their young. Sometimes I would take my bike and pedal the 'five mile round', through the village, round past the Arncot road to Boarstall, and back to Studley. I often slept in late, much to the disapproval of my father, and was not able to reconcile – even to myself – the fact that I was so active at school and such an idle mooner back home.

I also missed my elder sister Jo, now living in digs in Oxford. She had finished her secretarial training and had tried out for various posts, including transcription work for the novelist Joyce Cary – who, when she called at his house in Park Road, had already filled the position, but kindly invited her to tea. Being barely seventeen she was thought by most employers to be too young, but eventually landed a job as assistant to a dentist in Keble Road. As she handled swabs and mouth-rinse, and passed tools to her boss, she often looked out across the garden to the back of Joyce Cary's house on Park Road, and mused how different her life would be if she had been hired by him. It was clear she would not be making a career in dental work.

Towards the end of August Father determined we should have another family holiday, though once again Jo, of course, was not able to come. Again we caravanned, this time hitching a bulbous little white job behind the old Daimler and heading north into Scotland. Passing through Shropshire within a day or two of setting out, my sister Jenny slammed the car door shut as I was getting out after her. My third finger was in the hinge, and when I cried out and the door was opened, the bone of the final joint was protruding. We rushed to the nearest cottage hospital, where a drunken locum was called in and attempted to set the finger without anaesthetic, but finally gave up in the face of my cries and sprayed ether on a mask to put me out in the most nightmarish way, while he continued to struggle incompetently. Encased in plaster the finger was still painful, but not enough to deter us from our holiday. We continued north, poking our noses into the Lake District, bowling quickly through what we saw as the blackened horrors of Wigan, crossing the border at Gretna Green, driving past and through the grim streets of postwar Glasgow, and camping by Loch Linnhe. We made it as far as Fort William before turning back east and south to Edinburgh. By this time my broken finger had showed no sign of settling down, and we drove into the emergency department at the Edinburgh Royal Infirmary, where an X-ray determined that the finger had not been correctly set. An efficient surgeon repositioned the poor inflamed digit under a general anaesthetic, warning us that it was possible the bone would not knit and have to be removed. My mother was mostly concerned that my piano-playing was at an end, and she continued to worry as we barrelled down the Great North Road, passing proudly through the town of Bawtry.

The chief family memory from this trip was Father's determination to drive across the Forth Bridge. We had the devil of a time searching for the entrance to it, and trawled for an hour or so up and down the streets of Dunfermline with that superb structure continually looming above us and the caravan bumping along behind, before finally arriving in an overgrown, cobbled and uneven wasteland right beneath the bridge, where the weight of the caravan on the back of the car sheared off the tap of the petrol tank. It was exactly at that moment, as we got out to inspect the damage, that an express train thundered past overhead, and Dad realized for the first time that the great Forth Bridge was a railway bridge – and only a railway bridge. We spent that night in the Dunfermline Arms – yes, with another aged waiter in black tie and tails – until the petrol tank was thoroughly dried out before being welded back together. A splendidly quixotic mistake on my father's part, but altogether an expensive one.

When I look back at my time at Radley it seems to fall into three periods in the classic Aristotelian manner: a beginning, a middle and an end. In my first term I had established my footing. I had learnt the ropes. I had quelled most of the fear we always feel starting out in a new world, and which was to repeat itself one way or another throughout life. Now, for the next two or three years – the middle – it was a case of making a mark, and of Radley making its mark on me.

For one reason or another, any mark that I was able to make in those years was primarily in performance. Our Warden John Wilkes wrote later: "I believe myself that Music and Drama are of more value, educationally, than most if not all subjects". He felt that in his time at Radley these were activities in which, along with rowing, the school particularly shone. I was lucky, then, to find myself able to immerse myself in both of them, and through them to meet and work with the mentors whose talents, personalities and generosity helped me to grow: Anthony Caesar, Peter Way, Christopher Ellis and Charles Wrinch.

Though X-rays showed my finger was now knitting well, it was still in plaster when I returned to school in September, and when the boys poured on to the sports fields for rugger practice in the afternoons, I was excused for the first four or five weeks. I was also hampered in my piano lessons, which was especially annoying because I had acquired a new teacher.

The previous term had been Mr Dussek's last as Precentor, and a replacement had been hired. It turned out to be none other than Anthony Caesar, who had befriended me during my abortive attempt at an Eton scholarship, and who had stayed along with his parents at Studley a few years before. It was natural that I should ask to be transferred to the care of a family friend for my piano lessons, and Mr H-C-B was understanding. As the new Precentor, Anthony was in charge of the choir, and began an energetic revival of it, with the help of his youth, humour and musicianship. He also took over the Madrigal Society, which I had been invited to join, and which met in the evenings every two weeks or so to sing Elizabethan madrigals in parts. The Society, like the Choir, brought together both senior and junior boys, and also enlisted the services of some dons and dons' wives who liked to sing, which made it a still pleasanter social occasion. The following summer we even rehearsed Delius' eight-part madrigal *To Be Sung of A Summer Night On the Water*, and sang it memorably one warm July evening beside College Pond, among the mosquitoes.

This second term also saw the beginning of my involvement with Radley drama. The parts of women were played by junior boys in those days, and for my first production I was cast as Gwendolen in the middle act of *The Importance of Being Earnest*, thus beginning a lifelong love of that matchless play. Then, for the Social Drama Competition the following term, I played Emily in a shortened version of Thornton Wilder's *Our Town*. "Goodbye world! Goodbye father and mother..." These dramatic activities took place in 'the old Gym', a cross-shaped and ramshackle corrugated iron building which was reputed to have been designed around 1860 as a prefabricated cathedral bound for Australia, but which William Sewell somehow bought off the docks and had transported to Radley. It was a place I spent a lot of time in during the next four years, and my acting friends and I learnt to love its odd and messy but unmistakeably theatrical atmosphere. A highlight of its year, incidentally, was 'The Don's Plays', written composed and acted by the dons, performed at All Saints' weekend, and offering the boys a wonderful chance to laugh at their teachers. Mr Hammond-Chambers-Borgnis was the musical genius behind the plays my first year, and even now I can recall some of his tunes. I can still see the very large cricket coach I.A.W. Gilliatt dressed as a fairy and opening the show with a prologue:

Not in the upper world reign I a queen
But in the demi-monde am I much seen.

There were other more modest chances for me to perform. Our form master – now Theo Cocks – would give us the job of learning a sonnet or other short poem to recite in class once or twice a term; an old Radley tradition known as "memoriter". And twice a year a contest called "Declamations", revived by our Warden from Radley's earliest days, was held for boys at various levels of the school, and in which any boy who wished could enter. The contestants had to memorise and recite one set poem or prose passage, and one piece of their own choosing. This was something I felt confident about, and was successful with several times on my way up the school – though our first adjudicator, in awarding me the prize for my section, was not entirely complimentary when he referred to my delivery as 'the Voice Beautiful'.

That adjudicator was Peter (P.D.L.) Way, an Old Radleian who was to join the Radley staff in 1952, and to become one of our principal English teachers. He also took on the major burden of producing the school's drama, and in the autumn of 1952 mounted *Romeo and Juliet* with a cast of the school's younger boys. To my huge delight he cast me as Romeo, and I had the rare privilege at the age of fifteen of being able to play one of Shakespeare's major roles in a full production. A fulsome reviewer in 'The Radleian' described my performance as 'wholly admirable', going on to say that I had the advantage of 'a voice of great beauty'. That damned Voice Beautiful again.

Peter Way had fought in the Italian campaign as a platoon commander in the 60th Rifles, and came back to Radley having read English at Oxford, and after a spell of teaching at Bristol Grammar and a year at an American private school. Not yet thirty, he was tall, earnest, energetic, fast walking, dressed in cavalry twill trousers with tweed jacket or blazer over discreetly-checked shirts and establishment ties, and he spoke English with a classy Radley-and-Oxford accent. He had the odd mannerism of not being able to speak and laugh at the same time: he would speak, and then he would laugh. Peter's passion for the drama energised Radley's dramatic productions. And his love of literature soon won those of us who were already caught up in poetry. He did not have the vatic thrill of Charles Wrinch, but his careful reading of texts, his sensitivity to words, his enthusiasm, were irresistible. It was through Peter's involvement with the Literary Society that we were to receive visits from literary luminaries during those years, including Keats' biographer Robert Gittings, poet Elizabeth Jennings, novelist R.C. Hutchinson and the famous bibliophile from Worcester College, Colonel Wilkinson (from whose talk I preserved and have always treasured one comment: "I have found through life that I have always regretted my economies and never my extravagances."). It was above all Peter's extraordinarily dynamic love of the school and of literature, and his devotion to the boys in his charge, that offered a model of dedication for us all.

The school at that time also had a Marionette Society, which performed in its own small theatre outside School, seating as many as a hundred. The marionettes were string puppets, operated from a gallery above the diminutive stage. The guiding light of the Society was Chris (C.St.J.) Ellis.)

Chris (he was always 'Chris' to the boys) had been brought on to the Radley staff by John Wilkes a few years before, to teach arts and crafts and beginning-level mathematics. Short and curly-haired, with a small, oddly-curved nose, an easy manner, a dazzling smile and a ready laugh, Chris was the most unorthodox don in Radley's Common Room. An Etonian like Wilkes, and a noted yachtsman, he had won the George Medal for bomb disposal during the war. He was a carpenter, a fine draftsman, a flautist, an inventor and brilliant improviser – and something of a subversive. He had the extraordinary knack of attracting boys around him, and was especially important to the ones who were not and never would be scholars, but who shone in activities which needed courage and improvisation, inventiveness and tenacity. Schedules never meant very much to him, and he would often deliver boys late to their classes after having taken them away on one escapade or another. He drove an ancient and storied truck, and later a splendid open Lagonda. He cut a romantic figure. I have never known anyone so much themselves at all times and in every situation. (A vivid memory fits in here. One sunny summer afternoon I was astonished to see Chris's battered old open truck departing down the driveway, carrying a party of dons and their wives in full evening dress, sitting on benches, four or five on each side. It turned out that they were off to Glyndebourne to see the opera!)

Chris had been asked to take over the leadership of the Marionettes a year or two before, and had immediately suggested that rather than doing puppet stunts the Society should mount a full-length opera or operetta. In my first year they presented *The Pirates of Penzance*. Designer for the production was A.J. (Tony) Walton, a sixteen-year-old boy at that time, who created not only magnificent stage sets but some really astonishingly creative character puppets. (He was later to become a celebrated stage designer in London and on Broadway, and for some years was married to his childhood sweetheart Julie Andrews.) While Tony's marionettes disported themselves in front of his miniature sets, the soloists and chorus stood in the wings behind the stage giving voice to the characters, accompanied by a small orchestra.

I was lucky enough to be asked to play the supporting part of Edith ("How beautifully blue the sky, The glass is rising very high, Continue fine I hope it may, And yet it rained but yesterday .. "), and so dipped a first small toe into the world of Chris Ellis. I was not a typical member of his cadre: he was mildly cynical about classical scholars, and had little respect for the Latin-and-Greek hegemony which still reigned at the school. But I did sing and act and play the piano, which slightly took the mould off my classical afflatus. A year or two later he was good enough to invite me to direct *The Beggar's Opera* for the Marionettes: the first time I had ever directed a theatre piece. Maybe it was helpful for my initiation into that heady world that all my actors were made of wood and unable to talk back. I am not sure that my production solved the essential bagginess of the play. But I was to have plenty of opportunities in the future to look at it again.

Chris also taught me for a term or two in his low level mathematics classes, preparing me for the 'O' level exam which I took at the age of fifteen, and with which I said goodbye for ever to scientific learning of any kind. I learned enough from him to pass, but Chris in a conventional classroom was like a caged animal. His element was the outdoors, was adventure, was making things, was total commitment, was saying yes to anything unexpected. Exams and marks and quizzes he had little use for. Charles Wrinch once said of Chris, wittily and well, that he played Ariel to John Wilkes's Prospero.

And then there was Charles Wrinch. Black-haired, high-browed and weighed down by large horn-rimmed spectacles, he wore a continual expression of surprise. He spoke with great emphasis and oracular authority; we loved to hear him talk. And because he could easily be distracted from his plan for the class by any number of red herrings, it became a game to push him off track and into rich diversions. He would wander away in a trance of associations and pace up and down between the desks, so caught up that I remember one class where I was able to take a photograph of him in full flight without his being aware of it – at least I think not!

It was in my first or second year that Charles taught Greek to our Classical Fifth form. He was at his best taking us through a passage of Homer or Thucydides, where his breadth of interest and his intense eye and ear for drama had full play. He found it harder to deal with the routines of learning grammar, but managed to find dramatic ways of getting us not just to learn but to feel the language. I remember well the day he began to deal with the Greek verb 'ιστημι', to stand. A stodgier teacher would have declined the forms of the word in all its different tenses, and expected us to learn and parrot them back. But Charles went another way: he actually acted out each tense in front of us. "'ιστημι(histeemi)' – I stand, I am standing..." and he planted his feet apart and jumped up and down heavily. "I <u>am</u> <u>standing</u>." He paused for this to sink in. Then: "'εστην(esteen)' – I stood, I stood" – and he thrust out his arms to

Percy Bawtree and family, 1909, one-year-old Raymond
in a dress on his mother's knee

McEacharn grandparents

Ray aged 21

Tessa, aged 21

Fake coat of arms of the Bawtree family – 'baa' tree

Ray's and Tessa's passport photos, 1938

The *Strathnaver*, Sydney-London 1938

Lyd Valley House, Devon

Jo and MB, Lyd Valley 1940

The River Lyd below Lyd Valley House

Raymond Bawtree, Captain,
Home Guard

MB in a Tavistock studio, 1942

Poole cottage

Jo, Tessa and MB with Puppy, Jenny and Squiggly, Poole, 1943
(note Tessa's wartime necklace of spiral poultry rings)

The Bawtree family, 1944

Langstone Manor, old entrance

Langstone Manor, west façade

MB with father on Piccadilly, 1950   MB in 1945, aged eight

Arthur Harrison, Headmaster at Marlborough House School

The Bawtree camp: Surrey, summer 1946

Studley Priory in 1950

Studley, east façade

Studley Priory kitchen
garden under snow

MB with mother at Henley, 1952

Charles Wrinch, Radley don

Radley College, Abingdon

MB (right) as Romeo at Radley, 1953

A worried MB at Radley in 1954,
aged 16

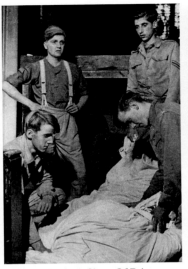

MB (right) in A Sleep Of Prisoners, Radley, 1955

Camping Italy, 1956

MB with Peter Cook and Jonathan Harlow on an English camping holiday in 1956

2/Lts Edward Jones and MB making use of local transport, Cyprus 1957

2/Lt MB, platoon
commander, 1957

Celebrating my 21st birthday on
Theodora, August 25 1958

Theodora in Vigo Harbour

Chris Ellis, Southampton 1959

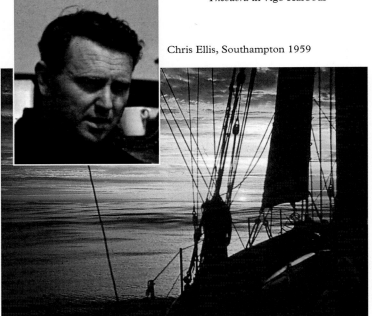

Homeward bound: sunrise on *Theodora*

Worcester College, Oxford (Iain Mackintosh)

Dressed for finals, 1961

Punting on the Cherwell, 1960

Photo op for Next Time Yes with Worcester Buskins, 1960; MB 3rd from left

With Vincent's Club, 1961

MB (left) as Lockit in *The Beggar's Opera*, Worcester Buskins 1960

MB (right) as Launce in *Two Gentlemen of Verona*, with Richard Hooper
as Proteus, Worcester Buskins 1960

MB (left) with Roger Mills in *That Was No Lady*, ETC Oxford 1959

MB 1962: young man going west

SS Arkadia

GREEK LINE

PASSAGE CONTRACT
TICKET

Nᵒ 119168

WESTBOUND

This passage contract is issued subject to all terms and conditions contained in coupon VII and subsequent pages of this ticket.

VERY IMPORTANT. The reservation(s) covered by this ticket should be confirmed two weeks before sailing, with any Greek Line agency listed on this ticket, preferably with an agency in the country of the port of embarkation. Failure to do so will make the reservation(s) liable to cancellation.

Ticket for Canada,
September 1962

the right, as though pushing the past away and down with a grimace: "I <u>did</u> stand, I <u>did</u> stand." Pause. Then: "'στησομαι (steesomai)' – I <u>will</u> stand, I <u>will</u> stand" – and he smiled excitedly and reached his arms upwards now and to the left, as though grabbing eagerly at the future. And so on, through the optative, the perfect, the pluperfect. His contortions in pursuit of the future conditional can be imagined, and of course we became more and more hysterical. But years later his dance of the tenses stays with me.

Charles, though, was more than a classicist. He had a deep and passionate love of poetry, and taught English as well as Greek. Naturally he was president of Radley's Poetry Society, which met every other Wednesday in the Chaplain's cosy rooms at the top of the Mansion. After writing a narrative poem about 'The Reverend Job' in my second year I showed it to the Chaplain, and he invited me to join the Society. It was a treasured home for those of us with poetical inclinations, bringing young and old boys together to sit at the feet of Charles, who in this temple had the authority of a high priest. (Charles, I realize now, was above all a divine conversationalist, ready to speak with seriousness, wit and knowledge on almost any subject, and always conveying a sense that there was a mother-lode of knowledge and of culture from which he was able to draw, and to which with diligence and effort we too could aspire.) Some evenings were devoted to our own poetry, and we would take turns to read our latest adolescent effusions. There would be a respectful silence after we had finished, and then Charles would speak first. He was always able to find something encouraging to say: noticing an image or turn of phrase here, a piece of alliteration or unexpected rhythm there. Others would then chime in, and finally, with much more assurance, we would read our poem again, before moving to the next piece. It was not only Charles' acute critical sense but his generosity to us all, his ever-ready sense of wonder and delight, which remain with me. "Extraordinary. Extraordinary... Really very remarkable in*deed*."

Other Society evenings would be spent on the works of well-known poets old and new, and Charles was never at a loss, knowing variant readings in different editions, or some fact of a private life, or sharing personal reminiscences of the more recent writers. I remember arriving at a meeting in late 1953, and immediately becoming aware of a hush in the room. I looked puzzled, and was informed quietly that Dylan Thomas had died in New York that day at the age of thirty-nine. Charles appeared stricken, as though a loved one had passed to the shades. "But he could never have reached forty," said Charles with characteristic certainty: "He could never have reached forty." A delicate reference to Dylan's alcoholism, no doubt, but also a tribute to the youthful vigour of "the force that through the green fuse drives the flower." Whatever had been planned for the evening was put aside, and in reverent homage we read "Poem in October", "Ballad of the Long-legged Bait" and "The Hunchback in the Park."

My own poems of those years, which still survive in a dog-eared manuscript notebook, show me writing at first in a rather flaccid five-foot metre, and moving slowly to a somewhat more muscular line, under the influence no doubt of Dylan Thomas and perhaps Hopkins. But the poems as I read them now, raw as they are and usually ending in a whimper, reveal two other elements I was hardly aware of.

First, at some time in the summer holidays of 1953, I changed my handwriting. Back in Marlborough House days my schoolmates and I had been introduced to Italic script by Arthur Harrison and his wife Muffet, who shared this passion with their friend Wilfrid Blunt – himself a fine calligrapher and later author of *Sweet Roman Hand: Five Hundred Years of Roman Calligraphy*. But true to my reluctance to learn physical skills of any kind – my odd belief (already mentioned) that if a skill did not come by instinct it was beyond me – I did not even consider the tricky business of training myself to write in a different way. It's perhaps a tribute to the education I was now receiving, or maybe simply a matter of growing up, that I now took on this task with the aid of an Italic sampler. My first efforts were painstaking and stultifyingly perfect, my poems suddenly recorded in a hand so archly beautiful that I think their content almost took second place. Warming to my work, I soon found myself writing my name on the front cover of exercise books with elaborate care, accompanied with extravagant and self-indulgent swirls. This in fact became such a habit that I even decided I had to wean myself from it: leaving the front cover to last in order not be hung up with the container for the thing contained. It's a wariness I am still conscious of even today. And though the florid perfection of that early campery is long forgotten, my hand did improve enormously for the better, and is even sometimes admired – on those rare occasions away from the computer when one's handwriting is still seen in anything more than a signature.

The other element revealed by those adolescent poems, full of flabby words like 'timeless' and 'joyous' and 'desolate' and 'indeed', is the pervasive presence of 'God' in one piece after the other. Evidently Radley's ministry was having its effect, and I was beginning to model my future self on the image of the God-loving, God-fearing young Mr Perfect, fighting the good fight with all his might. I was even persuaded in my second year to attend a fortnight's religious 'camp' at Iwerne Minster in Dorset, run by evangelical and muscular young Christians, up at – or fresh out of – Oxford and Cambridge. They included David Sheppard, at that time a schoolboy cricketing idol for his superb batting for Sussex and England, and much later to become Bishop of Liverpool. A new Radley don, Christopher Turner, was also among the staff: in fact he may have had something to do with my being caught up in the movement. I was to see a lot of him in my school career because he taught Latin, Greek and Ancient History, as well as coaching the First VIII. He was our form master for a year or more. He also served as the Social Sub-Tutor – the second-in-command – of my social, with bachelor rooms on the top floor, where he used to entertain us with tea and chocolate cake and symphonies on the gramophone. But for all his kindness I did not take to the hearty evangelical strain in the camp's religion, and when he invited me to return a second year, I declined, saying piously that I felt that they did not put enough emphasis on the Eucharist.

This High Anglican demurral, like my poetic preoccupation with God, probably had something to do with the fact that I was preparing for confirmation. Hands were laid on me by the Bishop of Oxford, I think in the winter of 1954, following a personal confession in Chapel before Charles Neate, sacramental and all ears in his black cassock. I can't think now what sins I might have confessed to, but apart from the usual petty unkindnesses they probably included some guilt for the sexual stirrings of puberty.

In this connection, it was around this time that I had a startling experience. I was developing prints in the darkrooms out in the Music School one evening, when I suddenly had a presentiment that it was getting late. The darkroom clock showed 8.15, but when I ran downstairs to check the clock in the hall it said 9 pm – long after the time I was due back in the social to prepare for bed. I was struck by a bolt of horror and panic. And at that very moment, for the first time in my life, I had a spontaneous ejaculation. Pleasure allied to fear. It's an odd thing, but since then, throughout my life, a spontaneous 'nocturnal emission' has nearly always been preceded by a moment of panic in my dreams, when I find I have just missed a train or a plane. Be that as it may, I was still a prepubescent child at the beginning of this middle period of my time at Radley. By the end of it I discovered myself to be a youth, and beginning to endure the private emotional turmoil of not knowing who or what I was. One of my poems around that time, in fact the last one to be recorded in my old hand, was dated July 25th, 1953, and below it the comment 'In despair.' I have no memory of what may have led to this self-pity. But I have an idea:

It may have been the result of great naivety on my part, but in my whole time at Radley I was never aware of any practising sexual activity between or among the boys. On the other hand I was highly conscious of amorous feelings, felt especially by boys of fifteen to seventeen towards boys two or three years younger. As a new boy I was aware of a house prefect in my social who made eyes at me in the bathroom, and I was very careful to avoid being alone in his company. A year or two later I fell myself for a pretty young fellow who happened to be a musician and chorister, so that our paths often crossed, and I was able to feast my eyes on his callow beauty regularly in Chapel and the Music School. These amours and crushes were not much a matter of shame if I remember. But I do know that I was deeply afraid lest I should find out that I was homosexual, and was much cheered up by having been told in our early sex instruction lectures at Radley (delivered by a Mr Noble, a visiting expert whose name gave rise to many a bawdy joke) that it was quite normal in adolescence for boys – and girls too – to experience amorous feelings and even physical desire for their own sex. It was something we would grow out of, we were told. I looked forward to that. Meanwhile I suffered the usual pangs of unrealisable desire. I remember once during the holidays receiving a pedestrian letter from the Admired One, and rushing out to the garden at Studley to read it – over and over and over. I suppose this was my first experience of the tumultuous feeling of being in love.

In spite of this emotional undertow, shared of course with absolutely no one, I managed to keep moving forward on the daily round and even the common task. I landed an 'intermediate' piano prize, as well as a junior poetry prize for a poem I now find shapeless and unreadable. The summer of 1953 also saw me and my contemporaries taking our 'O' level exams. I sat eight of them, I remember: I think they were Latin, Greek, English Language, English Literature, History, Physics, Maths and French. I succeeded in gaining at least adequate marks in all subjects – and thereafter dropped any further classes in either Maths or Physics. Thus I was separated permanently from the sciences, and found myself set irrevocably on the road of classical scholarship, with multiple classes in Latin and Greek, and with our History henceforward to be only 'Ancient History', from Homeric times to the fall of Rome. I don't remember even at this point questioning the direction of my studies, or even considering another. The trajectory leading to the classical programme of 'Mods and Greats' at Oxford was still the One True Path for those of us who had been battling with those two dead languages since we were small boys: I remember the surprise at discovering that one of my fellow scholars, Jonathan Harlow, had elected to specialise in History and English. It looked almost subversive.

It seemed to be assumed by our classical mentors that if you mastered Latin and Greek; if you could read the Odes of Horace and Virgil's Aeneid and the terse ironies of Tacitus; if you could decipher Homer and Thucydides and Herodotus and Xenophon and Plato in those beautiful Greek characters; if you could translate 'unseen' passages from both languages, and even turn English prose and verse into Latin or Greek; then somehow everything else in the world of learning and culture would be added unto you, not to mention a career in almost any field. We were learning (so we understood) to think, to analyse, to remember, to enter into the minds of people long dead, to be part of the long history of high civilisation in Western Europe.

At Radley in those days, this affirmation of classical education's supremacy managed somehow to avoid the pagan aspects of those ancient masters, and especially to skirt around the Greek celebration of homoerotic love. In fact, it somehow fed itself, with no apparent contradictions, into the moral earnestness of the school's Christian tradition. It's true that the most senior – and probably most pagan – of our teachers of Latin and Greek, Theo Cocks, was a child of the 1920s, an aging bachelor dandy, and a throwback to the world of Bertie Wooster; he, I suspect, was mildly cynical about the clerical regime he worked for. But our other classical dons – Turner, Wrinch and Vaughan Wilkes – were all devoutly religious, and so classical in the renaissance humanist tradition. They were also somewhat unworldly, all of them – beginning with Vaughan Wilkes himself. They were not exactly careless in their dress: Charles Wrinch in particular was fond of sporting a bright red handkerchief in his breast pocket, which he would take out and mop his brow with after a frenzied effusion. But they were old-fashioned, Wilkes in his dog-collar and the other two in their tweed jackets and grey flannels and ties. They were very much 'un-urbane': sincere, a little awkward, and high-minded. And so in fact were most of the other dons whose paths crossed with mine: Anthony Caesar, Peter Way, and in his very different style Chris Ellis. For all their public school and university pedigrees none of them had the smoothness and self-assurance in their social graces which I have always found unsettling. They were closer to St. Francis than to St. Paul.

John Wilkes left Radley at the end of 1953, to pursue a long-held dream of carrying out pastoral work. He became Vicar of

Hunslet, a sad working-class suburb of Leeds. For some reason I identified with his leaving, to the extent that I wrote a poem about it:

Trouble the world, cry break
to the sight of the
salt brick simmering,
Cry wash away to the
green summer seas
breaking over the trees
And the cricket bat knock of the long easy green
and the peace of the years...
and so on.

Wilkes' place was taken by W.M.M. Milligan, also a former Eton master, but of a very different stamp: handsome and charming, a Cambridge man, highly bred, immaculately turned out, with a distinguished war record in the Scots Guards, and displaying all the smoothness of manner which Wilkes lacked. His laugh seemed to have something manufactured about it; his kindness and warmth always tended to come across as a performance. But he was also a classicist, so we classical types went on being in royal favour, and continued to see ourselves as stumping up the road to the highest honours.

And Oxford was still the goal. Proximity to the University cemented its influence on us. We attended concerts at the Sheldonian Theatre. We were permitted to bicycle into the city on afternoons off, and if we won awards were allowed to choose our prizes at Blackwell's bookshop, rubbing shoulders with professors and undergraduates. Distinguished classical historians like Ronald Syme and Russell Meiggs were invited out to address us. And once a year Classical Declamations were held in Magdalen College hall,

open to students from local schools. We had to learn and recite a
set poem in both Latin and Greek, and were then handed a piece
of text in each language, with fifteen minutes to scan it before
reading it for the adjudicator, who more than once was Gilbert
Murray (already met with at Studley). Here I had the advantage
of my theatre experience, and two or three times came away with
the prize.

I remember one year in particular, perhaps 1953, when Charles
Wrinch drove the two or three Radley candidates into Oxford
early in his ramshackle car, because before the adjudications began
he was determined to take us along Addison's Walk to the Meadow
in Magdalen's gardens, in order to show us the rare snakeshead
fritillaries that were just then blooming. This was probably as good
a preparation for the competition as any other.

The Latin poem that year was Horace's ode 'Eheu fugaces,
Postume, Postume, labuntur anni ...': 'Alas, Postumus, Postumus, the
fleeting years slide by...' When the recitations were over and the
prizes had been awarded, Charles stood up in the audience and
asked 'Professor Murray' whether he would consider giving us his
own rendering of the Horace. Murray agreed, and we were to hear
that good old man, well into his eighties, reading this poem of
farewell to life and love, in a quavering voice. The fact that Murray's
wife had recently succumbed to senile dementia added pathos for
Charles, who knew this and was much moved by the line Linquenda
tellus et domus et placens uxor... 'We must say goodbye to land, and
home, and beloved wife.'

It was at the same event the following year that I met a fellow
candidate from Oxford High School. Her name was Pippa
Norrington, and I found her wonderfully attractive and intelligent.
We exchanged letters, and I was delighted to have something like
a girlfriend. It was only later that I discovered her father to be

President of Trinity College. I subsequently met this lively and charming man and his wife, as well as her two brothers Humphrey and Roger. Roger was working in a bank, but was shortly to leave it for what became his stellar career as a conductor. Pippa and I remained friends for some years.

I suppose the *mezzo del cammin* of my life at Radley could be placed, then, somewhere around the end of this year of 1954. By this time I was a young adult, and beginning to look outwards to the world. But chronology is never tidy, and there is some catching up to do before tackling the final phase of my rich and lucky schooling.

CHAPTER SIX

GANNETS AND FRIENDS

Outside the cocoon of Radley in those first years, the world outside, strange as it may seem, did go on. The Festival of Britain, Labour's brave effort to lift the country out of its post-war doldrums in 1951, ran its course during that summer, and although my own family never passed through its turnstiles, its landmark structures like the Dome of Discovery and the Skylon – a cigar shaped object floating high above the site – became iconic in our imaginations. I'm not aware that any parties from Radley visited the Festival, and we were no doubt influenced by the general right-wing feeling that the whole affair was a doomed Labour party initiative: Churchill called it "three-dimensional Socialist propaganda." Attlee's hope that its popularity would help his party win the next General Election did not materialise: the Tory party trounced Labour that autumn, and Churchill, now 77, was once again our Prime Minister. It is said that his first act was to order the Festival of Britain site to be demolished.

The King's death in February the following year brought Princess Elizabeth to the throne. Once the mourning for George VI was over, great play was given to the vision of the country entering a new Elizabethan Age, and this excitement probably cheered people up far more than the programmed gaiety of the Festival of Britain ever did. The Coronation was set for June 1953, and from the beginning of that year there were celebrations planned and rehearsed all over the country. Radley was not behindhand. At the nearby town of Abingdon there was a large mediaeval timber-roofed chamber (part of the semi-ruined Abingdon Abbey) which a local arts group had permission to develop. One member of the group was Charles Wrinch, and in late 1952 he recommended that Chris Ellis be hired to convert the space into an 'Elizabethan' theatre, with apron stage, brightly-painted scenic background and a gallery above. Chris brought boys from Radley to help with the woodwork, and he is rumoured to have been up on a ladder completing the painting of 'ERII' above the proscenium half an hour before lights went up on the first performance. One of the events put on that summer was a selection from *The Triumphs of Oriana*, a set of madrigals first collected in 1601 by Thomas Morley, and believed to be written in homage to the first Queen Elizabeth. The concert was presented on a sunny May evening by Radley's Madrigal Society under the direction of Anthony Caesar. I have no recollection of how we got there – perhaps we cycled in – but it was a beautiful occasion, and we eagerly and uncritically played our part in linking the glories of the old Virgin Queen to the new reign.

Back at Radley one of the cleaners, a German ex-prisoner of war with a background in window-dressing, decorated the whole college inside and out with banners and tassels, and with a huge royal coat of arms on the south side of the Mansion. Meanwhile we were busy preparing a concert of coronation music for the parents' day to take place at the end of May: *Pomp and Circumstance*, Handel's *Zadok the Priest*, Walton's *Coronation March* and Parry's heart-stirring *I Was Glad*... after which the school was to be sent off on a holiday for the whole of Coronation Week.

My sister Jo, who had by this time abandoned her white coat in North Oxford for a secretarial post in the office of the Royal Academy on Piccadilly, had suggested that she and I get together in London to watch the coronation procession. My father had taken the giant step of purchasing a television for Studley guests to watch the coronation (the set was banished into a room of its own outside the bar, with deck chairs from the garden set up for the occasion). But I was much more interested in going up to London for the thing itself.

I was wondering how to make the journey when my musical friend Richard Latham told me that his parents, who lived in Notting Hill Gate, were coming to our concert, and that they could take me with them to London when it was over. I did not know it at the time, but this fortuitous ride in the Lathams' little Ford Prefect spelled the beginning of a ripening friendship with Richard and his family, and even an opening up into the musical world of the capital. I spent that night with them at their little house on Ossington Street, just off the Bayswater Road: the first of many visits.

Jo shared much humbler lodgings with an old school friend or two on Stadium Street, at World's End, Chelsea, and I was delivered there the next day. Number Six was a mustily damp terrace house, as I knew well because I slept on the mustily damp carpet in the living-room – quite happily; I was excited to be away from school for a whole week, to be seeing my dear sister Jo in London Town, and to be sharing in the national excitement as we approached the big day. Suddenly, from out of a generalised mist of months and years, those next hours stand out with startling clarity.

Around eight o'clock on the grey, brisk evening of Monday June 1st, armed with blankets, extra sweaters, sandwiches, chocolate, apples and a thermos of tea, Jo and I caught the 22 bus up the King's

Road to Piccadilly Circus, where we met up with her current boyfriend, an Australian called Richard. The pavements were already peppered with people several rows deep, sitting on stools or deck chairs, or kneeling on newspapers, chatting, drinking, laughing, and singing. We knew that places like the Mall and Trafalgar Square, where the procession would pass twice – on its way both to and from the Abbey – would already be jammed, so we had decided to search for a spot on Piccadilly, where we would see the Queen pass only once, but where we could be sure of a view from the front row. Even so, we walked as far as the Piccadilly Hotel – almost to Hyde Park Corner – before we reached the end of the swiftly gathering crowd, and the three of us staked our place right at the kerb, in front of a chemist's.

It was growing dark and getting chillier. People kept milling past, and within an hour or two the pavement was filled to four or five rows back with cheery, beery folk. Seats of every kind popped up, blankets spread out, picnic baskets opened, and, with traffic already closed off, the sound of raised voices, and laughter and singing, echoed up the street: transistor radios were still a thing of the future.

Richard had brought a mickey of rye whisky which he was happy to share with us, but there were no glasses. He disappeared into the chemist's and came back having purchased a blue glass eyebath, from which we happily sipped the fiery liquor to keep warm.

Towards midnight we stretched out on the flagstones and tried to sleep. It was amazingly uncomfortable. After an hour or so the resourceful Richard got up and took off down a back street. In a few minutes he reappeared, telling us he had made a deal with the garage attendant underneath the Piccadilly Hotel. We could take turns to go back to the garage, where he would let us sleep in one of the hotel guests' cars. This was a highly priced establishment, probably accommodating a host of lords and ladies for the next day's celebration, which is why within a few minutes I found myself in the heated garage lying happily along the back seat of a sumptuous black Rolls-Royce. One after the other, the three of us each had an hour or two of patrician comfort.

At three or four in the morning it started to rain softly, and umbrellas appeared up and down the street. We did not have one, and sheltered ourselves under raincoats and newspapers. The rain continued sporadically through the morning, and it was still unseasonably cold: 52 degrees Fahrenheit, I seem to remember.

At five o'clock the first newsboys trawled through with their dawn editions, and stirred excitement up and down the street at their unexpected cry: 'Everest conquered! Everest conquered!' Hillary and Tensing had scaled the peak a day or two earlier, and the story goes that the news was held back until the day of the coronation, to add to the pride of the occasion. We certainly felt a little transcendent, partly no doubt from the whisky and the lack of sleep.

The morning went by fast enough. The coronation service, with Richard Dimbleby on hand to explain it to us in his hushed and reverent tones, was relayed by loudspeakers strung along the street on the Hyde Park side. *'Vivat Regina Elizabetha!'* Finally the newly-crowned Queen left the Abbey. The procession which made their way past us down Piccadilly must have continued for an hour or more, putting on display perhaps for the last time the wide reach of the British Empire, with Indian sepoys, colonial and dominion prime ministers galore, Queen Salote of Tonga, South Africans, Australians, Canadians, cavalry, infantry, gunners, marines, sailors, airmen. So many horses, so many landaus and carriages, so much livery, so many banners, so many marching bands, so many marching men – and even women. And it was the only time I ever set eyes on Winston Churchill: a big bald head seen faintly through his carriage window, with two fingers stuck out for his rude victory sign, eliciting a roar from the crowd. The Queen's coach, drawn by eight white horses, swayed along towards the end of the massive march- and ride-past, a low-slung fantasy of gilt encrustation and curlicues and crowns and tritons. Beside it, men walked in long scarlet coats. Inside it sat the heavily-crowned Queen, pale and smiling and waving the famous, much-parodied wave, husband Philip beside her. You did not have to be a monarchist to respond to the extraordinary aesthetic beauty and power of it all. And I was a monarchist: how could I not be?

When it was all over, we made our way up Piccadilly with the dispersing crowd, and the last memory I have of the occasion is sitting on the steps of Burlington House, drinking more belts of rye whisky – this time out of glasses Jo had rustled up from her office behind us. The liquor soon turned my young head.

The Coronation expedition, at a time when I was approaching my sixteenth birthday, seemed to mark the beginning of my venturing out into the world for the first time on my own and without my family. Yes, I was growing up. During the summer holiday which followed, I announced to my worried mother and father that I was taking off for a bicycle ride. The next day I set out, pedalling my old upright, three-speed black bike the sixty miles to Bath, where I stayed in a bed & breakfast in the town, with a window looking on to the Abbey and its chimes in my ears all night. By the next day I was down in the New Forest. And on the third day, overtaken by pouring rain, I made for Basingstoke, where I took the train back to Oxford and rode happily home. Later in the summer I was away again, teaming up with my old Marlborough House schoolmate Brian Knox-Peebles for a week's walking in the Lake

District. Apart from our responding joyously to the beauties of Borrowdale, that trip was chiefly memorable because Brian and I, in I don't know what post-coronation flush of national pride and concern, penned a joint letter to Winston Churchill, asking what we could do for our country. Brian eventually received a polite but stiff letter back from the Prime Minister's office, signed by the staff member who presumably was deputed to answer the letters of fans and crazies.

It was at the beginning of one autumn term of these middle years at Radley that a group of us got talking to a boy whose mother was Canadian, and who had just returned from a summer in Ontario. He talked of canoeing and camping out on the French River, of the breathless beauty of Algonquin Park, of the Indians he had seen, of the air and the freedom. He showed us the tasselled Indian leather jacket he had brought back, embroidered with beads. And he wore a red plaid shirt which gave him the look of a miniature lumberjack. His stories stayed with me for years.

My own ventures into the world became a little more venturesome. Early in the winter term of 1955, Warden Milligan asked me whether I would like to join a trip to Greece, organized by two classics masters from Westminster School. I told him I would love to, but that my parents couldn't possibly pay for it. Somehow he kindly organized the funds for me, and a few days after the end of term, armed with my first passport, I joined up with a couple of dozen classics boys from different public schools, on the platform at Waterloo and bound for the first time for 'the Continent'. Our guides and organizers were Theodore Zinn, a tall, stout, brilliant, malodorous polyglot with beads of sweat perpetually on his upper lip; Ted Craven, short and charming and a chain smoker; and Ted's wife, with thick spectacles magnifying her dark eyes, and full of kindly but exhausting brightness.

This was long before the days of cheap continental flights. We had before us the train ride to Dover and the ferry to Ostend, where we joined the Tauern Express for the four-day rail journey to Athens. To keep costs down no sleepers had been booked, and we were expected to doss down as best we could on the hard leatherette seats. With a few other boys I found myself in a compartment with the Cravens, and we eventually made ourselves a little more comfortable at night by hauling our luggage down from the overhead racks and filling the space between the seats, turning the whole compartment into a vast uneven bed, on which we slept a few hours at a time. But excitement outweighed discomfort, and as we chuffed through Belgium, Germany (Germany!), Austria and Yugoslavia, with passports inspected at every frontier, familiar names went tantalisingly by: Brussels, Liège, Köln, Stuttgart, München, Salzburg... I think we had to change trains unexpectedly in Serbia's capital, Zagreb, and remember Mr Zinn haranguing the stationmaster in Serbo-Croat, to our admiration. I'm not sure if it was on the original plan, but we also stopped in Skopje, Macedonia, for a night in a very spartan hotel, with supper in a collective restaurant – where, amazingly, Elgar's *Enigma Variations* were playing on the address system. A walk in the early morning led us over ancient humped bridges and past tiny mediaeval booths in which silversmiths worked by lamplight. Everything was drab and poor. Wan people looked at us curiously in our English schoolboy clothes. But they were wary. No one spoke to us.

And then we got back on board for the final run, crossing the border into Greece and heading down through Thessalonika to Athens, the alpha and omega of our classical dreams. As we steamed south we also headed into spring, arriving at last into a land of blossoming almond trees, and the gentle warmth of the Mediterranean.

We were booked into a simple modern hotel, the *Estia Emperon*, and that first night slept long and deep. Next morning began with a stroll through the market: the smell of Turkish coffee, combined with the exotic fragrance of Mediterranean herbs and spices from the Orient piled in open sacks in the warm sunshine outside the market stalls, was my first heady experience of the sensuous South. I was smitten, and still sixty years later remember the sensation.

Everything Greek was strangely familiar: we understood the terrain of the country well from our history lessons. We knew the names of the towns, and the hills and plains and capes and bays and islands. But the Greece we knew was the Greece of the millennium before Christ; modern Greece was tiresomely in the way. It was like touring England with a Domesday map in hand. In the same way we could read every word of the Greek newspaper but could understand almost nothing, while our very English pronunciation of names like Aegina (to rhyme with 'China') was a mystery to the locals.

It had been less than a decade since victory against Hitler in Europe, and in Greece only six years since the Greek Civil War had finally seen the defeat of the communist forces of the North – with first British and then American help. We boys knew little of this, and were unaware of the tensions and bitterness which still divided the country. Athens was full of small-business bustle, but we were very conscious of the poverty of the land and its people. Most of the roads outside the capital were narrow and unpaved. There were few hotels, and almost no tourism, apart from occasional clusters of Germans at the great classical sites, emerging from smart new coaches and being addressed in loud and strident tones by their professorial guides, thus confirming our childishly hostile view of the old enemy. We could not help thinking of them as the conquerors returning with no remorse to the scene of their old triumphs.

But it was in those same classical sites that we found ourselves back on familiar territory. For the first days we had the Acropolis almost to ourselves, paying our few drachmas to climb up more than once through the Propyleia into that amazing cluster of buildings. The glory of the Parthenon did not disappoint us, and we cursed the explosion which had ripped it apart in the seventeenth century, after two thousand years of perfection. From there we climbed down to the theatre of Dionysus. It was still an unrestored ruin with its Roman accretions, but we sat on its marble steps as Mr Zinn explained things to us, marvelling to be in the theatre of Aeschylus, Sophocles, Euripides and Aristophanes. We also visited the remains of the agora down in the town, and imagined Socrates shuffling around among the citizens with his tiresome questions.

We took a day-trip out to Cape Sounion to visit the Temple of Poseidon, and located Byron's famous signature on the base of one of the columns. Later we embarked on a tour to Tiryns, Mycene, Corinth, the scanty remains of Sparta and the deserted mediaeval town of Mistra. Then to Olympia, and across the Gulf of Corinth by ferry to Delphi, where we stayed a night in the one hotel, an old rambling single-storey building of great charm, where the ravishingly beautiful daughter of the owner was named Aphrodite. Waking in the morning to walk over to the valley where the ruins of Delphi lie, and looking out beyond them to the misty olive groves of the Greek landscape, I felt one of those strangely powerful and always remembered stabs of consciousness: ' I am here at this place. I am in Delphi, the site of the oracle, the ομφαλος γης, the navel of the earth. I am here NOW.' Later, as we boarded our bus after exploring the ruined treasurehouses and temple and theatre, we stopped beside the Castalian spring, which descends from the mountain of Parnassus, and from which the ancient poets drank to encourage their muse. It was a homely little flow of water gushing out of the rocks beside the roadway, but we drank reverently – at least I did. And as we continued on our way back to Athens I was even inspired to write a few lines of verse – in Latin for some reason:

> *Montibus in Graecis Delphos fundavit Apollo*
> *Nunc quibus in templis Zinn Theodorus adest.*
> *Huc Timidi veniunt, Edwardus grataque coniunx:*
> *Fors potare nimis diva furore jubet.*

('Apollo founded Delphi in the Greek mountains: now Theodore Zinn is here in its temples. Hither come the Cravens, Edward and his pleasant wife. Perhaps the priestess in her frenzy is commanding them to drink too much.' This must have been a reference to our guides' enjoyment of the local plonk.)

I even managed to convey my own swelling aesthetic excitement with one further line:

Pulchrius est aliquo viso quodcumque videmus – 'Each thing we see is more beautiful than anything we saw before.'

Our last weekend in Greece coincided with Orthodox Easter. One of its high points took place late on Easter Saturday, when thousands would bring tapers and climb the zig-zag track up the conical limestone hill of Lycabettus, which rises sharply out of the city of Athens in the same way the Acropolis does. At midnight a priest would come out of the church of St. George on the hill's crest, with a candle lit from the eternal flame. He would light the taper of the person standing nearest to him, with the words Χριστος ανεστι – 'Christ is risen'. The flame would slowly be passed from taper to taper, always with the same exchange of words: 'Christos anesti.' Gradually the light would grow, creeping down the wide winding path to the base of the hill. We were told we could either watch this beautiful sight from the city, or be up there among the mass of taper-holders. I chose the latter, and managed to thrust myself to within a few feet of the priest when he emerged from his church in his black stovepipe hat. Later we found our way to the cathedral for the midnight service, amazed at the hurly-burly of it all, so different from the well-tempered discretion of our own dear C of E.

One other moment survives the erosions of memory. We took a boat ride to the island of Aegina, and along the way listened to Craven and Zinn describing – and pointing out – the movements of the Greek and Persian fleets at the Battle of Salamis, in 480 BCE. Once on the island a few of us climbed up to the ruined temple. It began to rain softly, and as we sheltered under an olive tree a gnarled old goatherd limped by with his flock. He stopped and tried to talk to us, not understanding that we did not understand. But soon he untied a leather bag and drew out bread, black olives, home-made cheese and a bottle of *retsina*, to share with us. That ancient Greek meal in the rain, with the columns of the temple beside us and the goats grazing happily by, somehow fused the present day with the old Greece we knew. I have treasured the memory since, and occasionally still purchase a bottle of piney *retsina* in honour of it.

In the summer of 1955 I was away again for three weeks: hitch-hiking to Denmark and back with a couple of Radley friends. Passing through Husum, in Schleswig-Holstein, we earned ourselves a few deutschmarks helping to unload barrels of herrings from a fishing boat. In Copenhagen we tracked down Fleming Jørgensen, a Danish boy who had spent the previous year at Radley. We were welcomed by his family: his father and uncle had both been prominent in the Danish resistance, and they treated us like princes. In fact I still marvel at the extraordinary enthusiasm and generosity with which we raw young Englishmen, with the Union

Jack sewn on to our rucksacks, were taken to people's hearts everywhere in Holland and Denmark, as though we personally had won the war. In Germany, not so much.

My father had given me fifteen pounds for my three week trip. When I returned home I offered him the five pounds I still had in my pocket: even in those days it was astounding how cheaply the young could travel. Amazed, and as usual more generous than he could afford to be, Father said I could keep the change.

By 1954, the Props at Studley Priory Country House Hotel were beginning to flag. They had signed the lease on the property for a term of fourteen years, but the agreement included an option to break it after seven. The business had still not taken off, and as the end of March approached after an especially grim winter, I know the three of them had awkward conversations among themselves. There's no question that my mother wanted to bring the lease to an end. She was worn out from the work in the hotel, and recently had had to take on more and more kitchen duties because we couldn't afford another cook. Serving up meals four times a day, day after day, week after week, she had had enough. She referred to the guests as 'the gannets' – the gannet is described in *British Birds* as 'a greedy, voracious bird.' Once she told me that she thought of the guests as tubes: she kept shovelling food into the top of the tube, and every few hours they would need to be filled up again. She had also lost belief in the business. Though my father would never discuss finances with her ('shielding her from his worries') it was obvious that things were very difficult, that meeting payroll and other overhead expenses was a weekly challenge, that the manager of Barclay's Bank in Oxford – a Mr Dwelly – was losing his patience with Dad's small but persistent overdraft, and that we had reached the point where we could no longer afford to repair the

Daimler, which stood rusting in the copse beside the engine-house, brambles growing up around it. This meant that Whitbread's Car Hire had to take Jenny into Headington School every weekday, and bring her back in the afternoons. The humourless Mr Whitbread, wearing his suit and chauffeur's cap and driving a smart Wolseley, would also have to ferry Father to Oxford and back two or three times a week for shopping and banking, and all these journeys added up. There was a little bus which took the villagers into the city and back on Wednesdays and Saturdays for a shilling or two, but my father would not dream of riding in a bus alongside the village folk. When he wanted to save money he preferred to walk, clutching his binoculars and catching up with bird life in the hedgerows. It was four and a half miles to the outskirts of Headington, where he could slip on to a city bus for the last couple of miles without too much loss to his *amour propre*.

Wilma was somewhat equivocal about renewing the lease, but she loved her garden and her cows, and she spent almost more time with my father than Mother did, working beside him in the office and exposed to all the gravity of the financial state of things but also more aware of reasons for optimism. Strangely it was Father who had to endure the full force of their financial anxieties — meeting with the bank manager and creditors, buying provisions from grocers and butchers whose previous month's bills remained unpaid, occasionally even asking long-term guests to pay their monthly accounts a day or two in advance — it was Father who simply would not hear of giving up. The tenacious believer, he was for ever convinced that a corner was about to be turned, that prosperity was in their grasp. He ingeniously raised some capital by persuading some regular guests to invest a thousand pounds in the business, in return for which they would be able to stay for two weeks every year without charge. I know C.S. Lewis was one of these, and Sir Bruce Richmond another, and so I think was the Oxford philosopher John Simopoulos. There were more. But the money they handed over soon vanished into the blue to pay off overdue bills; Mother with uncharacteristic cynicism referred to the whole business as 'the blotting paper fund.'

One source of tension was that the more money was earned by serving meals, the harder my mother had to work. I remember one particularly tense evening. It was around 9.30. Mother had just finished scouring and drying the last pots and pans when my father hurried eagerly down the passage to the kitchen to say that a group of four had just arrived, that they were in the bar and would like bacon and eggs on toast with their beer. Mother protested: "No, no, Dad, please − it's too late." Of course Father had seen the occasion as a chance to bring in a much-needed extra pound or two: "We really do need the money," he said, almost timidly. Mother looked at him, then grabbed a frying pan off the shelf and banged it on the stove. She cut off a lump of lard and threw it into the pan. "Bugger!" she said. It was the only time, before or after, that I ever heard her seriously swear.

Of course, my father and Wilma won the argument, and the lease was renewed for a further seven years. But I believe in fact that the perpetual anxiety over money and the endless drudgery of running Studley Priory had already begun to put considerable stress on my parents' marriage, and that the decision was a blow for my mother. Her unfailing sense of humour was beginning at last to fail her. There was no fun in the enterprise any more. Not only had she lost heart in her own daily chores, she saw her husband drinking too much beer (though he was never drunk) and smoking a score or two of cigarettes a day. He was getting paunchy. His handsome face was more and more grey and lined; rings were forming under his eyes, and his hair was turning rapidly white. At night after the last guest had gone to bed we would gather round the hearth in the guests' lounge, where Mother and Wilma would knit, while my father would sprawl in the big armchair by the fire – and at once go noisily to sleep. When the rest of the family had finally gone to bed around midnight he would still be there, before dragging himself upstairs at one or two in the morning. I think I can say that Mother still loved the man she had married. But Father, though aware of Mother's unhappiness, could not bear to accept that their great venture had been a failure: his pride would not allow it. And so she was trapped. I think that around this time she had something of a nervous breakdown, and spent a few days in hospital. But she returned to fight in the trenches for another seven years.

By the end of 1954 I had been attending Radley for three years and more. The senior boys I looked up to when I first arrived had long departed, and those who took their places were gone too. I was now heading into that senior world myself, and coming along behind were droves of new arrivals. Some time that autumn Mr King elevated me and one or two of my contemporaries to the rank of house prefect, and we began to take a share in the duties of maintaining discipline and initiating newcomers into the odd ways of the school.

I was also approaching the next academic hurdle. In the summer of 1955 I was to take my 'A' level exams in Latin, Greek and Ancient History. Our classical teachers must have applied pressure on us more strenuously in the year leading up to the exams. I know we had to prepare Books 2 and 4 of Horace's Odes, a book or two of the Aeneid, some Tacitus, a book of the Iliad and some Thucydides. We had to continue writing and translating from both languages. I even won a prize for Greek prose. And yet, though strands of Greek and Roman history come wafting through the ether, I have almost no memory of any of these classes. As always, what I can recall is the pleasure of activities outside the classroom, and especially in matters theatrical.

In those days, as I have mentioned, Radley produced a Greek play in the original Greek every three years, and in the summer of 1954 Charles Wrinch – who had retired the previous year – came back to direct *The Clouds* of Aristophanes. Warden Milligan allowed us to stage it slap in front of his front door, where his circular front lawn served as a fine ορχηστρα ('orchestra'). I was cast as leader of the chorus, and also landed the job of the production's composer, writing in pseudo-Dorian mode – and as chorus leader having to sing much of it myself, accompanied rather thinly by a flute and violin. It was a pleasure to spend so much time with the great Charles. But I can't claim that the production did anything to alter my conviction that the comedic fun of most of Aristophanes is lost for ever to us – even in non-translation.

Late in the following summer term, after our 'A' level stresses were over, Peter Way staged Christopher Fry's *A Sleep of Prisoners*. I was lucky enough to be cast as one of its four actors, and even after so many years I look back on the whole experience with special affection. The play is set in a church where four British prisoners of war are being held by German guards, and Peter had managed to commandeer the Radley village Church of St James for our production. Over the weekends and long evenings of the summer months we would stroll down the driveway and out through the gates, meeting with Peter among the stone shadows of that beautiful 13th century building to put our play together.

All four of us were now senior boys, approaching or past the age of eighteen, and with the confidence of our comparative maturity. The fact that we were all playing the roles of soldiers had the effect of linking us up with our own futures: National Service was still in force in Britain, and the moment we left Radley we were expecting to be called up, to spend two years serving Her Majesty and drawing Her shilling.

Serving soldiers, of course, would not be speaking the language of Christopher Fry, which was highly word-conscious and decorative. But Fry's plays when I was at school were much in vogue. The *Lady's Not for Burning* had been commercially successful in London and on Broadway a few years earlier, with John Gielgud and Richard Burton in the cast. There was in fact a general feeling among *littérateurs* that Fry and Eliot and even Auden were finally restoring the poetic drama, which had been moribund since the closing of the theatres in 1642 – in spite of hundreds of efforts in the intervening centuries to revive that ol' Shakespearean magic. T.S. Eliot had cemented the modern revival with *Murder In The Cathedral* in 1935. Charles Wrinch and Peter Way at Radley certainly shared the current enthusiasm: Peter had directed an open-air production of Fry's *The Firstborn* at Radley in my second year. In fact the new movement, if it can be called that, fitted neatly into two of the school's guiding principles: the power of its classical tradition and the pervasiveness of its Christianity. The two are intertwined in Eliot's Thomas à Becket play, complete with its chorus in the Greek mode, its meditations on morality, and its story of Christian martyrdom. And though Christopher Fry discarded the trappings of Greek drama, most of his plays explore the great moral questions about the meaning of life, death, virtue and suffering inside a religious framework.

While we at Radley were living out the sophisticated and (dare I say) privileged-class dream of reviving religious poetic drama, and giving voice to Fry's characteristic poetic language with its strange mixture of vernacular and camp , it was ironic that, just one year later, John Osborne's *Look Back in Anger* would precipitate a genuine and lasting revolution in the British theatre. Fry's Corporal in a dream sequence of our play could spout lines like:

My heart breaks, quiet as petals falling
One by one, but this is the drift
Of agony for ever.

Quite clearly this was not the way corporals on stage would be talking from now on – or indeed ever talked in real life. Looking now at the poems I wrote at the time, I see how limited and self-preoccupied was their emotional range, and can't help feeling that we were living in an aesthetic cultural hermitage, decorating our feelings in pretty words and dreamy aspirations, and sheltered from the bitter realities of post-war Britain – or indeed of life. On the other hand, the school was protecting us in the same way that a happy family guards its children safe. There would be time enough, I suppose, for us to deal with bitter realities. Meanwhile, *A Sleep of Prisoners*, under Peter Way's guiding hand, made its way into a fine and telling production. As often happens with plays set in an army ambience, we developed a *camaraderie* which went beyond the usual team spirit. Cast as the dreamy, unaggressive Peter Able, I was in my element. And perhaps the Voice Beautiful was beginning to move towards tougher and more meaning-led expression.

It was the following summer holidays that took me to Denmark, and on my return I received the results of my 'A' level exams. I had passed them with reasonable distinction: a necessary prelude to the next academic hurdle, which was the scholarship exam the following December for entrance into Oxford. With Arthur Harrison's suggestion still whispering in my ear, I named Worcester College as my first choice, with two others in second and third place; I forget which. At the end of that same term I had been told that I would be made a school prefect and head of King's Social.

Just before the new term began again in September I spent some days back with the Lathams in London, as I had been doing since the Coronation expedition two years earlier. Theirs was the first and perhaps the only home I had been in where music dominated the lives and talk of everyone in the family and most of their friends. Mrs Latham was an accomplished pianist. Richard's father Dick was a Professor of Organ at the Royal College of Music, and their children Richard and Gillian were both budding musicians. The tastes of all of them were very much in the world of British music in the Elgar tradition. They loved Vaughan Williams and Gerald Finzi, and coped with Benjamin Britten, but the drastic musical rethinking of Schönberg and his disciples left them cold and scornful. Young Richard continued to share his favourite recordings with me, and their tiny comfortable house, with its etching of Brahms at the piano, its bursting library of musical scores and its photographs of musical luminaries, became for me a kind of divine refuge. I wrote a poem about it which records something of this:

9 Ossington Street

There are geraniums, geraniums
On the sill. There is an autumn sun,
And lights the white washed wall.
Music and light tell of the vastnesses
Of Man and God. Music and light
Playing in shafts and chords cross
criss-crossing the fullness and the deep
Across the white washed wall.

Here we are sitting, silently sitting,
Seeing or seeking into the seeing
of God, catching the drifting leaves
Of the minds of musical men.
Sad as this day, sighing
The dream of winter cold, we sit
And see or seek in ourselves
The warmth of music and light
Playing in shafts and chords, crossing
Criss-crossing the fullness and the deep.

Dick Latham was also the organist at St. Paul's Church, Knightsbridge, where he directed not only the regular choir but a Festival Chorus which presented oratorios two or three times a year. I had already been roped into the Chorus as an extra voice in Bach's *Christmas Oratorio* the previous December – where I had the excitement of seeing Ralph Vaughan Williams sitting in the front row with his silver ear trumpet. But my visit this time happened to coincide with a monthly event at the home of Vaughan Williams, where a group of his musical friends would assemble to sing madrigals under the maestro's baton, followed by a fork supper. Mrs Latham, who referred to him as 'Uncle Ralph (pronounced Rafe)' had already called his wife Ursula to ask if they could bring me along, and along I went.

We were met by Mrs VW downstairs at their beautiful Regency home in Gloucester Gate, where we were given a foretaste of the great man because his craggy head, sculpted by Jacob Epstein, dominated the hall. Led upstairs to their living-room, we were introduced to 'Uncle Ralph' and handed a sherry. Soon we sat down in a circle of maybe a dozen, and sheet music was passed out. I had been told that VW was getting deaf, and sure enough, when he made a mistake while giving out the starting note for each part in the madrigal, someone would correct it — too quietly for our host to hear. I was also warned that he would take the madrigals very slowly. And this he did: the sprightly *April is in my Mistress' Face* was funereal, I remember, and got even slower as it progressed. I was told afterwards that these evenings were in fact something of an ordeal for VW's friends because they were musically so frustrated, but they continued to attend simply because the old man derived such enormous pleasure from them. From the supper which followed I remember only the sight of VW sitting in a very low armchair, his hair like a silver thatched roof, and his whole front with its capacious *embonpoint* appearing quite horizontal from neck to knees, so that his supper tray perched totally level upon it.

Somehow — it happened so fast — I had become a young man. I had grown out of my adolescent anxieties and confusion — or had learnt to suppress them. And as part of this growing up I had begun to find friends among my near contemporaries; real friends. Richard Latham had left the school by this time, winning an organ scholarship to Exeter College in Oxford. But there were others in King's, like Richard Hale, who had come with me on the Denmark trip and was a promising artist, and the larger-than-life Noel Slocock, with whom I think I shared a study, and whose exuberant temperament, sporting enthusiasm and general *joie de vivre* made him a wonderful friend.

But now for the first time I had also begun making friends in other parts of the school. One of them was Jonathan Harlow. We had arrived almost together as entrance scholars, but he had taken his path into English and History, so that we saw less of one another in class. One day, though, we happened almost by chance to be in each other's company, and went for a long walk around the sports fields. We began to talk, and found that we amused and engaged each other more than we had expected. Jonathan, with his long face and slightly bowed head, had a pedantic and gently sarcastic manner. He spoke carefully, thinking as he went, and used a rich vocabulary. He had absorbed a great deal of knowledge and many ideas, and I suddenly knew that this was a friend that I would keep, my first genuinely intellectual comrade-in-arms. We exchanged long and interesting letters over that summer holiday. Jonathan wrote brilliantly.

We had another contemporary who was now becoming a friend to both of us. Peter Cook had arrived with Jonathan a term after me, and once our 'O' level exams were over he moved off into modern languages. But he had been making his mark on the stage since his first days at Radley, and recently had astonished our little world with his performance as Don Armado in Peter Way's production of *Love's Labour's Lost*. He had also drawn attention with his unique performances in comic plays and sketches, some of which he had written himself. To be honest, I always found his acting rather awkward physically, even self-conscious. But his force of character on the stage, his timing and his wit shone out in everything he did.

My first distinct memory of Peter Cook, though, was not in the theatre at all, but somewhere on the Berkshire Downs, where the Radley cadet force was conducting its annual Field Day. A mock battle was in progress, which meant that cadets were given their orders and then sent off in small sections into the hedgerows and ravines to scout for the 'enemy' and attack them with blank ammunition. I suppose there was a plan. Anyway, at one point in the afternoon a group of four or five of us found ourselves somehow cut off from the main action, and out of sight of the officer masters, who were chivvying the ranks elsewhere. Peter was with us. We sat down along a handy stone wall and rested our rifles.

The sounds of mock battle grew faint. We could hear the birds singing, and even bees and wasps and beetles as they buzzed past. Wild flowers glowed in the long grass. And in this suddenly surreal space Peter began to talk. It's impossible now to put a finger on the reason for the hysterics which started to overcome us, with Peter giggling quite as much as we. Perhaps that day was the first time that he had found that strange droning delivery of his, far back in the throat, while making remarks of blinding obviousness. "There goes a bee . . buzz, buzz, buzz. I like bees. Now there's nothing I like more than a bee..." and so on. Occasionally we chipped in with our own additions to the theme, and Peter enjoyed that too, building on them, improving them, turning them inside out, as he did his own. It was a *tour de force* which seemed to come out of nowhere, and we finally picked up our weapons and went back into battle with an overwhelming sense that what we had just experienced was more real than our military manoeuvres.

Perhaps, in fact, we had witnessed and participated in the genesis of Peter's developing style: some remark, or observation, situation or object was noted and laughed at, and then became a pretext for endless variations, each spinning off into further absurdity while we rocked with laughter. I often became a foil for his spiel, learning to ape his tone of voice and to follow him into his fantasies, and our shared fun brought us closely together over the next months.

When we returned to Radley in the autumn Jonathan, Peter and I had all become School Prefects ('Pups') and heads of our socials. This meant among other things that along with the other five 'heads of social' we had access to the supreme inner sanctum: the School Prefects' study, which lay beyond a stout and forbidding oak door off the covered passage in the middle of the school. 'Pups' Study', as it was known, had been a source of respect and fear during our whole time at Radley. It was where the Head Prefect administered canings for serious misdemeanours. It was where the great gods like Dexter had come and gone. And now here we were, gods presumably to the junior boys as we walked sternly through that door, but once inside behaving simply as another bunch of clever-silly youngsters. Our particular group of school prefects was different, though, from all others in the history of Radley, in that we had our own resident comic genius: Peter Cook.

It will be obvious by now that I was not a trouble-maker, nor any kind of a thorn in the side of the establishment, during my years at the school. I sought approval. I was friendly. I exuded team spirit. I took responsibility. I was loyal to the school and took it seriously. I was respectful to my elders. I also thought of myself as deeply Christian, praying every night and confessing my sins (including the occasional and it seemed unavoidable masturbation) and going regularly to Holy Communion on Sundays.

But all this rather numbing parade of apparent virtuousness is not to say that I was without guile or impertinence. We had all learned to imitate our teachers over the years, and had become adept in taking off the ponderous nasal tones of our own social tutor Mr Raymond T. King, the unctuous, pursed-lip manner of the Reverend Charles E.B. Neate ('I'm celebrating *myself* tomorrow morning'), and the guttural bray of historian Mr J.V.P. 'Rutch' Thompson ('Then it was that Louis put his spoke in the Hapsburg pie' was his oft-quoted and glorious mixed metaphor). The low, bubbling wheedle of the rotund cricket coach Mr Ivor A.W. Gilliatt, with his 'r's pronounced as 'w's and his barely-suppressed pederastic tendencies, was another favourite target.

But with Peter Cook we entered a whole new league. For Peter there was nothing and no one which was not food for his genial mockery. He was overcome not by the serious satirist's savage indignation but by helpless laughter at the absurdity of it all. The whole school and everything in it was a continuing carnival of ridiculousness. Peter's ridicule was cosmic.

At some point in that autumn term, though, Peter began to focus more and more on one *persona*, like a lens through which he focused his satirical view of the world about him. As school prefects we had now graduated to the high table in Hall, where it was our turn to sit around the polished oak board with its sparkling cutlery and be waited upon by Mr Boylett. And for reasons that will never be known or understood, it was Mr Boylett who became Peter's unlikely *übermensch*.

Boylett must have been in his fifties at that time: short and bowed, with grey hair around a balding pate, and a mouth that reminds me now of those Thurber mouths, open like birds' beaks. He would dress in shabby tails, grey waistcoat and tie, like a waiter in some Hungarian nightclub. Boylett worked with a fixed and affable smile always on his face – complemented somehow by a complete, utterly complete, absence of humour. However we teased him, he continued to smile, responding with remarks of sublime simpleness.

In our arrogant way we had never stopped to think twice about Mr Boylett. He was part of the landscape. But it was Peter who took painstaking note of the man. Boylett's humourlessness, his gentleness and his utterly literal simplicity were all reproduced in a brilliant vocal portrait, to which he and the rest of us added brush-strokes from one day to the next. Peter achieved the feat of looking at the world through Boylett's eyes and seeing it as a wondrous, inexplicable phenomenon. Peter was not cruel: his attention was even in a sense a mark of respect. Boylett, whom the rest of us ignored or passed off as a silly little man, became somehow mythologised. The more pathetic and simple the poor man was, the more Peter saw in him an absurdist superhero. It became hard not to giggle through our luncheon sessions with the Warden, who was not sure what it was all about.

It would be misleading, though, to suggest that we spent our entire time laughing our heads off. As head of King's Social I found I was for the first time a leader, and had regular meetings with our Tutor, Raymond King, on many matters of our administration. I was also in charge of my house prefects, and the group of us must also have met from time to time to discuss the running of affairs, and what to do about the 'difficult' boys in the social. But once again, these meetings and discussions have been utterly obliterated by time. I can remember only, and only too well, that in the course of the two terms that remained to me I had to administer two canings. Nothing, not even being a victim of it, could have more effectively turned me against corporal punishment.

One of the pleasures of those last terms at Radley was the amount of time we were given to study on our own, outside the structure of the timetable. It was I suppose a preparation for our university careers, and no doubt many hours were frittered away in foolishness. But the need to study for the Oxford scholarship exams in December concentrated my mind a fair amount: perhaps not enough, since in the event I failed to win more than entrance into Worcester College. I had the option of sitting further exams to other colleges in the next two or three months. But Worcester was where I wanted to go, and luckily my 'A' level marks were good enough to earn me a scholarship from the County of Oxfordshire. So my last term, from January to April, had no academic sword of Damocles hanging over me: I was free as the wind.

This was just as well, because in fact my hands were full. Chris Ellis had approached Peter Cook and myself in the autumn term and invited us to write a musical for the Marionette Society's next big show. Peter would write the book and the lyrics, and I would compose the songs. Peter delivered his script to me around the end of November, and once the Oxford exams were past, I set to work. I had written only two or three songs before this, but I had the confidence of the young, and turned them out pretty fast, so that when we returned to school in January I had a score to offer.

Chris had suggested that Peter write the dialogue in rhyming couplets, thinking that this might provide a form to cover up any amateurishness in the writing. Couplets were not really Peter's style, but he delivered. His script, named *Black and White Blues*, told the story of a jazz band, led by a Mr Slump, going out to Africa. I rack my brains to recall anything else about it, and thankfully have no memory of my music either: not a single ditty.

I had two handicaps in composing the music. In the first place, I was so naive as not to understand the basic form of the musical theatre song. My knowledge of light vocal music went only as far as folk ballads and Gilbert and Sullivan: so 'verse, chorus, verse, chorus' was the only shape I was comfortable with. Of course I knew some of the old 'standards' but, with my usual reluctance to analyse, or to follow a guide, I had never got the idea of the musical 'bridge' into my head. The result was that though I could usually create a good tune, the overall effect, when I think about it now, must have been clunking in the extreme, with few changes of key or tempo within any song. I also had no ability to reproduce the sheer rapidity of fast American-style musical numbers: my pace, even with lively songs, was I am sure unbelievably turgid – while of course jazz was for me an unknown language. Since the central group in the show was a jazz band, this was clearly a slight disadvantage.

Luckily, my ignorance was shared by most of the boys and their parents who came to watch the show when we finally presented it in March, a few weeks before my time at Radley ended. I was luckier than Peter because I played the piano for the show and was kept thoroughly occupied, whereas Peter suffered the usual fate of the writer in the theatre, whose work is done before anybody else's begins, and has little to do but to stand around offering suggestions, often politely declined. But at the curtain call Peter and I were stars, highly applauded as we came out in front of the miniature stage to take our bows. The true stars of course, as I know now, were the boys who made and manipulated the puppets from their platform above the stage. Some of them created a lifelikeness in their characters which was truly astonishing.

One member of that audience was Dicky Olivier, an Old Radleian and brother of the legendary Laurence. Married to Wilma's niece Hester and manager of his brother's estate at Notley Abbey, Dicky had become a family friend and often visited us at Studley. He was absurdly enthusiastic about *Black and White Blues*, insisting that he introduce it to 'Larry'. We produced a record of the show (which sold 400 copies!) and one evening a month or two later Dicky invited Wilma and me out to their cottage at Notley, telling us that 'Larry and Viv' might drop in for a drink. They did, and I had the delight of spending an hour or more in their rarefied company – tempered only by the excruciating embarrassment of having Dicky forcing them to listen to a track or two of our highly amateurish effort.

Black and White Blues was the fourth marionette show in which I had been involved, having missed out on an extraordinary *Magic Flute* in 1953, but having sung Robin Oakapple in *Ruddigore* a year or two later. Even at this distance I must pay tribute to the way in which Chris Ellis had developed the permissive creative ambience of Radley's marionette theatre of those days. It was one place at the school where anybody of any age could make a contribution, from the school prefect to the new boy. Many of the boys that became involved were not academically minded at all, but Chris gave all of them a chance to shine. Out of the woodwork appeared amateur electricians, carpenters, scene painters, costumiers, and puppet-makers, printers, singers and players: all drawn to the excitement of putting something together. It seems wrong-headed, when I think about it now, to make this kind of creative group effort a chance happening rather than a vital part of our education. But perhaps it was the whole activity's faintly subversive and improvisatory quality which was its great virtue.

I mentioned that in writing the music for *Black and White Blues* I was handicapped in two ways. My second difficulty was simply a matter of cultural snobbery. I had been brought up, starting at my previous school, to have a reverence for High Art, and though the writing of light music appealed to me strongly, and though I had a gift for a singable tune, I was beset by the sense that I was somehow letting the side down, and should be dashing off string trios and piano sonatas. I remember being so concerned about this that sometime that term I bicycled down to visit Charles Wrinch at his home in Radley village, and asked for his advice. I forget what he said, but I was to go on for some years writing songs that people enjoyed, so I suppose he argued me out of my silliness.

Strange the way memory leaves behind vast craters, with simply nothing to show for all those hours, days, weeks, months and even years in which I was presumably conscious and going about my business. Occasionally things come back by thinking hard, or flash into the mind unbidden at unexpected times. But most of the day-by-day events of those two last terms at Radley have sunk into oblivion, and I can only think that what survives does so, like good literature, because it has stood the test of time. The mind catches and holds what it wants to catch and hold.

I remember that we took very seriously the rugger competition held every autumn among the eight socials. Noel Slocock was our captain and star, a member of Radley's First XV. I was at my usual post at full-back, not having the speed to be a three-quarter and having successfully managed all those years to avoid ever being stuck in the scrum. I was only a Fourth XV laggard, but we had other good players. Our scrum-half was the remarkable all-round athlete Nick O'Shaughnessy. And with Raymond King himself as our coach we eventually made our way to the final.

Late on the night before the game, Raymond called Noel and myself into his study. He had been thinking constantly about our tactics for the next day, and I had never seen his laconic self so excited as he explained what he had come up with. His plan was simple. A full-back normally stays behind while the attacking three-quarters pass the ball along their line out to the wing, who with luck then dashes over the line and scores the try. Of course, each three-quarter is marked by his opposite number on the other side, and one of them will usually bring his opponent down before the wing gets the ball. Raymond's scheme was this: when our three-quarters got the ball and started moving up the field passing as they went, I was to come dashing forward outside our wing to be an extra pair of hands for him to pass to. I would be unmarked, and if I managed to snatch the ball could sprint over the line for a touchdown. Dashing and sprinting were not in my line, but Raymond was convinced that our opponents would be so surprised that I would breeze through. It was all somewhat unorthodox, and I am not sure that Noel, the classic rugby player, entirely approved. But we reckoned we should give it a go.

And – amazingly – it fell out exactly as Raymond King had predicted. We won the match, and I scored both tries! That evening, exultant, Noel, Nick and I went back out to the pitch in the dusk and out of sheer joy re-enacted the two tries in mime. I remember this replay more clearly than the game itself.

In my last term, down on the river, we also won the cup for Social Fours, under the expert coaching of Christopher Turner. I rowed at number three: I was no stylist but had a certain amount of strength, and as always in my sporting life I was at least dogged and tenacious. I also brought some weight to the boat: the records tell me I was now just under six foot and weighed 12 stone.

One other very different activity comes back to me. My second-in-command in King's that last autumn term was Richard Hale, who like myself was really more arty than sporty. We agreed that our social should not only have sporting events to bring us together, but that we should develop some kind of collective art project. After a lot of discussion we decided that we should take over the end wall of the upstairs library, spread thick paper over it, and turn it into a group mural in which every boy in the social, young and old, was encouraged to take part. Richard was to sketch out the basic plan, which I think was a landscape, and then, with paints and brushes provided, anyone who wished could add to it.

I cringe now at the recollection. How could we imagine that there would not be a single mischief-maker in the whole social to scrawl graffiti over it, to paint lewd goings-on in the bushes, or simply to tear the whole thing down? Nothing of the kind happened. I can't say that our enthusiasm was much shared even by our fellow prefects, but we all stuck to it and finished the job. I remember being more than relieved when it was over. In general, though, I believe that our social under my 'leadership' was a reasonably happy place, and we were all buoyed by our sporting successes.

For the rest, I can only remember being comfortable in myself, and clutching on to those happy months, fully aware that what followed would be very different. With the free time at my disposal I could do much as I pleased for much of my time. On one free day I took the Newbury bus out to the Ridgeway on the Berkshire

Downs, and walked along the ancient track for fifteen miles to the Vale of the White Horse, before coming down off the hills and finding my way back to school. Another time, and more than once, Jonathan and I, and maybe others, took a picnic lunch and bicycled off into the sylvan countryside around. I think some of these wanderings were in the spirit of Housman's *Shropshire Lad*, whose combination of landscapes and melancholy and grown-up 'lads' very much appealed to us: I wrote a poem or two in the Housman manner, and still have his Collected Poems, awarded for the David Raikes poetry prize as far back as 1953.

Back at school I would stroll down to the corrugated iron shed which served as the art school, and I think did some life drawing there under Chris Ellis' supervision. I practised for and even won a singing prize, adjudicated by the great Thomas Armstrong from Oxford. I also read a great deal, coming back to the English literature which my classical studies had somewhat separated me from and was still my first love. I very often shared books with Jonathan – in fact he often recommended them to me. One of them was Hilaire Belloc's *The Path to Rome*, published in 1902 and giving an account of his long walk through the French Alps to the Eternal City.

It was out of this over-written but inspiring work, with its author's own sketches and watercolours, that Jonathan and I hatched a plan. We would hitch-hike to Rome. But the date for this adventure would have to wait on one other event. We had entered 1956, and since in February the previous year I had reached the age of seventeen and a half, I was already eligible to be called up for National Service. While still at school I had no trouble deferring the date, and was tempted by the thought of staying for one more halcyon summer term. But I knew that with my poor father's finances (in spite of my scholarship covering most of the expense)

I could not justify the extravagance. Of course, like all my contemporaries at that time, I could choose to defer my service another three and a half years, and go straight on to Oxford, where I had already been assured of a place. But the thought of getting out of the academic world for a while was appealing, and since the thing had to be done, it were well it were done as soon as possible. So I had informed the authorities of my availability from the end of March, and some time in February was called down to Reading for my army medical, which I had no trouble in passing. A few weeks later I received orders to report to Cowley Barracks, Oxford, on May 26th. The wheels of a new and imperious engine were beginning to turn, as my golden last months at Radley slipped away.

But my call-up date meant that our sweet Roman plan could be put into effect: I had almost two months between Radley and the army. We decided that we should enlist two other comrades. I persuaded Noel to join us and Jonathan brought in his friend and a fellow school prefect, Roger Watson. The four of us spent many of my last evenings at school poring over maps, planning our journey in scenes reminiscent of *Three Men In A Boat*: we were about to undertake the biggest adventure of our young lives. For me, personally, it was also a kind of bonus extension of my time at Radley. Perhaps that is why I remember so little of my final days as a schoolboy.

A month or two after I left the school for the last time, I wrote this poem to record my going away:

Here alone, celebrating summer
Sit I now, sword tempered,
made. cast from the calm
Creator's hand, fault filled,
all goodness grudged, now

but steel to be sharpened,
proven in the fight.

Now to God's service and the summer
make I music, marriaging
the green — now take I
magics of imagination,
stirring mind and heart
premingled, jangling keys
of freedom and confines.

I was still imbued, as you can see, with the imagery of *Onward Christian Soldiers!*, though I am not sure it was going to help me much as I stumbled on to the parade ground in a real army. I also had occasion later to question the idea that I was a finished article, ready for battle. But so it seemed at the time.

What interests me, as I look back from over half a century on, is that I was educated by my two principal schools for a world which now barely exists. And yet my education prepared me, I think, to consider such a world, and even to help it spin.

My education was the best for the times. So what did it actually teach me, apart from the classics? Conventional good taste. Morals — being kind to others, yes, but also a sense of responsibility for others. My peers and I were educated just at the end of the colonial period, when there was at least a chance — which my good friend Jonathan took — of becoming a colonial administrator and sharing our supposed British morality and practicality with those 'less fortunate than ourselves'. What else was expected of us? It was assumed that we were all Conservative, and supported the established lines of authority from the King. Similarly, it was taken for granted that after Oxford or Cambridge (no other university was ever considered or even mentioned) we would find a gentlemanly niche somewhere in the settled world of the English hierarchy.

How did ambition fit into the picture? At both schools I was encouraged to be creative, to make things – whether plays or pictures or newspapers or music. We were also pushed hard into winning games, and developed the usual rivalries with other local schools. But I don't remember a wider worldly ambition ever figuring prominently. In fact, that might be a major difference between education then and now; our masters were not particularly interested, either at Marlborough House or at Radley, in our making a splash in the world. Once that university degree was gained, that was where their ambition for us ended. I suppose we were at the tail end of a time when gentlemen would retire to their estates on graduation and spend their lives on the land, hunting, shooting and fishing, with a little husbandry thrown in. In the 'fifties and 'sixties, though, most of us would have to find an occupation of some kind. If we were not connected with the movers and shakers and likely to become politicians, the professions offered a respectable future, and many of my contemporaries became clergymen, or doctors, or lawyers. Many more, in spite of absolutely no encouragement or professional training at school, became businessmen – some of them highly successful. We might teach at schools like those we had been educated by, but few of us were expected to be university academics: this was not a line laid out for us. Nor were the sciences expected to lure us, and those who moved in that direction were thought vaguely un ...un-something. Those of us who wished to continue being creative and avoid the tramlines of convention might write books or plays, or even paint, or run a theatre. A little more bohemian still, and perhaps we would even be actors. If we doubted the extent of our talent, we might at least find a job in publishing or in an arts service organisation like the British Council. When I asked Charles Wrinch about the idea of applying for a job at the Council, his reply was swift: "They do good work, they do good work, there's no denying it. But I have to say that anyone who goes into the British Council – well, one never hears anything about them ever again. They just – disappear."

For myself, at this age of eighteen and a half, I still had absolutely no idea how I would spend my life, and was totally unworried about it. I was sure of one thing, though. I did not want to disappear.

Postscript

Loaded up with rucksacks, and each armed with £25, the four of us crossed the Channel in the first week of April, found the road heading south, and sat down to wait. Many fruitless hours later we decided we must split up into pairs: no one, however generous, was going to pick up four hitchhikers. From then on we leapfrogged across France and into Italy, meeting one another at designated points – Rheims, Dijon, Avignon, Cannes, Genoa – and alternating our pairs. The more successful pair sometimes had to wait as much as a day for the unlucky ones to catch up, but they arrived eventually, and the whole journey was punctuated by anxiety, relieved by ecstatic reunions. I have a picture, one among a precious handful, of Jonathan and myself sitting in deckchairs on the beach in Cannes. I am smoking a pipe. Jonathan is writing postcards. And both of us are wearing tweed jackets – and *ties!* Another snap on a beach, this time somewhere near Nervi, shows Roger and myself (still with pipe), but this time we are wearing sweaters and *open-necked shirts*. I'm surprised we weren't arrested for indecent exposure. But this after all was Italy.

It took us ten days to reach Rome. I remember that for the last leg of the journey Jonathan and I gave up on hitchhiking and took the train, so that as we sped along those last kilometers we were free to experience in comfort the northerner's sensuous joy at leaving his rainy homeland and arriving in the warm south, with its ochre buildings and umbrella pines and sunshine and warm spring breezes and peasants and donkeys and oxen and – it seemed – endlessly happy people. I remember us pressing up to the window to catch our first sight of the dome of St. Peter's, glinting in the evening sun.

The four of us were soon together again, setting up our tents at the Villa Glori campground just off the Via Aurelia. We drank a lot of wine, we ate a lot of pasta. We talked and joked. We travelled the *tranvai* into the city centre and visited St. Peter's, the Sistine Chapel and the Colosseum. We walked along the Tiber ('father Tiber'), and spent time in the Roman Forum: my Roman history still fresh, I was buzzing with thoughts of the Caesars, and Pompey, and poor Cicero, making an effort to bring them alive again in that forest of broken walls and columns. It was more Ozymandias that came to mind. But I had now set foot in the two great classical cities, Athens and Rome, which had between them spawned all that ancient language and history which I had spent so many years trying to get under my belt. It was an epiphany of sorts.

I remember little of the journey back, except for a fair morning at Assisi, where Jonathan and I drank in the spirit of St. Francis. I suspect that my future was more and more hanging over me as we neared the shores of England.

For all its stresses, the Italian journey imprinted itself on all of us, I think. We would remember it for years to come. And I, the only one of us not returning to school for one more term, would soon have cause to look back on it as a golden time of true happiness, true freedom, and true camaraderie.

CHAPTER SEVEN

MARCHING AS TO WAR

Friday, May 26th, 1956: Cowley, outside Oxford. Some twenty young men between 17 and 21 are making their way by bus or car or on foot to a grim set of stone buildings in the lee of Shotover Hill, known as Cowley Barracks. Erected in the 1870s, its crenellated castle keep faces on to the road in triumphant *faux* mediaeval style. This is the headquarters and depot of the local county regiment, the Oxfordshire and Buckinghamshire Light Infantry; and most of the men are from one or other of the two counties. I am among them, and for the first time in my life find myself on an equal footing with men from every social background: farm labourers who had left school at 15 or 16; boys fresh out of grammar school or secondary modern; builders' apprentices and office clerks; mechanics and assembly line workers; and two or three public schoolboys like myself, who have never worked seriously a day in our lives.

We are none of us there because we want to be, but have been called up to carry out our National Service to the new young Queen, and to serve the commitments of the fading British Empire: two compulsory years before the colours. We are facing the immediate prospect of ten weeks' basic training, before being either deployed to the regiment's active Battalion, or shifted to some other military arm considered more suitable for our skills. A new life begins.

At that time the army called up a fresh intake every fortnight, so our barracks accommodated five intakes two weeks apart. We were shown to our barrack-room on the upper floor of the nearest block, allotted mugs and what I learned to call 'eating irons', and eventually pointed in the direction of the canteen to be served our 'tea'. Not a matter of scones and cucumber sandwiches, this was a solid evening meal, spooned and ladled out of aluminium baking dishes and vats. A mug of tea of course was available, but served with milk and sugar heavily mixed in, a drink which for the next two years I would have to learn to love. We sat at our own trestle tables, looking nervously at the other intakes ahead of us, full of assurance and cockiness: 'Get some in!' they would shout, jeering at us from across the hall. Even the group which had been called up two weeks earlier seemed infinitely senior to us, infinitely wise and knowing. We smoked nervous cigarettes, and went to sleep in almost total silence, all of us a little afraid among strangers in a strange place, and some of us sleeping for the first time in our lives away from home. Not so for me of course.

I remember few details of the next days, in which we were measured (roughly) and received our green berets with their bugle badge, our uniforms and boots and army kit; put through our first paces on the drill ground by the kindly but noisy (mostly noisy) serjeant (as my regiment spelled it) in charge of us; and introduced to our weapons: the .303 rifle, familiar to me from cadet days, and the Sten gun. We were taught how to make our beds without a wrinkle, how to clean our rifles, how to present our kit for inspection, how to salute an officer ('tip of the index finger one inch above the right eyebrow, palm outwards, thumb tucked in'), how to shoulder and present arms, how to march at the Light

Infantry rate of 140 paces to the minute (rifles at the trail), and a hundred other things now happily forgotten. From our corporals we learned how to 'blanco' our canvas belts and gaiters, how to polish our brass buckles, and all the secrets of developing a mirror-like shine on our boots. We were also warned, by those immensely wise young men two weeks ahead of us, of the kind of punishments which would be meted out if we failed to meet standards. These included 'jankers' (doing time in the guard-room cells) for serious offences like missing parade, but also more imaginative delights, like whitewashing the coal in the coal-heap, cutting the strip of lawn outside the officers' mess with a pair of nail-scissors, or cleaning the barrack-room toilet bowls with a razor blade. I never saw any of such absurdities carried out, and suspect our advisers enjoyed giving us rookies a scare.

In any case, all these strangenesses slowly became familiar, and with a building sense of security about what was required of us we began ourselves to grow assured and even cocky. We also began to make friends, and the talk after lights out became noisy and ribald. In the next bed to mine was a Gerry French, a mild and sweet-natured farm lad from a village on the edge of the Cotswolds. If I was having my first experience of social equality, so was he. He would ask me about my life, as I asked about his. At some point he said to me 'Mike, you're going to be an officer, you know that, don't you. Then you won't be able to talk to me like we're talking now.' He said it without rancour, and even with respect. I demurred modestly.

But the wheels had already started turning. At the beginning of our second week we were each interviewed by an officer about our future prospects. Those of us with 'A' level achievements would be steered either to the Intelligence Corps (taking a test to gauge our aptitude for learning Russian) or towards becoming a commissioned officer. I showed the right aptitude for languages, but when asked what I preferred I was quick to say that I wanted to be an officer and to serve in the home regiment. There was one particular reason for this: we had been told that the 1st Battalion of the Oxfordshire and Buckinghamshire Light Infantry, now stationed in Germany, was shortly to be sailing to Hong Kong. It was one of the most coveted postings in the army, and sounded to me like the very finest place in which to serve out my time.

It seems my preference was approved, because by the end of the second seemingly endless week I and two or three others found we were to be transferred to Strensall, five or six miles outside the city of York, where potential officers from all the Light Infantry regiments were brought together to continue their basic training for the eight weeks that remained. So after goodbyes to my new mates, and a snatched and surreal twenty-four hours of leave back with my family at Studley, I donned battledress once again, shouldered my khaki kitbag, and rode the train north.

Thus after only two weeks my first and only experience of true classlessness in England came to an end. At the time I was happy enough to be launched in the direction of a commission. But I have since often regretted that I did not have the chance to spend more time becoming friends with those lads from the city of Oxford and the shires around. Most were kindly boys from the country, though the more urban and tougher types had arrived wearing the Teddy Boy gear which had begun to appear in the streets of England's cities, with drape jackets, stovepipe trousers, thick brogue shoes and duck's arse haircuts. These glad rags had disappeared into lockers on our first evening, and any surplus hair had been shaved imperiously away the following day, leaving them and all of us looking equally like convicts. Teddy Boys were a particular target of our NCOs' scorn.

And so to Strensall. It was the home depot of the King's Own Yorkshire Light Infantry, and it was here that I first became aware of the various other regiments making up the Light Infantry Brigade. Our serjeant was a short and supremely ugly pirate from the Duke of Cornwall's; our small, stout Corporal was from the Durhams, and was the first Geordie I had ever heard speak – for him our boots were 'bew-itts'. My new fellow soldiers had all achieved 'A' levels, and many of them were bound for university after National Service; one or two had already graduated. They were a good crowd, and our small contingent – fifteen or sixteen – developed its own *esprit de corps* inside that windswept Second World War depot, with its glum rows of breezeblock buildings enclosed in acres of asphalt. Our NCOs here liked to think they were treating us as brutally as they would any group of raw recruits, but there was no doubt they were aware of the oddity of this: after all, when it was all over they might find themselves having to jump to our orders.

Though our basic training continued at Strensall much as it had in Cowley, we soon understood that we were also being groomed for an appointment with the War Office Selection Board (WOSB, known as 'Wosbie'), which would take place in the last week or two, testing our aptitude for command and either sending us on for Officer Training at Eaton Hall – or not, as the case may be. So alongside the dreaded bugle-call Reveille at 6.30, the marches and drilling and bayonet and target practice and instructions in the use of mortars and bren guns, we were given responsibility for directing small group tasks, introduced to basic battle tactics, and tested for our competence in giving short, unscripted lectures to our fellow recruits. This made me more nervous than anything else; I realized that for all my youthful appearances before an audience I had never had to speak without a set text. Making a fool of myself was the greatest terror, though I found I was getting better at coping with mockery.

Weekend passes allowed us to take the double-decker bus into York for a stroll round the Shambles, a look inside the gorgeous grey mass of York Minster, several beers in a pub, sausage and chips in a local café, and even a film. And one weekend I got permission to take the train to Leeds, where I had arranged to visit my old teacher and former Warden of Radley, John Vaughan Wilkes, who had now taken up his position as Vicar of St. Mary's Parish Church in the industrial suburb of Hunslet. Once again, I found time away from the enclosed world of army life a strange experience – especially now, butting up against the very different certainties of my old school, though set in an alien environment. The Vaughan Wilkes family kindly put me up for the night in their vast Victorian vicarage, cluttered with children's bikes and toys. Wilkes took me up to St Mary's for Compline on Saturday evening, and for a few minutes – in my battledress and steel-shod boots – I was back in the shelter of that beautiful Anglican rite: "Keep me as the apple of the eye; hide me under the shadow of thy wings." I saw little of Hunslet, but enough to sense its sad air: it was one of those northern communities which had once been a noisy, smoky, thriving producer of manufactured goods in great array, from railway locomotives and steam rollers to glass and ceramics and beer. But the great industrial engine was now faltering, leaving behind its usual debris: acres of primitive row houses with outside privies, a depressed and quietly desperate population, and a murky future. Youthful crime was rife. The High Anglican rites of St. Mary's seemed to have little to offer the people of Hunslet; its soaring Victorian roof looked down on empty pews at Sunday mattins. Vaughan Wilkes had chosen the Parish because he was determined to break away from the easy life of southern England. But I sensed the challenge was defeating him, and was not surprised to hear a few years later that he had moved south again, to the sleekly comfortable living of Marlow-on-Thames. Humankind has a hard time bearing such despairing reality for very long, if they have a chance to escape it.

Back in Strensall our training was coming to an end, and we were being sent south, in groups of four or five at a time, to Barton Stacey outside Winchester, the headquarters of the War Office Selection Board. The rumour was that they simply wanted to ensure that you knew how to hold your knife, and how to pass the port the right way. But this seemed not to be the case. We had to sit exams, show our skills at map-reading, give a ten-minute talk, lead a group over a ravine making the best use of a tree, a log and a length of rope, and other fierce tests of our knowledge and leadership qualities. The climax came with an individual interview by the commanding officer. My turn arrived, and I marched into his office giving my smartest salute − never very smart, I'm afraid, but energetic at least.

"Oh, sit down Bawtree," said the major, picking up my file. "How are you enjoying WOSB so far?"

"Oh. quite a lot, sir."

"Good. good... Oh, I see you were at Radley."

"Yes, sir."

"Jolly good school. My two boys are there. In fact I was up there last term and saw a fascinating puppet show they put on, called Black and White something or other. All written by the boys. Marvellous. Did you see it?"

"I, er − I wrote the music for it, sir."

"Did you really? My word! Cracking good show. Well, that'll be all, Bawtree. Good luck." He stood up and shook my hand.

"Goodbye sir, and thank you." I saluted and clattered out.

Who is to say that art has no purpose? Within a few hours I heard that I had been accepted for a commission. Not only that, but a good mucker of mine, an Old Etonian, who had journeyed south from Strensall with me and who certainly knew how to pass the port, was turned down.

Our basic training over at the beginning of August, we were granted two weeks' leave, and I took the train back south to Oxford for a blessed few days cradled in the beauty of Studley Priory. The hotel business had settled down to something of a routine, and my parents and Wilma, game as ever, were in the midst of their busiest month. Proud of his son's humble army career so far, Father allowed me to sleep in late, and was careful never to call on me for assistance, although I still enjoyed helping him out in the bar and socialising with the guests. The peace after so many bugle calls, so much shouting, so much crunching of boots, so much chivvying, so much obeying, was ineffable.

But there were plans already afoot for another adventure. My time in Strensall was made a lot more bearable by the steady arrival of long, rich letters from friend Jonathan, and as soon as he knew of my impending leave he began to arrange a week's camping holiday for August. He enlisted our Rome confrère Noel Slocock – who was even able to contribute his mother's Hillman Husky – and also, more improbably, Peter Cook. Peter, who had left school at the same time as I, and who had been able to avoid National Service due to childhood asthma, had spent the summer earning pennies as a beach photographer in Lyme Regis, and was only too ready to stop snapping and join his old Radley friends. And so it was that the group of us assembled at Studley in the second week of August, before taking off for the open road. We headed west to the Wye Valley and the Forest of Dean, then north to Shropshire, where we climbed Wenlock Edge and explored the Cluns with Housman in hand, then back south again to Dorset and the New Forest, before finally returning to Oxford to deposit me at Studley.

This was positively the last chapter of our book of Radley days, and to say that it was a happy time would be to understate the case. A handful of Noel's photographs survive to pinpoint a few moments, as we pore over maps before setting out from Studley; as we picnic beside the Wye, or camp in a high wind under the lee of a hill with me amateurishly strumming a ukulele. Above all, as with our last months at school, I remember chiefly the laughing – from morning to night. Peter was not much of a camper but more than earned his place as court jester. Noel was our driver: he and Jonathan were the practical ones. The fact that I had just come out from ten weeks under the heel of the British Army excused me from some chores. But there seemed to be not an instant's irritation among us, and we all did our share of pitching in. The pale ale and Benedictine made the evenings especially warm and fuzzy – except once for me when I stepped woozily back from our campsite in the dark and fell four or five feet into the River Wye, a scene straight out of Charlie Chaplin which gave all of us enough to laugh about for hours and even days.

My friends went motoring on for another week or two, Noel enlisting other friends like Nick O'Shaughnessy to take the places of those of us who had to leave the party. A month or two later the original foursome had gone their separate ways: Jonathan into the Royal Artillery and Noel to the Coldstream Guards, Peter directly to Cambridge. As for me, my blessed leave was soon over and I must report back to Cowley Barracks, with orders to proceed to Eaton Hall, Cheshire. I had now been promoted – or rather moved sideways – to that anomalous rank of officer cadet. Henceforth I wore white 'gorgets' on my lapels, and would be called Mr Bawtree

– addressed as 'sir', but not saluted. As the Regimental Sergeant Major at Eaton Hall was soon to bellow at us: "I call you 'sir' and you call me 'sir': <u>you</u> MEAN it!"

Eaton Hall, the Cheshire home of the Dukes of Westminster, was an extravagant Victorian Gothic pile set amidst what must once have been magnificent ornamental gardens. But the whole place had been requisitioned by the government in 1939, first as a convalescent hospital, then as the wartime home of Dartmouth College and finally from 1946 as an officer training establishment. Its high hall and triumphal marble staircase, once the scene of sumptuous gatherings of the local and even national aristocracy, now echoed with the metallic ring of army boots. Much of the grounds and stable yards had been turned into an enormous parade ground, though the terraced gardens to the east of the house still gloried in their lawns and fountains and rose beds and box hedges: a wonderful discovery for me after two or three weeks in residence, made even more attractive by the fact that a walk through them led directly down to a quiet pub on the back road below the estate, beside the River Dee. It was there with one of my new officer cadet friends, one Simon Coningham, that I got seriously drunk for the first time in my life, and still remember us joyously cavorting and somersaulting up through the Duke's formal gardens back to the Hall in the moonlight.

As with previous training establishments I had been involved with, I remember little of the day-to-day routine, unless it involved the emotions – mostly either of fear or of ecstatic joy. So I can recall the huge bulk of Regimental Sergeant Major Desmond Lynch, with his World War Two medal ribbons, and his uniform perfectly tailored to follow with no apparent strain the lines of his enormous girth. It was enough to spot him on the horizon to set up a dizzying pain of terror in the stomach. Will he see me? Have I done anything wrong? Are my boots clean? On the parade ground he was even more fearsome. I remember mustering for drill one morning, and realizing just as his inspection party approached that I had forgotten to attach my green Light Infantry lanyard. If he noticed its absence, I would be quick-marched off to the guardhouse holding my rifle above my head in both hands ("hup! hup! hup!"), and ordered to put myself on a charge for being incorrectly dressed. But the great man swaggered on past, his eye no doubt caught momentarily by someone else's dereliction. I was safe – till next time.

But I also remember, after unrelieved toiling and moiling, the day that I arrived in the canteen near the end of my second battering week to find some regimental band installed there and playing their hearts out. I was so overcome by the power and delight of it all that tears sprang to my eyes. It was not as though they were giving us Beethoven or Mozart, but I was uplifted to the very soul by their popular repertoire: that good old rouser the *March of the Dam-Busters* has never sounded the same to me since. It was as though those cheerful bandsmen were assuring me that there was still a world out there where harmony reigned king.

It was not long after this that harmony came to my rescue once again. The Duke of Westminster's family chapel had come with the estate, complete with pipe organ and room for a hundred or two ducal retainers. Eaton Hall's padre somehow heard that I was a pianist, and sought me out to ask if I could play for the thanksgiving service which accompanied the following Thursday's Passing Out parade. I was able to let myself into the chapel and practise for a couple of evenings, and on the day of the service was relieved of drill duties and able to acquit myself reasonably enough, even managing a few foot-pedal notes for Parry's *Jerusalem*. It was enough to earn me the job of resident organist of Passing Out services for the duration of my time there, and since a contingent of newly-commissioned young officers was sent out every two weeks, there were many exercises and parades for which I was excused every alternate Thursday. I was even permitted to attend their receptions. Again, who is to say that art has no purpose?

In the months since I began being introduced to the delights of military life, world events had been moving forward in their usual perpetually ominous way. Anthony Eden had succeeded the ailing Churchill as Prime Minister the previous year, and had been facing a growing crisis in the Middle East. Gamal Abdul Nasser, Egypt's new leader, had seized the Suez Canal in July and hoisted over it the new Egyptian flag. Once the lifeline to Anglo-India, Britain's prize possession, and still important as the main conduit for Europe's oil, the Canal was seen by those who had financed and built it – France and Britain – as theirs by right. They were not amused by this Arab insolence, and the old generation running both countries were making warlike noises while we young conscripts were learning how to be authentically warlike at Strensall and Eaton Hall. I still assumed that our regiment was soon leaving for the peaceful pleasures of Hong Kong. After all, we could always go round by the Cape.

World affairs continued to seem far away even when Israel launched an attack on Egypt through the Sinai Desert. But then, returning from a strenuous march late one early November afternoon, we glanced at the evening papers which were delivered to the Hall every day. They bore a mammoth headline: UK PLANES BOMB CAIRO!

For the first time, with a sudden shock, I connected what was happening in the Middle East with our own situation. A few days later we read of the landings at Port Said by British and French airborne troops: the Israel invasion had simply been a pretext for western intervention. Here we were being prepared for leadership roles in the British armed forces, and here looked like the makings of a new war, in which we would surely be involved and would probably lose our lives. The whole ill-thought adventure, failing to garner American support, ground to a halt a few days later, after Nasser had sunk forty ships into the canal and the United Nations – through its envoy, Canada's Lester Pearson – had the unusual experience, then or since, of actually bringing a war to an end. But the cessation of hostilities continued to have its effect within the army: seasoned soldiers saw it as a deep humiliation, and even our callow contingent of officer cadets, though relieved, also felt somehow cheated of our chance at death and glory. It affected as well the future plans of my own regiment: the 1st Battalion had been moved out to Cyprus at the end of the summer, and now I heard to my disappointment that the Hong Kong posting had been permanently called off, and that instead the 1st. Battalion of the Oxfordshire and Buckinghamshire Light Infantry would be stationed in Cyprus on security duty for the rest of their overseas tour.

Meanwhile our training continued. That November, in what seemed like an odd preparation for the Mediterranean, we were trundled off to Battle Camp at Trawsfynydd in North Wales, where we learned to be subjected to live ammunition fire, and to dig and live in trenches – as though gearing up for the First World War. The weather was very Welsh, and for at least two days and nights we worked and slept in our dugouts under slashing rain and through freezing darkness. But I remember less of the wretchedness, and of the simulated battles we must have gone through with live rifle fire and mortar shells zipping above our heads, than of the fabulous train journey to get there, courtesy of the Welsh Coast line which passed directly through a gate of Conway Castle on its way to Llandudno, and then wound its slow, chugging way through Snowdonia to our little train station at the slate mining village of

Blaenau Ffestiniog, where we changed for Trawsfynydd Camp. Rain and fog and all, it had been my first transcendent sight of the Welsh mountains.

Once we returned to the relative comforts of Eaton Hall there was little more to do but to drill and drill for our own passing out parade under the scorching eye of RSM Lynch with his Irish brogue ("Lep Ri' Lep Ri'! Heads up now! Nothin' to be afraid of – flowers smell the same to them as they do to you!"). The final ceremony took place if I remember on December 4th, and my dear mother managed to leave her cursed kitchen at Studley and make her way up to Chester to sit in her latest homemade finery, watch the passing out parade, and see me transmogrified into a second lieutenant. Someone else was roped in to play the organ.

Christmas was less of a family affair than usual. During the previous summer Jo had applied for a secretarial position at the Food and Agricultural Organisation (FAO) in Rome, and with the help of the Royal Academy's testy president Gerald Kelly, who wrote on her behalf to FAO's Deputy Director-General (an Englishman), her application had been successful. She had left her post as Exhibition Secretary at the Royal Academy at the end of October, and taken the train to Italy. Arriving in Rome on November 5th, she was at once told she would probably have to return to Britain, since war had broken out in the Middle East. But the ceasefire followed soon after, and Jo settled in to the city which was to become her home for the next thirty years and more. Which meant that she was not home for Christmas.

My young sister Jenny was there, though, having just returned from her first term at Wycombe Abbey school, to which she had won a scholarship. She was now fourteen, bright and still a loner, and not easily to be connected with. After my four months of steady disciplinary grind I probably spent much of my leave asleep, and not connecting much with sister, parents or indeed anyone. I have no memory of the next month or so, though it must have included visits to Cowley Barracks to have a pip put on to my uniforms, and into Oxford where I was measured for my 'Number Ones', the dark green dress outfit which I would be wearing on formal regimental occasions. I must also have paid a visit to Radley, since I remember being given a regimental 'Sam Browne' belt by a well-known Old Radleian governor of the school, Mr (later Sir) George Mallaby; the Oxford and Bucks sported its own special leather belt with straps going over each shoulder like braces. They were hard to come by and expensive to purchase, and I was grateful for the generous gift.

A shadow fell over that Christmastime, when I heard that our schoolfriend Nicholas O'Shaughnessy, now head of my old social and just designated as Senior Prefect of the school for the following term, had come down with polio while he was preparing to compete for Radley in the annual Public Schools Rackets cup at Queens' Club in London. Word passed among his friends as to how he was doing from day to day. He was partially, and then totally paralysed. He was in a coma. And just before the end of the year this fine sportsman and lovely young man succumbed to the ravaging disease, which within a year or two would be conquered by the Salk vaccine. It was the first death of someone I had been close to, and I returned to my duties in the army still very much shaken by the loss. I wrote a poem for him: *Eagle, oh eagle, where are you flying now?*

Early in January I received orders to report to my ship on the 30th, and as the date approached I began packing for the voyage, rapidly filling up my old blue school trunk, and painting a new address on the top as instructed:

2/Lt. M. BAWTREE
1 BN OXFORD & BUCKS L.I.
via TT ASTURIAS
SOUTHAMPTON

It still sits in my sister's lumber room in France, still so addressed.

I rode the train down to Southampton – travelling first-class, courtesy of Her Majesty, in recognition of my new exalted rank as a subaltern – and remember arriving at the dockside and seeing families with children gathered there to wave farewell; but I recall little else before we hooted our way down the Solent and out to the Channel. Since the War Office had only recently given permission for spouses to join their husbands in Cyprus, the troopship had a fair complement of officers' and warrant officers' wives, as well as a clutch of raw young officers like myself. The Oxford and Bucks female contingent included Sheila, the wife of our Battalion's commanding officer, Lt.-Col Anthony Read, and the decorous warmth which sprang up between us then kept up throughout my military service, and for years beyond.

The rumour soon ran round among us that several of the wives simply couldn't wait for their conjugal embraces, and were fair game for the handsome young officers on board. But like most of these boastful male fantasies, there was little substance to it in my own experience. Besides, I viewed marriage as a sacred tie which I would not dream of straining. I was still entirely inexperienced sexually and certainly had no idea how to begin wooing thirty- or forty-year-old women, whom I regarded more or less as I regarded my mother. Charm was another thing, and I was no doubt able to be attractive to them, though I would have run a mile had they made a move towards me. Meanwhile we would assemble in the lounge every evening at cocktail hour for many gin and tonics and a great deal of banter, returning after dinner to our favourite corner in the lounge, to play pontoon and swallow a bucketful of whisky. The women would eventually retire, and we young and not-so-young bucks would then carry on putting down a few more snifters, then horse around out on the deck or run down the gangways shouting and singing, until finally retiring drunkenly to our cabins, dreaming of the conquests we wished we had made. It was a new life for me: though I was still only nineteen it was the first time I had some kind of equal standing as an adult among other adults. I was technically no longer a schoolboy. I was also beginning to learn that adults behaved surprisingly like schoolboys.

While we were living it up in our not very splendid but at least officially first-class splendour, the sergeants and warrant officers and wives were well segregated from us on a lower deck and carried on in their own way. And then, far below decks, lived hundreds of 'Other Ranks' in the ship's holds, which had been converted into airless and wretched sleeping quarters. The vessel was in other words the floating epitome of a rigid hierarchy: patricians at the top of the heap, strolling the upper decks with their ladies and taking the air; aspiring status-holders on the lower decks with their less patrician ladies; and the lumpen proletariat kept conveniently below, far out of sight and mostly out of mind.

As officers, though, we were each given responsibility for one of the holds, and would pay occasional officerly visits to them to see how 'the chaps' were doing. This was a pleasant enough chore until we arrived in the Bay of Biscay. True to its reputation the Bay unleashed a massive winter storm upon our ship, which lurched its way through mountainous seas, pitching and tossing for three days and nights, and making most of our womenfolk and many of the officers spectacularly seasick. Feeling I had to visit my men at the height of the storm, and not suffering badly myself, I made my way down and down, ladder after clanging ladder, until I arrived at their quarters, lit by a single naked overhead bulb crazily swinging. It was a descent into hell. Packed tight in the bowels of the tossing ship the poor boys were being swirled around like dregs in a bottle, sick and green every last one of them. I shall never forget the sight of a dustbin full to the brim with vomit. The smell was unspeakable. I managed to exchange a few words with one or two miserable souls able at least to speak, and then fled up and away to escape being sick myself. On my next reluctant but dutiful visit I saved the embarrassment of retching by managing to hold my breath for almost the entire time. Poor fellows.

By the time we steamed through the Straits of Gibraltar into the Mediterranean all was calm again, and *mal de mer* loosed its hold on the unfortunates at all levels, who began once again to believe that life was possible. The sun shone, the sea flowed Prussian blue, turning wine-dark as the sun fell into the west. On our starboard side the African shore lay distant and amethyst, sending up a sultry, scented breeze as we churned slowly by.

We laid over for four or five hours in Valletta, and had a few hours to go ashore, where a group of us visited the Cathedral of St. John, built for the Knights of Malta, and then basked in the mild winter sun on the terrace of a cafe, drinking the local beer and cracking pistachio nuts. Soon it was back to the boat for the last two-day run to Cyprus.

Early on the morning of February 10th we dropped anchor off Limassol, which had no harbour deep enough for the *Asturias*. Open lighters, steered like dodgems by eager Cypriots (whom I at first looked at warily as potential enemies), came zooming out from the shore to surround the ship and ply for custom, and our luggage was roughly and laboriously dropped into them from the cargo hold, followed by those of us who were disembarking. Uniformed officers and serjeants from our own regiment and others were there on the dockside to greet their spouses and carry them off to their married quarters. Lorries from various units, painted beige (for deployment in the desert?) and each with its guard, picked up their soldiers and ferried them away with their kitbags, while Land Rovers, staffed by armed escorts, were on the dock to meet us new young subalterns with our trunks and suitcases, and drive us through the town and up to our camp on a low hill a few miles north. Along the way we were casually informed that on that very road, two soldiers had been killed the previous week by bombs hung in the carob trees and remotely detonated.

On the voyage out, to prepare us for our new posting, old Cyprus hands had treated us to lectures on Cyprus past and present. We were presented with a complex scenario. The island's ethnic troubles had in fact gone back hundreds of years, with its population divided between Greeks and Turks on a ratio of about four to one. Since the early 19th century the Greek Cypriots had worked to throw off centuries of Turkish Ottoman rule and bring about *enosis* – the union of Cyprus with Greece. In the 1870s, with Turkey's agreement, Britain had taken control of the island's administration – ostensibly to prevent it falling into the hands of Russia. But it remained technically part of the crumbling Ottoman empire until the first World War, when Turkey had come in on the side of Germany and Austria. At that point the British government voided their treaty with Istanbul and declared Cyprus a British colony – though they first sneakily offered it to King Constantine I of Greece on condition that he brought Greece into the war on the side of the British; an offer which he, educated in Germany and married to the Kaiser's sister, understandably refused.

In 1925 the British had claimed the island as a Crown Colony, which precipitated major unrest and riots among the Greek population, culminating in the burning down of Government House in Nicosia in 1931. Greek leaders working for *enosis* were at once exiled, political parties banned, and an all-Turkish police force set up. Municipal leaders were thenceforward appointed by the Governor-General, and the flying of both Greek and Turkish flags was forbidden.

The war brought the unrest to a halt, but in 1946 the new Labour government in Britain offered to invite Greek and Turkish Cypriots to sit down and develop a new constitution for the island. In what was designed as a conciliatory move they also pardoned the exiles of 1931. But the Greek Cypriots were angry that there was no mention of *enosis* (union) in the new plans, and the Orthodox Church of Cyprus weighed in on their side, as did their rivals the communist party (AKEL). When Bishop Makarios was made Archbishop of Cyprus in 1950, he had made it clear he would fight for the achievement of union with Greece.

Meanwhile a new figure entered the scene. Georgios Grivas, a colonel in the Greek army but by birth a Cypriot, became vocal in Athens on the *enosis* issue, and in 1951 visited Cyprus for talks with local leaders and with Makarios. Unlike Makarios, who at the time still believed in a political solution, Grivas favoured armed struggle. By 1955 Grivas had formed the National Organisation of Cypriot Fighters (EOKA) and In April of that year the group launched a series of attacks on police stations, military barracks and government installations in the capital Nicosia, as well as in the major towns of Famagusta, Larnaca and Limassol. Hundreds of British servicemen and police were killed, and it became clear to the British that the Cyprus issue had gone beyond the capacity of the local police force and must now become a full military operation. Field Marshal Sir John Harding, fresh from his successes in Malaya, was brought in as a military Governor-General. The army beefed up its forces on the island, instituted harsh security measures and worked to flush out the EOKA 'terrorists', who continued to have sporadic successes ambushing or sniping at Army personnel. Harding attempted to negotiate with Makarios, who was officially distancing himself from Grivas and EOKA, but the talks broke down, and in 1956 Harding had Makarios exiled to the Seychelles. This was the scene into which we had steamed in February 1957.

Polemidhia's Buckingham Camp, home to the 1st Battalion of the Oxfordshire and Buckinghamshire Light Infantry since the previous December, had at some point been tacked on at the far end of an older British Army encampment now occupied by the Royal Engineers, and through which we must travel to reach our own. Ours was an almost entirely tented camp, its khaki tents pitched in row after row up a gently inclining and very stony slope. Each tent accommodated four light infantrymen. Duckboards over the earth floor helped to keep beds and feet and kitbags out of the rivulets of water which streamed down the hill during winter showers. At the lower end of the hill stood the Officers' Mess, a breezeblock hut roofed in corrugated iron and housing a lounge and a dining-room. Clustered close to the Mess were the officers' washing facilities and DTL (deep trench latrine), and their sleeping quarters. Unlike our soldiers we each had a tent to ourselves: an iron bedstead, a chest of drawers, a table and chair, a washbowl and a small bedside stand. Primitive wiring looped its way from tent to tent all over the camp and gave us shaky lighting at night – also powering our wirelesses and the occasional gramophone. From the flap of my tent I could look over the barbed-wire perimeter fence and down the valley to the Greek village of Ayios Phyla, where a doleful church bell would occasionally sound; and to the dry and chalky white hills beyond, with carob and olive trees dotting the landscape.

I was posted to 'A' Company, commanded by Major H.J. Sweeney MC, inevitably nicknamed 'Tod'. Company Headquarters was simply a large white tent divided into two. In the front office gentle Company Serjeant Major 'Ally' Gater held uncertain sway. The commander of Number One platoon, Richard Bradshaw, was to be demobilised in a few months, and within a day or two of my arrival he started handing me over his command. Which was why, not many days after that, I was standing soon after dawn on the passenger seat of a lorry, head and shoulders sticking out through a hole in the roof of the cabin, clutching a loaded Sten gun and looking very intently indeed at the carob trees, as I led our 36 men down the road to Limassol for our first foot patrol.

No. 2 platoon had just been taken over by the recently arrived Edward Jones, commissioned into the Oxford and Bucks from Sandhurst: a loud, laughing, swash-buckling powerhouse who was to become one of my closest friends. And No. 3 was already in the hands of none other than George Metcalfe, who had been my schoolmate in Cornwall at our age of five, and who had also been at Radley, though our paths had rarely crossed. Noisy, impulsive, still a stutterer, and in the view of many of our fellow officers – and his own soldiers – slightly daft, George was nevertheless a torrent of energy and fun. Tall Edward's high spirits, raucous laughter and high professionalism, with short Richard Bradshaw's Sienese good looks, his solemn manner dissolving into giggles, and his huge admiration for the regiment's history and heroes; all this made for a joyful chemistry among us. (Richard had recently returned from a mysterious secondment which had taken him for a few weeks to the Canal Zone shortly after the British and French invasion. It was fifty years before he was able to tell me that he had been the driver and general dogsbody for a secret service team of four which had had instructions to kill Nasser. They had three alternative methods. One of them was to smuggle into his palace a poisoned box of his favourite chocolates. Needless to say, neither that nor any other of their crazy schemes worked out, and they were lucky to leave with their lives.)

It was soon clear that my joining 'A' Company was in fact a wonderful piece of luck. Our Commander, Tod Sweeney, now in his early forties, had led one of the platoons that landed by glider behind enemy lines in Normandy to capture Pegasus Bridge in the early hours of D–Day, 1944: an operation which had already taken its honoured place in the annals of the regiment. Of medium height, with curly hair just beginning to grey at the temples, a lean face, eyes ready to laugh, a beaky nose and a full moustache, Tod had an avuncular attitude to his young officers and his company, and it was not surprising that we came to revere him and worked hard to avoid his disapproval. He was highly intelligent and well read, enjoyed classical music, and possessed a strongly analytical mind. Nothing further from a Colonel Blimp could be imagined. We soon discovered that Tod was also a faithful though undogmatic Roman Catholic, and were taken aback at learning that he had been a novice Benedictine monk who had discarded his monkish habit at the start of the war to enlist against the Führer, later meeting and marrying his wife Geraldine. He had won his Military Cross when he was wounded on the push towards the Rhine. He had served with the regiment in Palestine after the war, and then in Germany, and by now had four young children.

Tod had just rejoined the regiment after two years seconded to the Canadian army in Manitoba, and had returned to Europe bringing a bulbous and chrome-laden 1955 Plymouth sedan in two shades of green. This splendid vehicle, which he had shipped to

Cyprus, set him apart from the crowd, and gave him a uniquely racy image among our senior officers. His family's eager accounts of camping all over western Canada and through the Rockies maybe helped to stamp on my imagination the idea of the boundless world of that great dominion to the west.

It was not long before we persuaded Tod, on some company operation up in the hills above Limassol, to recount to us one evening by the camp fire the story of the capture of Pegasus and Horsa Bridges in Normandy, and of the bloody campaign that followed. At that time these exploits seemed to hail from the very distant past, and it's odd now to remember that the war had been over for no more than a dozen years.

There was no formality among the officers of the Company. Tod was 'Tod' to us from the beginning (though 'sir' in front of our troops), and we were George and Edward and Richard and Michael to him. In fact this was a delightful characteristic of our unusual regiment, in which officers all referred to each other by their first names, with the single exception of the Commanding Officer, who was 'sir', or 'Colonel'. I heard later from friends in some other regiments how stiff and unwelcoming their units had been to young subalterns, who were required to address anyone of field rank (major) or above as 'sir', and who had to stand up any time a major entered the mess, and speak only when spoken to. National Service officers were treated with particular contempt. None of that nonsense in the Oxford and Bucks, and we learned it had always been so.

The Battalion's task was to maintain security and protect police stations and other government installations within Limassol, and also in the local region, which stretched at a radius of some twenty miles along the coast east and west of the town, and up into the hills which reach north towards the Troodos mountain range in the centre of the island. The 'enemy' were groups of EOKA guerillas that we believed were holed up in hides somewhere in the hills, or perhaps hidden and looked after in the tiny, almost mediaeval villages which dotted the landscape. From these hideouts they would occasionally launch raids or ambushes in Limassol or the country round.

Our operations took three main forms. First, we would conduct town patrols, in which small groups of armed soldiers would 'show the flag' along designated streets in Limassol, both by day and night. We were taught to be on high alert, and I learned early on to be minutely aware of movement along roof-tops and down alleyways, in front and behind us.

Secondly, there were a number of specific sites which had to be guarded. Chief among them was 'MilPol', the headquarters of Limassol's British military and police forces, located in a requisitioned villa on the edge of town, and an obvious target for the EOKA fighters, as the prime local symbol of our hated regime. There were other locations out in the countryside, including one I remember at Asgata, a small copper pyrites mine where explosives were used to dislodge the mineral from the mine face. The dynamite was stored above ground in a securely locked and barred shed. The whole site was enclosed in a barbed wire fence with sandbag emplacements for sentries, and the guarding platoon lived in a corrugated iron hut within the enclosure; blindingly hot and dry in the summer months. Asgata was up in the hills in what looked like moon country, and I remember my platoon guarding it for as long as two weeks at a time. Every few days Sjt. Price and I, with an armed escort, would accompany the manager to the explosives shed, where we would together count out the sticks of dynamite to be used on that shift. We would then lock up the shed and descend the long steps into the mine. We would watch and recount the sticks as they were inserted into the holes which had already been drilled for them. The fuses were attached, and we would retire to the surface with the manager, detonator in hand. We would hear and count the explosions going off underground, and then leave the miners to their work. Obviously all these explosive materials would be valuable to EOKA, and the lonely mine was highly vulnerable to attack. Hence our presence in what seemed one of the most tedious guardposts in the world. We played cards, we read, we listened to the armed forces radio, we played guitar, we drank copious draughts of the Keo orange juice which was delivered to us in crates every couple of days from Polemidhia, along with ice and other rations. Never once were we attacked. The only excitement I remember there was that famous early October night of 1957 when the Soviet Union launched its Sputnik, to the shock and awe of the West. We were able to follow its track above the mountains in Cyprus's brilliant night sky: the first time we – and the world – had ever seen a man-made satellite in orbit.

Thirdly, there was the cordon-and-search operation. 'A' Company was sent on one of these a month or two after I arrived, centred on the village of Kellaki. The company was dropped off before dawn a mile or so away, well out of earshot of the sleeping villagers. We then stole silently through the stony fields and olive trees around the village until it was fully cordoned off, a soldier every few yards. Checkpoints were set up on all the roads leading in to the village. All the male villagers were then rounded up and led into a hastily erected barbed-wired compound at the schoolyard, from which they were brought out into the school one at a time, so that the security police who accompanied us on the operation could inspect their papers against the known records of EOKA members. We also made a house-to-house search, to be sure that all males had been routed out.

Of all the regular activities carried out by the our forces, the cordon-and-search was for me the most invasive. Our regiment was gentle and polite – even notoriously so – but still we had to march into the humble, dirt-floored homes of one family after another, the wrinkled old crones dressed in black and looking ahead impassively, the children crowded at their mother's skirts and watching us timidly as we lifted up their few sticks of furniture, opened boxes, searched behind chimneys and up in the rafters. Polite as we tried to be, I am sure we made no friends.

By springtime I had assumed full command of my own platoon, and we had already taken our turn at all the various kinds of regular operation the Battalion was faced with. In addition to these duties, we were required to keep ourselves in good physical shape, and our Battalion's second-in-command, Major Charles Mason, before long instituted a schedule of marches: we were wretchedly unfit, he decreed, and must henceforth undertake one five-mile march every week, and one twenty-five mile march every month. I remember only one of these marathons, when in the height of the hot summer 'A' company was transported far up into the hills, to set out in the cool of midnight and make our way to a beach at the coast. Each platoon, fully equipped with backpacks, rifles and ammunition and with their bren gun sections carrying an even heavier load, was dropped off at a different starting point. It was the platoon commander's job to find his own route. Unfortunately the maps we were given were full of inaccuracies, and it took me and my serjeant a while to find our way out after a few false starts. But in those early hours I mainly recall the slant of moonlight through the trees, the heavy scent of mock orange blossom and thyme and sage, the whiff of resin from the pine trees, and above all the quiet murmur of streams and irrigation channels and glimmering weirs as the precious water puttered and bubbled down the valleys. Since then I have always been drawn to the sounds and sight of what Housman calls 'brooklands' – especially at night.

It was a long haul, but at least it was steadily downhill. By six o' clock the sky was already light, and the sun was soon showing its fiery face over the hills to the east. As the men of my platoon became more and more exhausted, the temperature rose swiftly. By eight o'clock the stronger soldiers were helping their limping comrades along, even carrying their weapons and backpacks for them. I took my turn with the men's rifles too, and chivvied everyone along, trying to hide the fact that my own feet were painfully blistered. What drove us on was the occasional glimpse of the blue sea ahead: 'thalassa, thalassa!' Just after nine, with the sun now scorching us, we stumbled on to the sandy beach. No orders were given, but in one unanimous surge we all dropped our kit and our weapons, stripped naked and threw ourselves into the water. That would have been the perfect moment for EOKA to launch a deadly attack. But they didn't, and it was the best swim I can ever remember. It was followed up by a two-day holiday on the beach, sensibly arranged by Tod Sweeney.

At some point that summer I was sent up to Nicosia on a week's 'fire course', to learn the basics of firefighting and control, finishing up with a dramatic day in the Troodos forest, where we watched a 'controlled burn' being cleverly managed and extinguished. Naturally, as soon as I returned to Polemidhia, Colonel Tony Read designated me as the new Fire Officer for the Battalion. This was generally reckoned to be what they called a 'cushy number': I had a small section of three or four men to work with me in the event of a fire, and we congratulated ourselves on having avoided some of the more arduous duties being handed out at the time. Strangely enough, I was finishing my lunch in the mess that very day when

I heard the bugle call sounding for 'Fire!' My fellow officers chuckled as I grabbed my belt and beret and ran out, picking up a red bucket of sand at one of the fire stations and doubling to our meeting-point, where my section quickly joined me with their buckets and an extinguisher in hand. It was a fire in the cookhouse, if I remember, and it was not long before we successfully doused it and dispersed. We were observing summer working hours at that time, which began with a drill parade at 7 a.m. and ended at 1 in the afternoon, when most of us retired to our steamy tents to sleep off the heat of the day. I drifted away happily for my siesta, and was just dozing off when to my astonishment I heard the bugle-call for 'Fire' sounding again. I put on my boots and clattered out to join my fire section once more – who all thought as I did that it must have been a joke. But no, there was a small and rather suspicious fire just behind 'C' Company headquarters. We did our job again before much damage was done, and once again dispersed.

The next day, the fire call sounded three times, each time signalling a fire in a different area of the camp. The day after, it blared out five times: 'ba-ba-ba-ba-ba-ba-ba-ba- bu-uh bu-uh!' Most were pretty minor conflagrations – a smoking waste-paper basket or a bundle of rags somewhere. But once a whole sleeping tent went up in flames. Luckily all the inmates got out in time – my fire course had taught me that a tent is reduced to nothing but charred embers in about four minutes flat.

There were another three fires the following day. People by this time used to come diving out of their tents just to enjoy the sight of my poor section and me clumping heavily by at the double on our way to a new outbreak. It was obvious that some arsonist was at work, but we had to run to no less than twenty-seven fires in ten days before the culprit was finally discovered, calmly setting a new blaze in the rubbish dump. He was an otherwise perfectly ordinary soldier, and we were all thoroughly surprised. He was of course court-martialled: I was called as a long-suffering witness. Found guilty, he was sent back to England right away. Which was perhaps the whole object of the enterprise.

The legend of the British *sahib* donning evening dress for dinner in the jungle is not without foundation. You would have thought that the Battalion's rapid deployment to Cyprus the previous year would have meant that only the bare necessities for active service would have been transported alongside it. But space had obviously been found for a special crate carrying a fair amount of the regimental silver. We drank our beers and shandies in the officers' mess from engraved silver tankards, some of them dating back to the nineteenth century. And at our first formal mess night, as we sat down in our 'number ones', I was amazed to see the amount of elaborate silver pieces which were displayed along the whole length of the dining-table. Our chinaware and cutlery bore the regimental crest. And we were served by reasonably well-trained mess waiters: infantrymen who had been lucky enough to be chosen for mess duty. As I later found out, the serjeants' mess had their own proudly-guarded silver collection. The 'Other Ranks' of course must make do with their enamel mugs, enamel plates and eating irons.

Even as young officers, we were all entitled to the services of a personal batman, chosen from our platoons, who woke us up in the morning with hot water for shaving, shone our boots and brass, fetched our laundry from the *dhobi*, and generally looked after our basic needs. This was all very gratifying – and I was once saved by my quick-thinking batman from the terrible indiscretion of oversleeping and missing a parade – but I must confess that I was in general quite simply embarrassed at being cosseted in this way. Discussing it with my friend Edward, I found that he felt the same way, and one day we approached Charles Mason and told him how we found it unnecessary for ourselves and demeaning for the soldiers who attended us. Charles was outraged. "Look, you young idiots," he told us, his face red and his big belly quivering with indignation, "You are in one of the luckiest positions in the world, where you have your own servant to do your bidding. You'll never ever have such a privilege again. For God's sake, enjoy it – make the most of it – and don't come to me snivelling about workers' rights. You are officers, damn it all – and don't ever forget it!" We retired somewhat shamefaced, our social consciences beaten out of us – at least for the moment.

Major Charles Mason was in fact a much more complex character than this Blimpish incident would suggest. He was a powerful presence: tall and stout, loud-talking, combative and dismissive, with a fund of anecdotes from the war and from his service in Africa. I have never forgotten the mess night when for no reason the chat around the table happened suddenly to fall silent, and in the lull Charles Mason's voice boomed out: "I once knew a White Russian in Addis Ababa..." The laughter which greeted this splendid opening went on for a full five minutes, and I don't think he ever got a chance to continue his story. But Charles was also moody: he was perhaps even a manic depressive, though we would not have known that designation in those days. In a black mood, and if he decided that he did not like you, he could cut you down with a terrifying ferocity. One of his *bêtes noires* was Major David Wood, who commanded Support Company. David, like Tod Sweeney, was a war hero, having commanded a platoon and been wounded in the Pegasus Bridge raid, but he was something of an old woman in his over-meticulous attention to regulations, and in his almost servile attitude to officers senior to him. Charles would bully the poor fellow almost to tears.

Within a month or two of my joining the Battalion, I for some reason became the apple of Charles Mason's eye. He was almost menacingly nice to me, and everyone including myself was mystified at his attentions. The high point came on August 25th, when to my utter amazement Charles brought a cup of early morning tea to my tent and wished me a happy birthday.

It was perhaps as a result of his exaggeratedly high opinion of me that when the Colonel of the Regiment, Major-General Sir John Winterton, came out to Cyprus for a visit to the Battalion in April, I was appointed to be his *aide de camp* for the days of his visit. I accompanied the General from the time of his arrival at Nicosia airport on an Air Force plane to his departure four or five days later. He inspected the Battalion on parade, and then went out to visit our detachments in the countryside – including the benighted Asgata copper mine. Along the way I took a photographic record of his tour with the new 35mm Minolta camera I had bought at an Armenian shop in Limassol, some of the photos finding a place the following year in the regimental chronicle for 1957.

Winterton had been the Allies' Governor of Trieste after the war, when he was described to me by a Serbo-Croat years later as 'the most hated man in the city': the cross-border and ethnic complications of the region were evidently a nightmare to sort out, but from what I saw of the General there was an inherent pig-headedness in the man which I imagine did him no service in a task calling for extreme sensitivity and skill. The culminating episode of his Cyprus tour, and one on which he laid great store, was an official visit to Governor-General Harding at Government House in Nicosia. I was told to pack my bag for a formal evening with the Governor-General, but also to include my bathing trunks. When our staff car arrived at the door, our cases were whisked off and we were brought in to meet Their Excellencies for a cup of tea. I still remember the delight of sandwiches and cake in stately, comfortable surroundings, with the gentle clink of good china and silver spoons, after three months under canvas. Going upstairs afterwards to dress for dinner, I found my shirt, socks and underwear, looking ratty from months of tent living, had all been removed from my scruffy and hastily-packed suitcase and meticulously laid out on the bed by an invisible valet. No matter, I said to myself: I am a working soldier, in from the field. I drew a long hot bath and revelled in the luxury.

The Oxford and Bucks had some representation at Government House: the ADC to the Governor-General (himself a Light Infantryman) was the regiment's very poshly-named Captain Seymour Thistlethwayte. He and others joined us for a highly formal dinner, which must have been pleasant, though I remember nothing of it, and nothing much of the Governor-General except that he looked a little like Lawrence of Arabia: short, lean, handsome and the picture of a successful soldier. I better remember his vivacious and bosomy wife Lady Harding, who next day took me with her and Seymour to Kyrenia, where I water-skied (inexpertly) for the first and last time in my life: hence the bathing trunks. Lady H. zoomed around the bay like a professional, with Seymour at the wheel: it was my first sight of that beautiful sheltered harbour on the north coast of Cyprus, though not my last.

That evening General Winterton flew off home, and I returned to Polemidhia and the now familiar routines of camp life. It had been a fine interlude, and I seem to have managed it without any major screw-ups, since, when the new Governor-General Sir Hugh Foot paid an official visit to our regiment many months later, I was attached to him also as ADC for the day, my most memorable duty being to pull off his long and incredibly sweat-gummed boots after he played a chukka of polo with some cavalry unit outside Limassol. I think that Foot, an international diplomat, had seen service in

India, which would explain his familiarity with polo. It also explains why the officers' mess decided to prepare an elaborate curry lunch for him. One of our officers with Indian experience supervised activities in the stifling, corrugated-iron lean-to which served as the mess kitchen, and when the meal was served it turned out to be the very hottest curry anyone had ever eaten. We were already suffering under a burningly hot day, and within twenty minutes every face around the table, including the Governor-General's, was beet-red, with sweat pouring off our temples. In his remarks after the meal Foot observed with professional diplomacy: "I don't think I would have liked it any hotter than that."

The year 1957 was the centenary of the storming of the Cashmere Gate at Delhi by the 52nd, during the Indian Mutiny. The incident featured as one of the regiment's battle honours, and on the precise anniversary, September the 14th, the Battalion decided to mount a re-creation of the battle. A Delhi Gate of wood and hessian was hammered together and erected on our parade ground on the edge of the camp, and our historically-minded Adjutant Bill Chevis provided the narration for a kind of *son et lumière* event, with an evening frontal attack against a vigorous native defending force (did they wear turbans and black their faces? I expect so), enlivened with rockets, blank ammunition, fireworks and explosions, all accompanied by the regimental band playing urgent bugle-calls, and a handful of final triumphal marches as darkness fell.

The Indian Mutiny was a short-lived but very violent uprising against the British domination of India, and is now regarded in India as one of the first brave and honourable revolts against the Raj in the century-long struggle for independence. Our regiment was in general an ethical and even liberal-minded body of men, but I can remember no hint of squeamishness about the celebration: in our highly partisan history lessons at school we had all been taught so much about the savagery of the mutiny and the horrifying treatment of men and women in the Black Hole of Calcutta, that we still saw the reaction of the Army as a righteous fight to restore law and order and the sensible British way of doing things.

Nor do I recall any preparedness to draw comparisons between that far-off colonial struggle and the work we were currently engaged with in Cyprus. Here we were, after all, in another country far away from our own, attempting to put down the justifiable struggle of Greek Cypriots for union with Greece. Britain of course wanted to hold on to the island as a gateway to the Middle East and a launching pad for military operations there. Our own ostensibly justifying point in the struggle was the opposition of Turkish Cypriots to any suggestion of *enosis*, but there is no doubt we leaned on that Turkish opposition, having created an all-Turkish police force, using Greek-speaking Turkish interpreters as spies and informers, and honouring Turkish leaders by attending key religious ceremonies in their mosques. Greek and Turkish Cypriots, after all, had been living side by side for centuries in reasonable harmony, with even a certain amount of intermarriage: British policies had set the two communities at each other's throats for ever. From being straightforward defenders of imperial power we had now renamed ourselves as impartial peacemakers and peacekeepers, without whose firm hand sectarian violence would break out, with untold misery as a consequence. It was a story which has been repeated the world over: Hindus and Moslems in British India, Protestants and Catholics in Ireland, Palestinians and Israelis in Palestine. And, as elsewhere, partition (*taksim* in Turkish) would a few years later become the only option. In 1974 Turkey would invade Cyprus on behalf of the Turkish community, with the northern coastal region becoming the *de facto* Turkish sector of the island.

In 1957, of course, the island was still one, and the short drive from Nicosia through the mountain pass and down to Kyrenia provided a blessed release for those living in the capital or in the dusty plains around it. In August of that year I had the opportunity to experience the region first hand, when Tod Sweeney rented from Cyprus's Director of Antiquities and his wife a house which they had built high on the mountains above Kyrenia, two or three thousand feet up from the sea. Tod and Geraldine invited Edward Jones and myself to stay with their family for a long weekend, along with the ebullient Major Denis Fox and his wife Pat. Denis, now commanding Headquarter Company, had been another of the platoon commanders who had glided in early on D-Day to capture the bridges over the Orne river and canal, and ever since then he had been Tod's close comrade and friend. The house we shared that long-ago weekend was built in the local Greek style, with white stucco walls and flat roof with a parapet to catch the rain. It was set in a wild garden adorned with almond and fig trees and a huge ancient Greek amphora. Up a few stone steps sat a luxurious outdoor privy topped by a miniature Byzantine dome. The house's simple furnishings had been gathered from the area: wooden-made and hand-crafted with a natural peasant elegance. From the dining table on the terrace outside the house you looked out over the Mediterranean, and on a fine day you could glimpse Turkey no more than forty miles away. On an outcrop of rock just above the house stood the famed castle of St. Hilarion, whose spectacular ruins are said to have provided the model for the castle in Disney's *Snow White*.

To bathe we had a long way to go, heading down the winding gravel driveway to where it joined the Nicosia road, and then on down the hairpin-bent road to the shore, where there were superb and more or less unpopulated beaches. After our swim at Snake

Island we would head into Kyrenia's sultry midday for drinks at the Octopus Bar, buy our groceries and beer and wine, and then drive back up into the heavenly cool of our mountain home. Whenever I imagine paradise on earth it is this beautiful place which still comes to mind.

Some time that first summer the Government began a long overhaul of the British Army, as part of which they announced compensation rates as incentives for senior officers of field rank to retire and re-enter civilian life: there were far too many of them left over from the war to be accommodated in more senior ranks within a steeply reduced force. This was quickly dubbed the "Golden Bowler" programme, and many of our own majors finding they were eligible spent the year studying the rates and considering their options. I decided to write a song about them, and having recently acquired a guitar at the music shop in Limassol set to work. The result was *Oh, 43rd and 52nd Gentlemen*, which with some diffidence I sang at a mess night. It seemed to go down extremely well, and from then on it was a regular request. It was subsequently orchestrated by Bandmaster Kenney and I understand was played on regimental evenings for years!

Flushed with minor success, I produced another song, this time about our regimental heroes and their often-repeated war stories:

When I hear all the tales I've heard
Of the 52nd and the 43rd,
I think as I'm supposed to think
That all young subalterns stink:
You're not a man unless you won the war!
You're not a man unless there's something of the war you saw;
You're not a man unless you've done it all before:
You're not a man – unless you're a bore!

And so on. If my first song had been mildly cheeky, the second – though in a spirit of fun – was close to being insubordinate. But it was well received and became another favourite request – even in the serjeants' mess. I recorded the songs with piano when I returned home the following year, and can still hear my youthful baritone pumping out rather prettily through the scratches of fifty years.

I managed to get invited to the Sweeneys' paradise a second time in late August, this time with George Metcalfe, and it was on this second visit that Tod, George and I cooked up the idea of putting together a pantomime to entertain the troops the following Christmas. George, who I think made the original suggestion, was to write the book, and I, fresh from my modest successes with my satirical songs (not to mention *Black and White Blues* at Radley), was to furnish the music and lyrics. We decided to base our show on the story of Aladdin, and George's first draft, heavily adjusted to reflect our military life, was ready by October: *Aladdin And His Wonderful Lamp (Pressure)*. I started churning out songs soon after this, and in November we began fitting our rehearsals round our army duties. In the opinion of the ever caustic Charles Mason, it was really the other way round, and I think it was about that time that Charles began to take a dimmer and dimmer view of his former golden boy Michael Bawtree. His dim view had even expanded to cover the whole of 'A' Company and even its company commander. We were thought to be taking our military responsibilities altogether too lightly.

In fact since the spring of that year life had been made a good deal easier and freer for the units stationed in Cyprus, as the result of a truce called by EOKA. Technically this was their response to the liberation of Makarios from his exile on the Seychelles in March 1957, though he had not been allowed to return to Cyprus. More probably it seems that with the increased activity of British forces on the island EOKA was feeling the heat, and that they used the freeing of Makarios as their justification. Their cessation of bombings and ambushes enabled us to loosen up some of the security measures restricting our own freedom of movement. But the British in no way cut back on their efforts to locate and capture EOKA fighters. We continued to guard facilities, and to engage in cordon-and- search operations through the rest of that year. We also continued to hunt EOKA members down within the town of Limassol, with the help of a little pocket manual issued to all officers and containing names, descriptions and photographs of EOKA suspects: the more important of them were code-named 'Bluebirds'.

At some point, when the theory got about that individuals from EOKA gangs in the hills were sneaking down into town on weekends in search of a little fun, it was decided that all the brothels and doss-houses of Limassol were to be searched on a single Friday night. For this delicate operation 'A' Company was chosen. Perhaps this was Charles Mason's way of ensuring that our theatrical activities were being kept sternly within bounds – though in fact it was seen by other Companies as a dream commission, and we were much envied. In our briefing from Tod we officers heard with astonishment that there were sixty-five locations to search. We were divided into groups of five, each under an officer or serjeant, and each group was given a hand-drawn map showing our targets. The plan was to surround each location in turn, demand entrance, round up all the males on site, and then wait for our security police to come and inspect their papers. On my own list I had one doss-house and two brothels.

We assembled around 11 pm that night, all of us, as instructed, wearing not boots but street shoes. Tod attracted much attention and amusement by arriving on parade in those suede shoes with thick rubber soles known by us all then as 'brothel creepers.' We were transported down to the edge of town, where we divided into our teams and set out stealthily for our various destinations, in and around Limassol's provocatively named Zig Zag Street.

My group located our first site, and after sending two soldiers round to the back to prevent escapes from the rear I drew my revolver and knocked at a huge and ancient door, demanding entrance. There were protests from inside, but eventually we heard bolts drawn back and a large-breasted and angry woman well into her sixties, heavily made up, with loop ear-rings and long greying hair loose down her back, appeared in the doorway. Behind her was a spacious, high-ceilinged room smelling of sweat and cheap scent. It was lit by two or three candles, and a vast double bed took up much of the available space. The bed was covered with gaudy coloured wraps, and under the wraps was a small and very frightened man, covering himself up to the chin. Setting a soldier to guard the door, I entered the room and ordered the man out of the bed. He was reluctant, pointing to his trousers on the floor. I picked them up and handed them to him, and after some struggles under the blankets he emerged more or less clothed, and gibbering with fear and humiliation. I gestured for him to get out his identification papers, and we then waited five or ten embarrassing minutes before a security police officer arrived on the scene. The man was soon cleared, and muttering apologies (*'signomi, signomi'*) we left them to it. I have a feeling that the night's excitements had been irretrievably dampened for the poor pair.

Our next stop was another brothel. It was on an upper floor. A sad old woman led us up to a landing furnished with a few tatty armchairs and a sofa. From there a passage wound off into the dark, from which led three or four small rooms curtained off, each holding a bed and some scanty bedding. We searched the whole place and found no clients. But a staircase led up to another floor.

I climbed up with another soldier into a low attic with four or five small pallets, a sort of dormitory. Sitting on one bed in the corner, lit by a bare bulb overhead, were four terrified young girls, scantily dressed and clutching on to one another. The oldest was no more than sixteen, and they were all plastered with theatrical make-up: orange lips, rouged cheeks, mascara'd eyelashes. I gave them a smile to calm them down – unsuccessfully; and after looking perfunctorily under the beds we thankfully descended and on down into the street. It had been a shaking moment, and I will never forget it.

In fact, fun as it had all seemed at the outset, I found those two visits deeply upsetting. If a cordon-and-search was invasive, our sudden thrusting into the nightlife of the town was highly intrusive, and the hate and fear we aroused in innocent people were fully justified and abhorrent to me. Our last address, a primitive doss-house with eight or ten men roused out of two small rooms smelling of sweat and urine, was less troubling. And by chance one of the men's papers revealed him to be a Bluebird. He was led away by the security police for 'questioning'. I was proud of my catch at the time.

These security policemen, who worked out of the MilPol villa, were a small and somewhat sinister group of Englishmen, presumably from MI6. None of us much liked working alongside them. Nor were their ways our ways. One night my friend Captain Charlie Simmons heard shouts and screams coming from the shower-rooms in the grounds of the villa, and drawing closer he heard the thumps of a club hitting flesh. Charlie was outraged, and next day reported the incident to our Commanding Officer Tony Read. Nothing more was heard from the showers at MilPol, but no doubt the police simply moved their operations elsewhere. Information-gathering, it has been called, and the methods of gathering it by so-called world powers have not much changed in fifty years, for all our talk of international human rights and the Geneva Convention.

Charlie had become a good friend of Richard Bradshaw ever since they had represented the regiment skiing in Germany the year before, and since Edward and I were colleagues of Richard's in 'A' Company, the four of us became something of a team. In September Charlie had become Intelligence Officer (in succession to Captain Bob Pascoe, who had been posted back to England to continue a stellar army career which would eventually land him up as a full general and a knight). A short, softly-spoken fellow with a long rather dolorous face but a radiantly warm smile and an infectious, slow laugh, Charlie could not be bothered to be very smart in his turn-out, but he was highly intelligent and had a wry sense of humour. He loved animals and birds, and for some months, in his tent next to mine, had been nursing a crow which was injured and unable to fly, and had now become very much attached to its saviour. Charlie was soon nicknamed 'Crow' by Richard, who for some reason was called 'Bugsy'. Fifty years later the names were still being used by the two of them.

Work on *Aladdin* continued through the autumn, but there was time in October to take off for a week's leave. Richard had long left the regiment and the Army, but Charlie, Edward and I decided to make a flying trip to Jerusalem. We caught a plane from Nicosia to Beirut, where we took in a luxurious but almost deserted nightclub before being whisked off to the mountains east of the city for a very short night's rest, followed by an early morning flight to the Holy City. We were in fact to visit Old Jerusalem, which at that time was part of Jordan. We stayed in the hostel attached to the Anglican Cathedral of St. George's, just outside the walls, and the first night we strolled down in our tweed jackets and ties through the Damascus Gate built by the Crusaders and into the labyrinthine alleyways of the ancient city. The Arab merchants seemed pleased to see us, and we eventually hooked up at a café with a wise old guide called Mehmet, who took us round during the next few days to the various holy sites. I have a picture of the three of us on the roof of the Church of the Holy Sepulchre. We visited General Gordon's Garden of Gethsemane, took a taxi to Bethlehem to see the actual spot where Christ was believed to have been born, and climbed the Mount of Olives to see the footprint in the stone, from which He is thought to have launched Himself into Heaven. We took another taxi to the Dead Sea, where Edward floated (and I to my regret did not) before we drank beers at the Lido Bar: I still have the bill, for 9.90 piastres. And on the way back we passed the entrance to the huge refugee camp at Jericho where over a hundred thousand Palestinians had been stranded for a decade. It is strange to think that the little children we saw playing there, if still alive, will now be old men and women who have lived their whole impoverished lives in exile from their homelands.

All three of us at that time, I think, were still believers in the decorous faith of the Anglican church in which we had been brought up, and had come to Jerusalem with the excitement of pilgrims to the Holy Land. In the very un-Anglican world of Cyprus our own Church had come to seem more a badge of nationality than a faith, and I imagine we were keen to regain our religious bearings. In the event, though, the experience for me was quite different. In the city which was equally holy to Jew, Moslem and Christian, the Church of England seemed even more of an imperialist sect, even – or perhaps especially – with the irredeemably English Victorian Gothic pile of St. George's Cathedral at our backs. Christendom's record as a whole in

Jerusalem was none too savoury either: we were amazed to learn that the various Christian denominations could never agree as to who should have the honour of keeping the key to the Church of the Holy Sepulchre, so that it had been guarded for hundreds of years by members of a Moslem family whose prayer mat we saw just inside the low entrance door. To sweep the Church floors, we were told, the Copts, Roman Catholics and Orthodox Christians all had their territories, and fights had broken out over the centuries whenever jealously guarded boundaries were overswept. Religions and their various fiercely opposed creeds, I was coming to see, were an excellent way of dividing people and peoples. The city itself was bisected by a high wall separating the Jewish city from the Jordanian. Our passports allowed us into Jordan, but if they had been stamped with Israel's visa we would never have been permitted to land – and *vice versa*. Jericho's refugees were in flight from Israel, which had possessed their homes in the name of the Jewish state. It seemed that religious fervour of any colour so often manifested itself as a licence to hate, to expel and to kill.

Nor did our visits to the Holy Places do anything to cement my personal faith. The birthplace of Christ in Bethlehem, and His place of crucifixion and tomb in Jerusalem, were all encrusted with the icons and marbles and gilt and mosaics of the centuries, set about with candles and censors and flowers. Priests and people knelt and intoned. But none of this, astonishing and ancient as it was, seemed to have much to do with the loving kindness which Christ had preached. Too many vested – and vestmented – interests, it seemed, were in play. My gradual weaning away from the church of my fathers and from the Christian faith in general had its beginning, I believe, in this extraordinary and wonderful week in Jerusalem.

We returned to Cyprus to find that one of the men in Edward's platoon had died in hospital of peritonitis. Sadly I heard that the soldier was none other than Gerry French, who had slept in the bed next to mine in our first two weeks of basic training, and whose sweet disposition had made such an impression on me. Gerry, attended by all his friends from 'A' Company, was buried in the British cemetery in Nicosia, with full military honours. I hate to think what medical negligence might have led to his untimely death.

A week or two later the Battalion bid farewell to our commanding officer Tony Read, who left us in early November to command an Infantry Brigade in Cyprus. He was replaced by the kindly Colonel Andy Martin. Of all the officers I served with, Tony Read had the most commanding presence, the most natural authority and the greatest self-assurance. Not surprisingly, he went on – like Bob Pascoe – to become a full general and a knight, and when I last saw him and his wife Sheila in the 1970s he was serving as Governor of the Royal Hospital Chelsea. His command of the Battalion in Cyprus was exemplary. He was tough but fair, made good judgements, earned the respect and affection of all his officers, and kept firm control of the behaviour of our soldiers in their dealings with the Cypriots. I heard years later that when the Oxford and Bucks Battalion finally left in 1959, the locals, even the Greeks among them, were genuinely sorry to see it go.

As December approached 'A' Company found itself more and more involved in the preparation of *Aladdin*, and Second-in-Command Major Charles Mason, no longer reined in by a more powerful boss, became more hostile than ever. But we were allowed to persevere, and in fact the whole thing became an increasingly regimental affair. Bandmaster Kenney was orchestrating my songs and rehearsing them with his band. His wife helped us with make-up; and his young daughter Anne stepped up as the romantic female lead Princess Lotus. Transportation officer Jack Howland was roped in as Lotus's aging female sidekick Honeydew, and David Wood became the Genie. Two of 'A' Company's new subalterns took roles, and so did our company commander Tod, who sold new lamps for old under the name of Kushi Ollie McKeefik, 'an evil contractor of doubtful but half Scottish parentage'. Edward Jones took on the Dame role of Aunt Annie Twankey. The Signals Platoon provided the lights, and a note in the programme tells us — I think with unintended irony — 'The donkey in Act II appears by courtesy of the Intelligence Section.'

At the dress rehearsal David Wood, who was to appear in a flash of lightning when Aladdin rubbed his pressure lamp, lost his eyebrows and nearly had his face blown off when the signals officer put far too much magnesium in the pan. — David used to say afterwards that his life had been more in danger in our pantomime than in the landings at Pegasus Bridge. But in spite of the usual last minute crises we were more or less ready on the night. We played to a full house of soldiers and they laughed a lot. Edward (who in years to come would also be a General and a knight and even Black Rod for the House of Lords) knocked out the house with his rendering of "I like my little drop of brandy". The lead romantic song "Cool Girl" seemed to charm them all — judging by the catcalls — and Jack Howland was magnificently hideous and wonderfully funny in drag. We were only sorry, very sorry indeed, that Charles Mason unfortunately had another engagement and was unable to be with us.

Christmas Day saw the officers serving turkey and Christmas pudding to the soldiers in the dining-hall, and Boxing Day found most of the officers' mess and their ladies dining out in jolly fashion at a restaurant known as 'The Slab', on a rocky outcrop of the shore a few miles east of Limassol. A few days later the year of 1957 was finally put to bed, and after seeming hopelessly in the future ('roll on death: demob's too far away') my date of departure from Cyprus and the Army was suddenly round the corner.

Early in the New Year I was obliged to hand my platoon over to a new subaltern. It had been a happy time with No. 1 Platoon, 'A' Company (the 'Fighting First' they called themselves proudly), with my ignorance and inexperience slowly ripening into something like assurance, and my serjeant always on hand to get me out of trouble firmly but respectfully. It was obvious that like most of them I was not and never would be a professional soldier. But I was clearly not a bastard: I cared about them all and made them laugh and usually made decisions they went along with. I also played my guitar as we sat around the campfire out in the field, and accompanied sing-songs comic and sentimental: *Danny Boy*, I remember, was familiar to us all. But it was also the time of skiffle, with songs like Lonnie Donegan's *Rock Island Line* and *John Henry* as popular items ('A' Company had its own skiffle group, with ukuleles and washboard accompaniment). American romantic singers such as Bing Crosby, Frank Sinatra and Perry Como were only on the edge of our consciousness, and Elvis still further away round the corner. The Beatles were still schoolboys. My songs from *Aladdin* were of course in the old vein, and much appreciated when they arrived on the scene.

To while out the rest of my time I was seconded to Charlie Simmons in the Intelligence Section. My chief and still vivid memory of those days was a patrol which Charlie sent me out on, accompanied by our Turkish interpreter Osman, signaller Corporal Chadwick, and a donkey: donkeys under Charlie's command of the Intelligence Section seem to have been essential equipment. We were deposited after dark up in the hills north of Limassol, our donkey loaded up with food and bedding for a night or two in the field, and with radio equipment to connect us with Charlie at home base.

The object was to try and locate EOKA fighters who might be in the area. Osman's Greek-speaking – as well as his English – was flawless, and his sallow looks and aquiline nose helped him pass without question as a Greek Cypriot. Chadwick and I, on the other hand, if seen from anywhere closer than half a mile, were unmistakeably Anglo-Saxon. We set up our rudimentary camp well away from the villages, made wireless contact with Charlie, and then set out on our mission.

We had two targets. One was a tiny monastery, the other a lonely farmhouse. Our story was to be that we had come down from the Troodos mountains and were trying to locate the local EOKA group, because we had weapons and messages for them. Did our informants know of a group in the area, and if so could they help us locate them? The monastery, like all Greek churches and establishments, had been suspected for a long time of supporting EOKA, and of protecting and even harbouring fighters. And the farmhouse was far enough away from other houses for the farmer – if he was so disposed – to be able to give us information without being spied on by his neighbours.

It was after midnight and under a full moon that we approached the gleaming white walls of the little monastery. Chadwick and I settled down in a ditch a hundred yards away, covering Osman with our rifles as he went forward to the outside door and rang the bell. After a few minutes a monk came to the door. There was a whispered conversation, and then the locks were turned and Osman slipped inside.

A nervous ten minutes followed, and our respect for Osman's courage grew as we realized the danger he had walked into. What if EOKA members were in the monastery and he was led directly to them? Would he be able to stand up to their suspicious questioning? If not, he would certainly be shot.

Finally he emerged and the studded door closed behind him. He strolled casually down the track to a pre-arranged *rendez-vous* out of sight of the monastery, and a few minutes later we joined him there and heard his news. He had come back empty-handed. The monk he spoke to had been cordial but guarded, perhaps sensing a trap. He suggested that Osman return the next morning to speak to his superior. Until then, there was nothing he could do.

After a quick snack of chocolate and orange juice we crept quietly over the fields to our second target – the farmhouse. Once again Chadwick and I hid where we could cover Osman, and he went forward. Once again he roused the household and disappeared inside. This time, though, he emerged and came right over to our hiding place to tell us that the farmer was going to lead him to a hide among the terraces on the hill above the farm – that he was just putting on his boots and would join him shortly. I realized that Osman was going to have to make the visit to the hide on his own, once again putting himself into a potentially dangerous position. But there was no way we could accompany him. The brave fellow seemed unperturbed, and said he would see us back at our encampment in an hour or two. The farmer came out of his door, Osman joined him, and we watched them till they disappeared into the shadows. We then returned to our camp, and Chadwick radioed the news to Charlie.

Osman showed up fairly shortly afterwards and reported that, yes, the farmer had shown him the entrance to a hide up among the carob trees. As soon as Charlie received this confirmation he got busy, and by six in the morning the Battalion's duty company had arrived on the scene and was surrounding the area. We joined up with them, and led by Osman approached the hide. We removed the earth and brush concealing the entrance and with revolvers at the ready lifted the cover. The hide was empty.

This was the closest I ever came to a military action in my fifteen months in Cyprus. During that time I had never fired a shot and never been shot at. Nor had I ever seen anyone else shooting or shot. Of course incidents did occur during that time, but for most of the British forces stationed here it was a peaceful posting. I remember sitting back in the mess one evening with a gin and tonic and picking up the day-old *Evening News*. A huge headline across the front page screamed FEAR SHAKES TERROR ISLE. I wondered idly where this was, and read on to discover that the TERROR ISLE was our own tranquil Cyprus. Terror, of course, sells newspapers. Tranquillity does not.

Early in May my service in Cyprus finally came to an end, and after several drunken farewell parties I packed up and was driven to a camp in Nicosia, where I was to wait for an Air Force transport plane to fly me home. It was a strange no-man's-land, in which I knew no one and lay sweltering in my tent with only clouds of flies for company. Finally the call came and I climbed aboard a Bristol Britannia transport for the journey back to Britain. The four-prop plane was bare-boned with all its ribs showing, and the noise was shattering as we slowly edged our way west over the Mediterranean, stopping briefly to re-fuel in Malta before heading off again into the night. We landed at Hendon Airport at seven o' clock in the morning after a fourteen-hour flight (!), and I will never forget the ecstasy of stepping out of the plane into a damp, luxuriously green English May morning, and at once hearing a joyous blackbird sing. I was home.

My discharge took place at Cowley a few days later, and although I remained a reservist for a few years (I believe I was actually promoted to full lieutenant in the Territorials) I never again graced or disgraced a drill ground or an army camp. My military days were over, and the world was all before me.

CHAPTER EIGHT

BOTH GOOD AND TRUE

While the troopship *Asturias* was plunging its way through the Bay of Biscay in February 1957 on its way to Cyprus, I did not think that eighteen months later I would find myself back on that same bay, this time in a dead calm, and celebrating my twenty-first birthday. I had been out of the army for three months, experiencing for the first time in my life the sense of complete freedom.

But first there had been Studley to come back to. Returning joyfully after fifteen months away, I was happy to be welcomed home greedily by Father and Mother. Throughout my time in Cyprus (as indeed throughout my long years away at boarding school as I was growing up), Mother had sent me a loving and newsy letter almost every week. Wilma also wrote, and just occasionally my father would fill a page or two in his careful copperplate hand. So I was not out of touch with goings-on at home. But I could soon see what was carefully omitted in everyone's letters: that Studley Priory had finally ceased to be in any way a pleasure for the dear 'Props'. There was now no money to pay a cook, and my mother, gritting her teeth, produced four delicious meals a day, day after day, month after month, year after year. Wilma's zest and optimism had finally started to fade under the hard work and endless worry. My father, grown paunchier and more white-haired, his hands yellow with nicotine, wrestled daily with the accounts, which resolutely refused to give him comfort. Like many of his generation and social status (whatever that now was), he was dogged by the fear of bankruptcy, and prided himself on never having had a cheque returned because of 'not sufficient funds'. But the ritual contortions he went through to avoid this intolerable fate seemed almost worse than the alternative, and for the first time I became privy to his ways and means when I accompanied him on his trips to the city.

Father could no longer afford to run a car, and now depended on old Mr Beckley from the village, who brought him into Oxford to do the shopping for the hotel. On the way into town he would place his order with the butchers along The Plain near the foot of Magdalen Bridge. He would then be dropped off at Barclays Bank on the Cornmarket, where he would pay the weekend's cash and cheques (sometimes substantial, sometimes paltry) into the hotel account. He would then order the rest of the groceries at Palm's in the covered market, and perhaps a case or two of wine from the vintners.

Around one in the afternoon he would arrive hot and thirsty at the Mitre Hotel on the High, settling into the leather armchair at his usual corner in the front lounge. The barman, Charlie Crouch would appear: "The usual, Mr. Bawtree?" "Yes, thanks Charlie"; and he would take a first grateful swig at the tankard of Mitchell and Butler's Best Bitter placed before him. He would then take out his bank deposit book. He had one hundred pounds in overdraft privileges at the bank: any cheques putting him above that figure would be rejected. A rapid calculation would tell him how much his shortfall would amount to at the end of the working day. Then, putting away his wretched documents, he would sit there, reading one or two items in his *Daily Telegraph*, but concentrating on the crossword.

Over the next hour he would order a second and perhaps a third pint. Occasionally he would be joined by the Mitre's manager, Percy Gravett, always eager to chat in his gossipy way about the hotel business. Finally, soon after two, he would call for Charlie. "Charlie, I'd like to settle up..." – looking at his watch – "oh, I don't think I have time to get to the bank before three: would you mind cashing me a cheque for £25, and taking the drinks out of that?" "Of course, Mr Bawtree, no trouble at all." This was a regular request, and no cheque of my father's had ever bounced. Leaving a ridiculously handsome tip for Charlie he would gather up the cash, tuck his worn leather briefcase under his arm, and start up along Turl Street at his usual rapid gait, hair flying, knitted tie in place, trousers slightly too short, shapeless green tweed jacket flaring awkwardly behind him.

At Elmer Cotton's (the sports shop) he would greet his friend the manager and purchase a carton or two of Players' and du Maurier cigarettes, along with a dozen ping-pong balls and maybe some billiard cue chalk. As they totted up the bill he would look at his watch and ask them to cash a cheque for £25, less the cost of his purchases. "Of course, Mr Bawtree" – no cheque of his had ever bounced. Stuffing the cash into his briefcase he would continue fast-stepping up the street, repeating the same routine at Alden's the stationer's at the corner of the Turl and Broad Street. Heading into the Corn he would pick up some dry-cleaning on Ship Street – and cash another cheque. At last, just before closing time at 3 pm, he would bustle into Barclays (trying to avoid the eye of manager Dwelly) and deposit his sixty or seventy or eighty pounds cash: enough to cover his shortfall. Relaxed now, he would meet with Beckley in the public bar at the King's Head on Market Street, where he paid for the two of them to gulp down a quick half-pint. Beckley would have already picked up the orders in the market, so they would then drive down the High, stop to pick up the chickens and pork and beef and sausages at the butcher's, and finally sail home to Horton-cum-Studley, the day's work done.

To suggest this was a cumbersome way of extending his overdraft would be putting it gently. The next day, of course, all those cheques for £25 were likely to be presented at the bank. Unless a departing guest had paid a fair-sized bill, or unless a large party of diners had swollen the hotel revenues, Father would have to find some way of covering the new shortfall; and sometimes this meant another round of unnecessary purchases, another handful of cash to plug the hole. And of course the interest he paid was in those very purchases. In the passage outside the kitchen at Studley was a row of tall green-painted cupboards. Open one of them, and you would find it stuffed with ping-pong balls, ping-pong rackets, billiard chalk, arrows for archery, *Tatlers*, *Fields*, *Country Lifes* and *Queen's* magazines, and hundreds and hundreds of cigarettes. It was not the smartest way of doing business.

But, as I have already suggested, Father was at heart no businessman. His continued determination to run a hotel for 'respectable' folk made him reluctant to go after people who had more brass than class. Thirty miles north of us was Birmingham, which was now beginning to thrive in the first resurgence of prosperity after the war. But a Brum accent grated on Father's ears, and though he served the odd Midland businessman courteously and put up with him and his family and friends, he made no move to have them return. He was also of his generation in worrying about Jewish people becoming members of the Studley Priory Country Club: "they're perfectly nice people but…" When our wonderful grocers the Palms came out to the hotel for tea or dinner he would be warm and friendly with them – he genuinely liked them – but he was clearly uncomfortable with the fact that they were not only grocers but Jewish. Only towards the end of his life did he seem to get rid of these prejudices, which he had inherited from his Victorian father and indeed from the quietly racist society around him.

While I was home I would happily volunteer to help out Father in the bar, where I enjoyed talking with guests as they came and went. C.S. Lewis ('Jack' to his friends) was still dropping in regularly, now more and more often bringing with him his newly-found love Joy, who adored the place, and would battle her way through to the bar on her two canes every Sunday morning. I enjoyed lingering behind the counter when C.S. and his friends were in full spate. Occasionally I would find myself alone with the great man, and worked hard to entertain him. I remember telling him of Churchill's comment back in the 'forties when the austere Labour Chancellor of the Exchequer Stafford Cripps walked by: "There but for the grace of God goes God." It was his kind of fun, and he laughed inordinately.

The only way I could spend time with Mother even now was by sitting under a shelf in a corner of the kitchen while she prepared the next meal. Her spirit and doggedness was extraordinary. I cannot think I could ever have gone on so long – years! – doing something I so much disliked. I am still amazed to think of the organisation and the imagination required to produce so many meals: a brilliance approaching genius. It was taken for granted, I'm afraid: her place, after all, was in the kitchen. With no kitchen help, she had to clear up after these affairs as well – scouring out the frying and roasting pans, washing up the ladles and strainers and whisks and tablespoons, and putting away the left-overs. She was sustained from morning to night by cups of tea from the massive teapot permanently on the hob: as many as thirty-two a day, she once laughingly calculated. Changing the regime, Dad would occasionally come through with a welcome gin and tonic from the bar. He worked hard too of course, but a lot of the work was simply being in attendance on the guests. Not the same thing.

If I wanted to chat with Wilma, I would walk with her to the cowshed for the afternoon's milking – done by hand of course. She often used an old wooden yoke to carry two pails of milk back to the house. Sometimes I would do this for her. The milk would be deposited in one of the slate-countered pantries along the passage from the kitchen, where it would be passed through a hand-operated separator to produce our prized Jersey cream, a popular accompaniment for Mother's mouth-watering pies and cakes and mousses.

I was happy to be back. But home was not after all a very happy place. If I helped the Props around the house I was soon bored and frustrated: if I did not, I felt guilty. So it was not long before I was beginning to make plans for my summer. Since my army pay (which I think had amounted to £32 a month for me as a second lieutenant) was no longer finding its way to my bank account, I started looking for a new source of income.

I was lucky. Through one of our new guests I landed a contract with Nielsen's Market Research, based in Headington outside Oxford. It was a six-week summer job touring Wales and the western Midlands in a company car – a lowly Ford Prefect. My research project was targeting farmers, and the farms had been chosen at random from co-ordinate points on the ordnance survey map. I found my way to one farm after another, often far out in the wild, and came armed with a questionnaire for the farmer and his wife. The questions, after establishing the acreage, specialisation and employee numbers of each farm, asked (among other things) what kind of fertilisers they used on their crops, what tractors they drove, what they fed their livestock, what farming magazines they read, and whether they listened to the Archers.

I visited thirty or forty farms, sat at innumerable kitchen tables, caressed or fended off countless dogs, cats and children, admired scores of cows and horses and sheep, and thoroughly enjoyed my encounters with many hardworking people living tough lives – interspersed with the odd tweedy gentleman farmer, of course, and his tweedy lady. These were early days for market research, and the whole exercise was very personal and direct. The arrival of a cheery young man from far-away Oxford was a welcome distraction, and I sensed that they even felt privileged to have been picked out for the survey: they had not yet been harried to death by telephone campaigns or bombarded by television commercials, and the thrusting internet was decades in the future. Many of them had no television set, nor any possibility of reception. Nor had the motorways cut swaths through their neighbouring countryside. It was in fact almost the last moment at which genuine isolation in rural Britain was possible.

I also enjoyed being put up by pubs and small hotels along the way. It was before the age of the brewery-owned or chain-owned establishments, and long before the pretentious gourmet attractions of later years. The pubs were still the natural gathering place of locals from all walks of life, still sporting their class divisions into 'saloon' and 'public bar'. Many were the strange couples who had decided to set up in *The Star of Wales* or *The Moon and Sixpence* after the war, and scratch a living from beer and beds. My happiest memory was spending a night at a fourteenth-century inn at Rhydspence on the banks of the River Wye, where I mingled with shepherds and farmers over a game of snooker. One old hand was keen to teach me some Welsh, and coached me in a phrase until I got the hang of it, while his cronies sniggered. I then asked what it meant. "Seven kinds of a bugger," he replied.

On a couple of my days at home I went back to visit my old school at Radley, and was able to pick up my friendship with some of the old schoolmasters who were still important in my life – including Chris Ellis. While I had been away Chris had bought a sailing boat called *Theodora*. Fifty years old and one of the last wind-powered Bristol Channel pilot cutters (her original name was *Kindly Light*), she was a graceful 70-foot vessel of some 35 tons, and Chris was busy scooting between Radley and Southampton to fit her up in time to take part in the Cherbourg-to-Corunna sailing race being held in early August. Chris invited me to join him on the boat. He had already put together a full crew of eleven or twelve for the race itself: a mixture of Radley boys, old boys and masters, boys from one or two other schools, and a woman friend of his (Celia, I think) to serve – surprise! – as ship's cook. But three or four of them had to leave at the race's end, and he suggested I find my way to Corunna and join them there, sail round the coast of Galicia and then back to England. It didn't take me long to make up my mind. My summer job would be wrapped up by early August; I would have enough money to hitch-hike out to Spain, and also to make my contribution to the voyage – £1 a day if I remember. I knew nothing about sailing but was happy to learn. This was an adventure I could not turn down.

Just before I left, I received my first, jolting communication from Oxford since I had returned from Cyprus: a brief, dry letter from the Senior Tutor and senior classicist of Worcester College, Mr Bryan-Brown, informing me that on the first day of my first term in October I would be required to sit an exam testing me on two books of Homer's *Iliad* and two books of Virgil's *Aeneid*. I looked at the letter in dismay. I had not thought about Latin or Greek for two years, let alone kept up either language between army patrols. Could I bear to immerse myself once again in the whole frowsty business?

For the first time ever, I considered changing the field of study which had been more or less wished on me since the age of eleven. What about switching to English? Apart from being sure that its three-year programme would be a whole lot less grinding than the four-year 'Mods and Greats' laid out for me as a classical scholar, I genuinely loved English literature, read poetry, had acted in Shakespeare and knew many of his sonnets by heart. After a day's tense thought I wrote back to the College, requesting permission to change my degree programme to English Language and Literature. I left for Spain before I could receive an answer, but I felt reasonably confident, and was exhilarated by the prospect: it was the first time that I had attempted to engineer a major shift of direction in my life. There would be others.

Chris had put me in touch with Peter, another would-be sailor, and the two of us crossed over to France and hitch-hiked down the west coast together. Once over the border at San Sebastian, in Franco's Spain, we gave up on *heigh-ho for the open road*, and finished the journey by train. We spent most of the time sitting on our rucksacks in the corridor: it was the end of some sacred holiday, and there were conscripts everywhere returning from leave. The army presence, and Franco's ubiquitous armed police at the stations – looking in their shiny black hats like walk-ons in a comic opera, but menacing for all that – gave us our first and almost only taste of fascist Spain. Arriving in Corunna we took a tram down to the harbour, and there, nestling in a berth just off the stone wharf, was *Theodora*.

The next enchanting three weeks took us at a leisurely pace around Cape Finisterre, and down the north-west coast of Spain as far as Vigo. Along the way I began to pick up some of the basics of sailing. Every operation on the heavy sails was of course done by hand and muscle, and I learnt to join in the raising and lowering of the mainsail and the jib – or the elaborate khaki-coloured hemp squaresail rig when we enjoyed a following breeze – and to take my turn steering the vessel and standing watch. We put in at coves and bays and alongside small fishing-village quays. We made cheerful contact with local sailors as we went, and once were also lionised by some of the most beautiful and sexiest young girls I had ever seen, whom Chris was quick to invite on to the boat for a day trip. They came from wealthy – probably fascist! – families, brought paella and fruit and bottles of red wine with them, wore flowers in their hair, and draped themselves about the deck in ways no English girl I had so far met would dream of. We were all heavily smitten. The temperature of the boat rose considerably during the day, and when we said a final goodbye to them as the moon rose, there was a collective sigh. *Adieu and farewell all you fine Spanish ladies...*

At Vigo we enjoyed the fun of a large town, and I even ventured out with Chris and a few others to see my first bullfight. I wish I could say I was shocked at the cruelty of it all, but must admit I responded most to the artistry of the killings. It was also in the harbour of Vigo, out of the blue of a quiet afternoon, that we experienced a sudden quirky gale, which rolled the boat over so fiercely that the top of the mast was underwater. At once the anchor started dragging, putting us in considerable peril from the rocky shore close by. I was able to see Chris at his skipperly finest, as he raised a sail, cut the anchor line, headed the boat round, marshalled us on the deck with boat hooks, threw over a second light anchor, and saved his beloved boat. We then trawled the seabed for a couple of hours with our dinghies and managed triumphantly to locate and bring up the anchor we had had to cut away.

The day came when we had to turn back north towards England. Courageous Chris was planning to take *Theodora* over the Atlantic that autumn, and needed to be back in time to fit up for the great journey. All went well until we entered the Bay of Biscay, when – as I have already noted – we were unaccountably becalmed, for one, two, three, even four days. *'The breeze dropt down, down dropt the sails…'* Occasionally Chris would start up the small auxiliary motor to move us along a little trying to find a breeze, but the fuel was too precious to waste for more than a few miles.

One reason that Chris had been happy to welcome me aboard the boat was that he had been pining for music, and was disappointed at the lack of musical skills and interest among the rest of the crew. An accomplished amateur flautist himself (he had played under Vaughan Williams' baton at the Leith Hill Music Festival), in Vigo he bought some penny whistles, and during the doldrums we spent hours in the wheelhouse of the boat playing simple duets, and the gorgeous fugue from César Franck's violin sonata. For my twenty-first birthday on August 25th, he engineered something of a ceremony. Our ship's cook, who I seem to remember was sick at the time, somehow managed to put together a birthday cake for me in her tiny galley, and with the crew assembled and me at the wheel I was given a collective present from them all: a most handsome Tomas guitar, which Chris had purchased in Vigo for me, and which I still have and occasionally play over fifty years later

The wind finally picked up. We cruised up the west coast of France to the Channel Islands, putting in for a couple of days at St. Peter Port, Guernsey, where we were feted by the famous Guernsey family de Sausmerez, whose son had been with me at Radley. And from Guernsey, early one evening, we sailed smoothly out of harbour without benefit of our little engine, proudly heaving up our sails as we went and earning, we hoped, the respect of the sailing community watching us from the shore. Our departure was perfectly timed for us to catch the famous Alderney Race, and the current ripped us with it around the Islands and catapulted us into the Channel.

What followed was the most memorable sail of our whole trip. With a strong and steady wind at our back, we raised one square sail after another: the stunsails on each side of the main squaresail, and then the topgallant sail above that – also with its two stunsails. I think there was even a royal topgallant up there somewhere. The boat flew. Sunset and dusk turned into a majestically clear wide night with a full moon, and I remember spending hours sitting on the bowsprit with the water churning darkly by, the gallant *Theodora*, every stay creaking and straining, achieving nearly twelve knots as it ploughed sweetly over the silver sea. By early dawn we were already skimming up Southampton Water and into our berth at Hamble, arriving in time for a last breakfast on board before the crew said its goodbyes and went its separate ways.

(Chris's plan to take 'Theodora' across the Atlantic took shape, and they set off in early October. They called at Madeira, the Canaries and Antigua, then sailed up the Atlantic coast to New York, and from there to Maine, New Brunswick and Nova Scotia. Sailing up the Bay of Fundy they even put into 'the world's smallest registered harbour' at Wolfville, Nova Scotia, where I now live. Only in the 'nineties did I learn from Chris of this visit, and think of it whenever I pass our harbour – now almost totally silted up.

In 1960 Chris and a colleague started the Ocean Youth Club, to introduce young people, boys and girls, to the world of sailing, as a means of enriching their education and their self-reliance. 'Theodora' was one of the two original boats in the scheme, which now, as the Ocean Youth Trust, has four centres in Britain and a fleet of sailboats: thousands of young people have gone through their programmes.

'Theodora' continued in active service until 1971, when Chris Ellis presented her to the Cardiff Maritime Museum. She remained there as an exhibit until 1991, when she was sold into private hands on the understanding that she be restored to her original condition. This has been meticulously carried out over nearly twenty years: the boat, once again bearing her original name 'Kindly Light', was re-launched in 2010, her hundredth birthday.)

Making my way home by train, tanned and fit and happy as perhaps never before, I found a letter waiting for me from the Provost of Worcester College. He wrote to let me know that my request to change my course of study had been granted, and that I had been accepted into the first year class of English Language and Literature. He also informed me that the aged Fellow of English, Colonel Wilkinson, had finally retired at the end of the previous summer. So my tutor was to be his young and freshly appointed successor, whose name, I learnt, was C.B. Ricks.

I was also informed in a separate letter from the Bursar that in my first year I would be lodged outside the College, in a College-owned house at number 6, Beaumont Street: this was no more than three hundred yards from the entrance to Worcester, and directly opposite the Ashmolean Museum.

So once again, for the fifth time in my twenty-one years, I found myself entering as a new member into an institution, with its own culture, its own rules, its own sense of itself, its own way of life. But college life at Oxford differed from them all, in that the opportunity to make personal choices, to make one's own way within the bounds of the institution, was part of the ethos of the place: not a major element in the schools I had attended, and the very opposite of life in the army, where your own personal choices and preference were drummed out of you from the beginning. Oxford was to give us a chance to self-fashion: to decide whether we were loners or *bons viveurs*, idle or industrious, self-deprecating or arrogant, showy or reserved, respectful or contemptuous. All around us were examples of these experimental possibilities: young men prancing around town in red cloaks, stern revolutionaries in jeans, prim conformists in tweed jackets and ties, wits, recluses, religious devotees, single-minded scholars.

For most of the freshmen arriving that year from all over Britain and beyond, the city of Oxford was also something to be grappled with. But Oxford was my home town. My parents lived seven miles away. I had been at boarding school four miles down the river. And I had served two years in the local county regiment. Both our family doctor and dentist had practices in Beaumont Street, and two doors away from my first-year lodgings stood the Oxford Playhouse, where my family had been among the audience in plays since the late 1940s. This was home territory.

Worcester College in 1958, with its three hundred or so (male) undergraduates, was a medium-sized college, and medium-sized too in its aspirations. It was for most of us, I think, a pleasant place to be. We did not expect Worcester to be at the top of any academic list, but not at the bottom either. It had a strong inter-collegiate sports tradition, but furnished no more than a handful who represented the university against Cambridge and won blues. We also had a vigorous theatrical life: the Worcester College Buskins were one of the liveliest of any college drama group.

Worcester's Provost was John Masterman, who had read modern history at the College before the First World War, and had been a fine cricketer and tennis player in his younger days. He was also an author, with two detective novels and a tongue-in-cheek Oxford guidebook to his name. A courtly bachelor of middle height, a little hunched, with short grey hair, sharp nose, pale face and half-moon spectacles, he was knighted within a year of my arrival, and it was only years later that his work in the Second World War as director of the Double Cross system at MI6 came to light. He ran the College with gentleness and occasional acerbity, and was widely praised for his astute judgement, particularly (dare I say?) in his choice of undergraduates for the College. In this he was also indubitably part of the old Oxford: he was keen to consider an applicant's character and his social, artistic and sporting skills as well as his academic prowess, and he felt some obligation to accept the sons and grandsons of old College members if their qualifications came close to the required standard. All this made it easier for public schoolboys to be accepted at Worcester: their social skills were more polished, their opportunities to develop sporting competence more varied, and their past lineage more likely to have been educated at a public school. If you applied from, say, Bootle Grammar School, and had a strong Liverpudleian accent, you had to be cleverer than the good oarsman or musician from Rugby – or, yes, from Radley. Was I a beneficiary of this policy? Maybe.

Worcester College was not one of the ancient ones: it had been founded in 1714, on the site of a much older establishment known as Gloucester Hall. Its main buildings dated from that eighteenth century founding, with a fine complex of library, dining-hall and chapel, and a graciously classical stretch of lodgings along one side of its principal quadrangle. But the money apparently ran out before the other side could be completed in the same grand style, so that the classical lodgings looked down on a humble but charming set of fifteenth-century buildings left over from the defunct Gloucester Hall, and known as the Cottages. Beyond and behind the Cottages stretched a noble sward of lawn leading down to a lake (embowered romantically by over-arching trees), and strolled over not only by dons and undergraduates but also by various ducks and geese of exotic breeds. Chief among them was a portly, red-combed, dyspeptic-looking Muscovy duck known as 'the Colonel' – named, of course, after 'the Wilk' (Colonel Wilkinson), who had just been made a fellow emeritus of the College, and enjoyed a choice set of rooms at the end of the Cottages, with his own private garden.

The College claimed a number of minor notables among its graduates, including the Cavalier poet Richard Lovelace from the old foundation, and De Quincey from the new: there was a set of De Quincey rooms in the Cottages – believed to have been the scene of some of Thomas's earliest opium debauches – and over the Wilk's mantelshelf was a fine contemporary portrait of Lovelace. But Worcester had produced no prime ministers, no Miltons, no Gladstones, no Archbishops of Canterbury, no High Admirals, no Darwins.

This, then, was to be my home base for the next three years: a good fit, perhaps, for my own fairly modest – though not negligible – ambitions. My scholarship from the County of Oxfordshire covered my tuition and my accommodation and living expenses at the College, and since the small residue of that old legacy from my great-aunt had matured on my twenty-first birthday, I must have had some funds in the bank. I have no memory of being short of money, and seemed to have enough for regular weekend visits to the pub. My time in the army, my education to that date, and my various travels on the continent, had given me confidence in my capacity to make friends, to develop my intellectual curiosity, to do reasonably well in my studies, and to have fun. And this, I suppose, was my agenda.

I soon managed to adjust myself to the timeline and expectations of Oxford's academic year – very different from that of the schools I had attended. Each of Oxford's three terms (named since time out of mind as Michaelmas, Hilary and Trinity) ran for only eight weeks, and vacations were correspondingly long: six weeks at Christmas, six weeks at Easter, and a luxurious sixteen weeks in the summer. But lest it be thought that we gambolled our way lightly through our Oxford careers, it should be made clear that the very shortness of Oxford terms meant that they were a pressure cooker of activity, and also that vacations were looked on as a time when we were expected to continue with a certain amount of private study: at the end of each term our tutors gave us a programme of work for the vacation, and examinations, known puzzlingly as 'Collections', took place on the very first day of term to see whether we had buckled down to it. The results of those examinations had no effect on our final degree, but simply gave our tutors – and indeed ourselves – a sense of whether we were taking our studies seriously. My County scholarship even gave me a 'vacation allowance' of £35 so that I would not have to take on a summer job! It has to be said that undergraduates, especially in their first year or two, tended to treat their vacations as holidays just as any other student would – at least until the last few days, when some hasty reading had to be done to prepare for Collections. But as the final examinations drew closer it was not uncommon for third- or fourth-year students to 'stay up' for at least a few weeks during the vacation, to read and study away from the pressures of term-time.

There were only two external tests of our competence in those days at Oxford: a Latin paper which had to be written by all undergraduates – even scientists – in the second term; and the gruelling final exams at the end of our three years, in which we students of English Language and Literature wrote nine three-hour papers in four and a half days. These final papers covered the whole gamut of English, from Anglo-Saxon poetry to the close of the Victorian period. (Victorian literature was in fact a new addition: until a year or two before, the curriculum had ended at 1830, on the premiss that everything since the Romantic poets – like Dickens, for example, or George Eliot, or Tennyson or Browning – had been written just too damn recently to be properly appraised. The new cut-off in my own finals was still only 1910, comfortably before any new twentieth century voices would have to be dealt with.)

For those accustomed to the shape of university study in North America, or to that of English universities based on the North American model, Oxford in those days – and perhaps still – was startlingly unlike. Our curriculum was set by the English faculty of the University. It included a few 'set texts' for particular attention – *Beowulf*, Milton's *Paradise Lost*, *King Lear* and *Twelfth Night* among others; but the whole thousand-year history of English language and literature was in our purview and open for study, and provided we became familiar with its major peaks and valleys we could choose any area of it for our own private explorations. The job of our tutor was to keep us on the path as we travelled through the various periods building our knowledge and our sensibilities. Lectures were given all over Oxford by English professors and fellows each term, on any subjects that the individual lecturer might choose. The lectures were not connected in any specific way with exams: they were there to attend or not to attend, as we wished, though the Faculty presumably saw to it that someone should cover the 'set texts' in the course of the year. Most unlike of all, the faculty members who set our final papers and marked them were not the same people as those tutors who coached us. That fatal conflict of interest which bedevils the 'course' system was happily avoided.

I have no memory of my first encounter with David Evans, the sad and heavily bespectacled young man who was to teach us Old English. But I still remember the first October meeting of us seven freshmen undergraduates of Worcester College with our new tutor in English, whose name, Christopher Ricks, was unknown to us all and to the world. Young and fresh-faced, fast-talking, and quick to laugh, he introduced himself and outlined our programme. "I think this term we shall start with the eighteenth century. Then each following term we shall concentrate on another period, not necessarily in chronological order, and gradually cover the ground over your nine terms." He would meet with us once a week, but in order to fit in all his students from the three years, he would give us one-on-one tutorials only every other term, alternating the following term with tutorials we would share with one other student. He would expect an essay from us each week, which we would read aloud to him at our tutorial. We then established our tutorial times, and he set our first essay topic: we should read Dryden's political satire *Absalom and Achitophel* – do some reading around it (he suggested a few critical works) and then "write me an essay on how Dryden apportions praise and blame among the protagonists of the poem." That was all. He then handed out the list of English lectures for that term, and I still remember my astonishment as he gave us his laconic recommendations: "Make sure you go to so-and-so: she's really excellent. Try what's-his-name on Pope and Swift. But you can give Professor X a miss – he's a terrible lecturer and has been giving out the same old rubbish for thirty years..." This was a whole new idea to me: not only that attendance at lectures was entirely voluntary, but that scholars did not necessarily have high estimates of their fellows, and that they were not afraid to share their views with their students. Within a few weeks I realised, in fact, that scholarship – perhaps especially at

Oxford – was a battleground: that no hostility could be so biting and so deep as that of an academic towards those he disagreed with.

There were other inaugural rituals, including a walk with our Senior Tutor to the Sheldonian Theatre, where the Vice-Chancellor addressed some hundreds of us gowned freshmen – in Latin of course – and pronounced us members of the University; and a gentlemanly talk with Provost Masterman welcoming us to the College. We were also each allocated a strangely titled Moral Tutor, one of the other Fellows of the College, to whom we could go for help if we had personal difficulties. But with these introductions and ceremonies over, we were now on our own for the rest of the eight-week term. I was tied to only two hour-long appointments each week, one in Language, one in Literature.

I soon made friends. My fellow lodger at 6 Beaumont Street, Jeremy Twynam, was in fact already an acquaintance, since he and his family were visitors to Studley Priory and had once even spent Christmas with us at the hotel. Tall, lean, red-haired and jocular, he was reading PPE (Philosophy, Political Science and Economics), so his studies took him in a different direction from mine. He was also a keen oarsman, which I was not. But lodging alongside we would see a lot of one another, and were soon close friends.

Members of the College were expected to don their gowns and dine in the College dining-hall, a gaunt and rather unlovely place, yet to receive its magnificent renovation of a later time. The food was unlovely too (Rog: "How did you find your steak tonight?" Ron: "I just lifted up my tomato and there it was!"). But College meals were memorable because you would find yourself sitting next to other undergraduates of all years and all disciplines. It was not unusual to be part of a group comprising, say, a music scholar, a physicist, a linguist and a philosopher. Conversation was often of trivialities, but often not. And if an interesting debate started, those involved often repaired afterwards to someone's rooms, where the talk continued – sometimes until the small hours of the morning. It was in Hall that we were able to open up to fields of study other than our own. And it was in Hall that we made our first friends: some of them to last a lifetime. For me, one of these was John Weston, a classical scholar fresh from National Service in the Royal Marines, and just launching into the 'Mods and Greats' programme which I had ducked out of. Another was David Kimball, Worcester's organ scholar, and a musician of consummate taste and stringency. John, articulate and perceptive, enjoyed the cut and thrust of debate. David, on the other hand, became renowned among us for keeping his counsel while we gabbers threw our conversational weight around – until, in a quiet moment, he would make one softly-spoken, perfectly-formed observation which made all our extravagant flights seem utterly juvenile.

I'm not sure how it began, but at some point in my first week or two I found myself being asked to meet with members of the drama club, the Worcester College Buskins. The two creative engines of the group were Roger Mills and Ron Heapy, both reading classical Mods and Greats, and both in their third year. Ron was that clever young man from Bootle, tall, black-haired and beaky, who spoke so fast and with such a pronounced Liverpudlian accent that it took me a while to understand a word. But he was immensely genial and energetic. Roger, curly-haired with owlish horn-rimmed spectacles, was witty and clubbable, with a beautiful voice and a laugh which carried all before it. They were soon joined by a designer, Iain Mackintosh, tall, Scottish and a touch imperious. And with them also at that first meeting was a Canadian undergraduate in his second year who was introduced as the Club's resident pianist and composer. He had come to Oxford from completing a first degree in Princeton, where he had been involved with the Princeton Triangle Club, famous since Cole Porter's days there for its musical comedies and revues. His name was Bill Glassco. Was he the first Canadian I had ever met? Perhaps. He was impressively tall and thin, with dark hair and a kind and sensitive face, slightly pitted from a youthful battle with acne. He was extremely modest, even diffident, in his manner, and I wondered what kind of music he wrote.

The Buskins were well known for their summer productions, which took place – weather permitting, and somehow it usually did – in the College gardens. During the previous term they had produced Anouilh's *Thieves' Carnival*. The summer before, Ron Heapy had directed *Toad of Toad Hall*. Now, they told me, they would like to keep the name of the Club in the public eye by putting together a musical revue for Christmas. With so much to deal with in my first term I was doubtful about having the time to write sketch material. But I was happy to act for them, and fresh from my musical projects at Radley and in the army, I would perhaps be able to write them a few numbers. Bill expressed interest, and after the meeting he took me down to the little hall where we planned to present our show, and where there was a small grand piano. He sat down, and began to play.

Within two minutes, all the confidence I had in my own gifts as a light music composer had drained away. Here was the thing itself. Bill's playing had infectious rhythm, his harmonies were enchanting, his key changes smooth and inevitable, and there was a forward thrust in his music which carried you irrepressibly along. His ballads were lyrical, and saved from being sentimental by their sly wit and unexpectedness. The 32-bar AABA construction of a popular song, which I had never mastered, was second nature to him.

After he had played for five or ten minutes (he played entirely by ear, and could not read music) Bill got up for me to take my turn. I felt I was a wash-out: his North American sophistication, the sheer tempo of his playing, had quite blown me away. I fingered through one or two of my old numbers, and Bill was kind and encouraging. But the roots of my song-writing efforts were still dug deep in church hymns and Gilbert and Sullivan, and everything I played sounded to me dismally pedestrian and, yes, boring. This was my first encounter with the sheer energy and drive of Broadway. I was to learn an enormous amount from Bill, and my playing over the years was to become a good deal more racy and harmonically interesting than it had been. But I vowed on that forlorn evening in 1958 that I would put my own song writing aside for ever. It is a vow I have more or less stuck to.

I did furnish one downbeat musical number for the Christmas show, but it was as an actor and singer that I seemed to be able to offer something to the Buskins, and from that evening until our Christmas premiere we spent almost every weekend putting together the kind of old-fashioned musical revue that we were all familiar with in those days: a musical number to start the thing off with a jolly bang, and then a series of comic sketches interspersed with ballads, songs and snatches – some of them comic and some sentimental. At that first show I made something of a hit with Bill's very sweet and somewhat fey solo number *Share My Tea*:

Someone to share my tea,
Someone who's there with me
At four o'clock every day:
She'll fill the kettle up
And rearrange my cup –
How I long to hear her say:
"How many lumps of sugar darling – one or two?
Just a tiny drop of milk – will that do? ... etc

This was not to be the last time I would sashay my way through that coy and woman-fearing little piece.

The show was held together by Ron and Roger's running music-hall routine, with Ron He's-A-Laugh Heapy spouting out deathless one-liners, and Roger Get-Out-Of-It Mills clutching his fiddle and itching to play: "I say, it's a fine day for the race!" "What race?" "The *human* race!" ... "Oh get away with you. Ladies and gentlemen, as you know I am a serious artist, and I would now like to play for you –" "You know, I used to be teacher's pet!" "You used to be teacher's pet?" "Yes, she used to keep me in a cage at the back of the classroom!!!" And so on. We were lucky too to have in the College a fine comic actor, Neil Bratton, who treated us among other things to a send-up of Field-Marshal Montgomery's solipsistic account of how he won the Battle of El Alamein. (The secret, said Neil, was that whenever and however often you came to the word "I" or "me", you gave it a thumping emphasis whatever the context. Result? You sounded exactly like Monty.)

One of the greatest joys of being at Oxford was that I did not have to participate in any sports, and was able to watch my friends trooping off to the rugby field or the river while I stayed cosily beside my gas-fire reading and toasting crumpets. I occasionally enjoyed a game of squash, and even in summer joined in a game or two with the Worcester Rustics, made up for the most part by the College's poorest cricketers, who drove out in cars to some Oxfordshire village to match up against the local side on an improvised pitch, with beer flowing generously at every pause in the play. (It was a rule that everyone had both to bat and to bowl. During my one over, I remember, a delivery of mine went somewhat wide and on hitting the ground disappeared down a rabbit-hole. The batsman almost suffered a hernia stepping out to the vanished ball, and the entire fielding team collapsed with laughter for about five minutes.)

Meanwhile, there were my studies to organise. Having decided on which of the term's lectures I would be attending and could fit around my tutorial times, I would bicycle out most mornings for a lecture at the Examination Schools on the High Street, or occasionally at other Colleges, adjourning afterwards with pals to the Cadena Café for coffee and cake.

The study of English Literature was at that period in the ascendant, and Oxford could boast a number of luminaries among its professors and fellows, including Helen Gardner, Lord David Cecil, Nevill Coghill, F.W. Bateson, J.B. Leishman, John Bayley and J.R.R. Tolkien's son Christopher. (C.S. Lewis had only recently decamped to Cambridge, after failing to win an Oxford Professorship, apparently because of prejudice within the University against his Christian views; they lost a fine and humane scholar.) The reigning queen of the humanities at Oxford in the late 1950s, though, was not English but linguistic or 'ordinary language' philosophy. J.L. Austin, perhaps its leading exponent, was in the last year of his life, but his disciples – and enemies – were scattered throughout the colleges. Gilbert Ryle ('*The Concept of Mind*') could be seen stalking down the High or the Broad below his amazingly high and broad forehead. I once played bar football with logical positivist and football devotee A.J. Ayer. My friend John Weston was taught by John Simopoulos and David Mitchell. Iris Murdoch tutored in philosophy at St. Anne's – in her spare time between novels. Peter Strawson, Geoffrey Warnock and his wife Mary were all teaching at Oxford; names to be conjured with in the struggle for meaning. Language, the uses and traps of language, occupied – and in fact were embodied in – many of our conversations. Since all of us talked – and talked a lot, this being Oxford – we were all conscious of listening in to our own words and the words of our friends – checking their logic and consistency, however trivial the theme. Though ordinary language philosophy sometimes tended (in the army phrase) to 'disappear up its own arsehole', it was an unforced discipline and probably did everyone's intellectual rigour some good, whatever their field of study.

There was one lecture in those years which attracted undergraduates from all disciplines. Edgar Wind, the art historian, had come to Oxford as a Jewish refugee from Vienna, and had been allowed to set himself up in the drawing room of his own little house on Beaumont Street to give seminars on the history of art – not normally a subject at the forefront of Oxford's interests, but presumably attractive to a few students from the Ruskin College of Art. But news of his scintillating seminars soon got about, and within a term or two he had to be given a small lecture room in Schools. Another term or two and he had to be moved to a larger lecture hall to accommodate the students that kept piling in to what was now his weekly lecture. Eventually he was allotted the largest lecture hall available, and soon outgrew even this 400-seat space. By the time I arrived at Oxford in 1958, he was having to give his lecture *twice a week* – in the Oxford Playhouse! A copper had to be on hand to control the crowds, with bicycles chained to every lamp-post within hiking distance, and road traffic jammed up along the street. It was an extraordinary tribute to the man's erudition and brilliance.

Dr Wind spoke with a strong but easily intelligible Austrian accent. When he entered from stage right, he took out his pocket watch and laid it on the lectern in front of him. He started at exactly five past the hour, spoke without notes, and illustrated his lecture with slides. He finished his last perfectly-formed sentence at the stroke of the next hour exactly fifty-five minutes later. He always received mighty applause. I must have attended two or three of his courses of lectures, though I remember only one of them, on the drawings of Leonardo da Vinci. But he opened a door into the history of art which for me has never closed.

Some morning during that first October I knocked nervously at Christopher Ricks' door clutching the carefully handwritten and no doubt laborious essay I had written for my first tutorial. It was the first of over seventy hours I must have spent with what turned out to be the prince of tutors. Memory doesn't distinguish these many tutorials from one another, but the combined effect of them comprised nothing less than the core of my Oxford education. Courteous, sharp, witty, caring, stabbingly intelligent, encouraging, mocking: the descriptors proliferate almost ad infinitum. And just as conversation with a brilliant friend or colleague goads us to our own best efforts, so Christopher's best attentions called out our own. Certainly my writing shifted to be more spontaneous, more fluent and self-assured, and my critical skills sharpened. I became better at being witty and serious at the same time, and was able to staunch my talent for pretentious bullshit, which Christopher could smell out a yard away. He became not only a mentor, but a friend, a dear friend. And so he has remained.

Reading one's own essay out loud to your tutor provides an actor with special opportunities, offering a chance to make the very best of his/her critical arguments by means of deft rhetorical emphasis and well-timed *drôlerie*. But of course it can also expose intellectual cheating and phoniness. Christopher was not to be dazzled by such histrionics, and I learnt valuable lessons in taste. It should be made clear too that he never gave an essay a mark or grade, unless for some reason – like running out of time in a two-man tutorial – he had to take it home, in which case it would be returned with a suggested grade somewhere along the line between α and β minus, along with acutely discerning comments in the margin. ("This is both good and true," he wrote once of a remark I made in some paper. Could it be a good remark but *not* true, I asked? A philosophical question if ever there was one, and the debate was lively. I seem to remember Christopher conceding the point.)

No memories of life as an Oxford undergraduate could efface the ineffable beauty of the buildings among which we moved and had our being: walking at night through the back lanes between mediaeval walls, the streetlamps staring mildly through the autumn trees, a soft damp rain falling, the line of festal lights in Christ Church hall, or Exeter, or Worcester, the shining flagstones, the clock bells sonorous or clunky, the night van on St. Giles' open for business (LOCAL BOY MAKES GOOD HOT DOGS), the red double-decker buses braking and revving past the Martyrs' Memorial, the far-off beer-happy cries, and the light of our own college porch to come home to, or to see glowing at the end of Beaumont Street: all this held us in its ancient arms.

So the brief Michaelmas Term drew to a close, marked for me a week before the end by the Worcester Buskins Christmas Revue *We Never Even Opened,* which we in fact opened twice to a small but well-packed house of our Worcester friends and Fellows, including our tricksy, diminutive Dean Harry Pitt (who was once subjected to a drenching from a watering-can by an undergraduate at the window of an upper floor, the student crying out "Grow, man, grow!"); Christopher Ricks with his wife Kirsten, and Christopher's distinguished predecessor (and one-time Dean) Colonel Wilkinson, who had a particularly soft spot for the Buskins and had seldom missed a performance for the previous forty or fifty years.

Christmas that year took me away from Oxford and away from home for a cheap and happy skiing holiday in Austria with my old army friends Edward Jones, Richard Bradshaw and Charles

Simmons. But I also spent time at Studley, and was sad to witness the increasing stress of the whole venture, and its wearing effect on my parents. I was glad to return to the excitement and stimulation of life at Oxford, although the stresses followed me when one day in early spring my Father arrived at my rooms and told me he was in deep financial trouble, and about to be sued in small claims court for the non-payment of a bill for hay. He needed a thousand pounds by the end of the week. He did not want any part of the small legacy I had in the bank. But did I know of anyone who could help?

There was only one person whom I knew could afford the loan, and whom I felt I could ask. I took the bus out to Radley, and walked down to the house of my old schoolmaster Charles Wrinch. We went for a walk along the river, where Charles pointed out the violets and primroses of the new year, while I explained the situation. "Of course!" he said promptly. I assured him that my father would repay the loan later as soon as he could, to which Charles responded, "Yes, that would be very nice, but I have found through life that when you lend money to a friend, you must always think of it as a gift." I returned to Oxford with a cheque, and a useful piece of wisdom. My father's situation was solved: but more importantly for him, his honour was saved. He was embarrassed at my success, but grateful too. In admitting his desperation and throwing himself on my resources, I felt he had treated me almost for the first time as an adult and an ally. I was proud to have helped him.

It was in that second term at Worcester that I also made an important decision of my own. My faith in Christianity had gradually faded since I had left Radley, and there came one night in February or March when I went down on my knees beside my bed in my room on Beaumont Street and told God that, using the intellect and feelings he had given me, I had reached the conclusion that 'Our Father in Heaven' did not exist, and that the concept of 'sin' was mistaken and unhelpful. I hoped he would forgive me if I was wrong, but from that night onward I would no longer think of myself as a Christian and a church-goer, and I would no longer pray to him or ask to be forgiven my sins. I see now a certain amount of double-dealing in talking this way to the God I had ceased to believe in, but I suppose I felt I owed it to Him to make some kind of apology. Whatever the suspicion of having had it both ways, I know I felt a whole lot better for having crossed that Rubicon, and walked out into the street the next morning surprised by a new kind of joy.

With the Christmas revue I had become a Worcester College Buskin, and though I amassed a large number of other friends, it was the Buskins that became my intimate family for the first two years of my time at Oxford. In my second term, during which I sat and passed the obligatory Latin exam with little difficulty (given my classical upbringing), we produced a concert performance of *Iolanthe*, in which I stood sentry as the humble but godlike Private Willis. In my first summer term, after an Easter vacation that included a week of canoeing down the River Wye with Radley friend Noel Slocock and new Worcester friend John Gretton, I was invited to direct the Buskins production of *The Beggar's Opera*, but was then cast as Constant in the University's Experimental Theatre Club (ETC) production of *That Was No Lady* – and so reduced my involvement in the Worcester production to playing – over-playing – Lockit the jailer. My friend David Kimball was the show's rigorous music director, and Humphrey Norrington, a Worcester man and brother to my friend Pippa, displayed his beautiful tenor voice (if not too much flexibility as an actor) in his elegant playing of Macheath.

That Was No Lady was the Experimental Theatre Club's musical version of Vanbrugh's *The Provok'd Wife,* and was performed at the Oxford Playhouse, with original music by Herbert Chappell, and a cast which included my Buskins friend Roger Mills, Kenneth Loach, and – playing opposite me – one of the most beautiful, intelligent and marriageable young women in Oxford ('girls' we would have called them) called Caroline Seebohm. It was also directed by Ron Heapy and managed by Iain Mackintosh, so the Buskins had something of a stranglehold on ETC that summer of 1959. I'm not sure that the show was much of a success, although Loach's performance as Sir John Brute brought the highly partisan house down every night.

Iain Mackintosh, though, already had his sights set further afield. He had discovered that the 150-year-old Kenton Theatre, in Henley-on-Thames, was free for the week of the Henley Royal Regatta, and offered to book it on behalf of the Worcester College Buskins, who would entertain the rowing crowd with a revue, soon to be titled *One Over The Eight.* The revue would be based on our modest success the previous Christmastime, but would bring in more talent, not all of it from Worcester. Having pinned down the services of the home team of Ron, Roger, Neil Bratton and Michael B, with composer Bill Glassco on piano, he also secured the services of a choreographer, Rex Nettleford by name, who had come to Oriel College as a Rhodes scholar from Jamaica. Iain arranged for the Buskins to take over a barn and some outhouses two or three miles outside Henley, and it was there that the company was to assemble a few days after the end of that riotously happy and larky summer term.

The last and largest festivity of my whole first year was the Commemoration Ball in June, which it was Worcester's turn that summer to host, and which took place under marquees in the gardens from dusk to dawn, with three or four bands, oodles of food and champagne and dancing, and a fair amount of dalliance by the lake and in the shrubberies. All of us had to go to the ball with a partner – tickets were sold per pair – and for most of my friends who had steady girlfriends this was no challenge. But I was still lagging behind in the girlfriend department and had no Oxford lovely in my life. With my heart in my mouth I asked my stage lover Caroline Seebohm whether she would be my partner for the evening, and to my amazement she accepted, giving me instant status among my circle of friends but making me highly nervous in case I should be expected to walk her off to the bushes for kisses and embraces I felt unqualified to offer.

The Buskins were called upon to furnish a midnight cabaret for the ball, and I was asked if I would approach my Radley friend Peter Cook – who by this time was making a name for himself at the Footlights in Cambridge – and invite him to join me for a twenty-minute show. He agreed, and my stock rose even more respectably for having snagged him. In the event our little two-hander was only marginally acceptable. Peter had already launched into his own private brand of writing and performing, which was just beginning to make its mark. I had been left behind since Radley days: my stoogework and piano-playing were from a less caustic era, and we failed to pull the two styles together in the few hours we had to rehearse. I'm not sure it mattered: by midnight most of the crowd were too drunk to care.

A week later the Buskins company – actors, musicians, cooks and bottlewashers, stage and house managers, stage designer, painters and publicity folk – travelled down the Thames Valley on motorbikes, in dilapidated cars and an old London taxi. After visiting the Kenton Theatre in Henley town, we found our way among the fields to the barn which was to be our home for two weeks. As the sun set we claimed our sleeping places in the hay of the barn or in the sheds nearby, setting out our personal stuff wherever we could find a hook or a nook. The kitchen with its propane stove was set up outside and somehow our cook Alan Carter was able to put together a robust meal for us all, which we ate greedily in the moonlight, lit romantically by lanterns and candle lamps. We sang and played guitars and drank the beer we had been sure to bring with us.

The warm air that first happy moonlit night, and in fact for our whole stay, was heavy with the scents of midsummer, and I don't think I ever remember a more beautiful and seductive natural world than the one we happy band, like the 'Good Companions', inhabited there among the fields beside the river. It was also the first time in my life that I was to experience the joy of working at theatre not in between other obligations but with my whole heart and attention. Because of our single-minded dedication to the show, and with the help of our sparkling composer and pianist Bill Glassco and our resourceful and patient choreographer Rex, we also managed to bring it to a high finish, and it was well attended by the townspeople and even some of the rowing crowd – especially after they had been knocked out of their various competitions in the Regatta. Iain immediately booked the space for the same period the following year.

As soon as we were free from Henley I was determined once again to take the path to Rome, where sister Jo was now thoroughly settled into her job at FAO and busy making a life for herself – Mother had visited her there the previous year during a snatched two weeks from Studley. I was lucky to be commissioned to drive the car of a Worcester friend called Simon Brown to Paris, which got me well along the route – though introducing me at the same time to the terrors of driving round L'Etoile. Jo met me at Termini station in Rome, and a week later we were back there to greet my mother and young sister Jenny off the train from London. Thus began three or four weeks of sight-seeing in the high heat of an Italian summer: swimming at Ostia, touring through Umbria and Tuscany, and finishing up with ten days in a summer *casa* in the seaside village of Ansedonia. It was a joyous time for me, but perhaps even more for our mother, finding herself back in Italy and quickly falling in love again with the country and its people.

I returned to England with, it seemed, few cares in the world. Some time that September I acquired an elderly, dark green Velocette motor-bike for £50; a very gentlemanly, quietly purring machine with three gears and a less than hurtling top speed of 60 miles per hour. It was not the most reliable way of travelling on long trips, but for scooting round Oxford or out to Studley Priory it was ideal, and allowed me more freedom of movement than ever before.

Some time towards the end of that month I took the train up to London to stay with my friends the Lathams, and to see the new musical revue *Pieces of Eight*, with Kenneth Williams and Fenella Fielding. There was a particular reason for this: the chief writer for the revue was Peter Cook, who had somehow managed to launch himself into the professional theatre with this show while still a Cambridge undergraduate. I was dazzled by the success of my good friend Peter. I was also conscious of how his career was leaving me further and further behind in his wake. He seemed to find himself quite at home amongst his stars, and in the seedy haunts of Soho where we went for a meal. I found myself then – and really for ever after – simply awed by London, thinking of myself as a simple country bumpkin oohing and aahing in the big city. For all Peter's kindness and friendship, his apparently effortless self-confidence continued to outpace me.

Self-confidence... I recently heard from a fellow undergraduate from Worcester who wrote regretting the fact that we had not seen much of one another while there, and that he thought he had been intimidated by me at Oxford because I was 'so self-confident and stylish.' Yes, I had established myself as something of a force at the College that first year, with my performances on stage and also with my talkativeness and enjoyment of fun. I had shown a certain intellectual grasp too, delivering a paper on Tourneur's *Revenger's Tragedy* for the Lovelace Society, of which the president of the Junior Common Room (JCR), Duff Hart-Davis, was also President. Some time in my second term Duff approached me to say he would like to nominate me as his successor as JCR President for the following year. Would I stand?

It was a flattering suggestion. The President of Junior Common Room was a kind of Head Boy of the undergraduate body, chairing undergraduate meetings, serving as spokesperson with the Senior Common Room, and representing Worcester in various gatherings outside the College. I reflected on the suggestion for a day or two, but in the end I told Duff that I thought a much more suitable candidate would be my good friend John Weston. John was nominated and eventually elected.

So why did I decline? I don't believe many guessed that behind all the *bonhomie* and apparent social ease which I had developed over the years, and which flowered at Oxford, I had harboured since Radley a secret *malaise* which kept threatening to disempower me. For all my hearty friends at school, in the army, and now at Oxford, I knew that I was still in bewilderment about my sexuality. I was courteous with girls, I liked girls, I found them beautiful. But I had no instinct for pairing off with any of them, and if they flirted with me I would back away in terror. On the other hand I could not deny to myself that I found good-looking men quite as beautiful and perhaps even more attractive. This was the secret I kept locked up in my breast: my acting skills on stage were as nothing to the brilliance with which I dissembled my confusion, and I like to think (perhaps mistakenly) that no one knew of it. But for the rest of my time at Oxford the battle between my two selves – between my continued attraction to men and my fervent desire to grow out of this and become 'normal' – became more and more intense. I simply did not want to be queer. Nor did I want my good, close friends to think that my friendship with them was somehow covertly sexual. It was not: I was sure of that.

These were the thoughts and feelings that wrestled within me as I puttered into the city on my more or less trusty Velocette, to launch into my second Oxford year.

(Kenneth Loach, our Sir John Brute in 'That Was No Lady', soon gave up whatever acting career he may have been contemplating, to turn to the cinema, where of course he has become one of Britain's most celebrated film-makers.

Rex Nettleford, our Henley choreographer, returned to his native Jamaica, where only three years later he founded the National Dance Theatre Company of Jamaica. He went on to work for Jamaica's Prime Minister Manley, and edited his speeches. He wound up as Vice-Chancellor of the University of the West Indies. He died in 2010.

Simon Brown became a barrister and then a distinguished judge, crowning his career as one of the five Law Lords, and a member of the newly established Supreme Court,

Duff Hart-Davis became a prolific writer: naturalist, biographer, novelist and a journalist with the Independent.)

CHAPTER NINE

THE RUNNING TIDE

In those days Worcester College undergraduates – unless they were scholars – could have rooms in College for only the second of their three years. Somehow, through the good offices of Duff Hart-Davis and his room-mate John Gretton, I was able to inherit from them the very finest rooms in College for my own second year. They were called the Somerset Rooms (named after a former Fellow of Worcester) and sat on the first floor in the very centre of the eighteenth century pile on the north side of the main quadrangle. The high and elegant principal room was still graced with some of de Vere Somerset's carpets, furniture and good paintings, and its two lofty windows looked commandingly down over the quad to the Cottages on the southern side. At the back, two bedrooms gave off from the main room. My room-mate for the year was my friend Jeremy Twynam, and we had the extraordinary privilege of being looked after by our kind and fatherly scout Harris, who made up our beds, washed up our dishes and kept our beautiful room clean and tidy. It was not long before our new and spacious headquarters became a centre of activity and fun. My own *bonhomie* and gregariousness continued unabated, well-matched with Jeremy's.

Under Iain Mackintosh's prodding, the Buskins soon got

together once again to plan a new revue for Christmas. We had lost Bill Glassco back to Canada. But we also corralled some new talent, including a new comic actor in Hugh O'Shaughnessy. We rehearsed a couple of evenings a week if I remember, and on Sundays.

It was some time during that term, though, that I began to find myself enjoying more and more the company of a group of three or four friends who had nothing to do with the Buskins. Their acknowledged heavyweight was organ scholar David Kimball, with whom I had already worked on *The Beggar's Opera*, and whose air of modest authority continued to exert its power in our countless talks far into the night. Alongside David there was Andrew Baker, son of a Congregationalist minister, Malcolm Booth, a physicist from Birmingham way, and Roger French from Ashtead, Surrey, who I think was a chemist. (It was usual to refer to undergraduates by their area of study, as though they had already arrived in their profession: 'physicist', 'doctor', 'classicist', 'chemist'.) We all shared a love of classical music, in which David was our guide and analyst as we listened to the LPs which each of us brought from our collections. Malcolm, stocky and pugnacious, opened my eyes to some of the basic laws of physics, which I had left far behind me when I was fifteen. Laid out as they now were by an enthusiast, I began to see not only their beauty but their good sense. Through the gentle, moon-faced Andrew I began to learn more about Congregationalism – the denomination my grandfather had been born into – which led me to understand really for the first time that like Andrew I came from a family of Dissenters, of Nonconformists, with all the exclusions that this until quite recently involved.

And then there was Roger French. Roger, I confess to myself now, was surely the ulterior motive for my involvement with this group of friends. Roger was a quite remarkable beauty. Blonde and blue-eyed in a classic Nordic way, he was also perfectly formed in every feature, and moved with the lazy grace of an athlete. He was reticent, and in fact so contained that you were never sure what he was thinking. But this only added to his allure, along with his dazzling smile and contagious laugh. I had eyed him curiously from afar in our first year, but now found myself more and more under his spell – to the point that I would know the pattern of his lectures and tutorials, and from the vantage point of our wide windows over the quadrangle would be looking out for him passing on the way to and from his rooms.

I was beginning – helplessly it seemed – to yield to the power of this sexual attraction. I wrote a poem:

A passion like no other ever
Binds me to place and hours
Dragging my feet and time
Against all powers.

For this I forego and forget
Sitting to reason love
– Reasoning worse for the ache
But comfort of.

With every nerve of my being I wanted to touch and embrace him. And yet, and still, I kept this *'passion like no other ever'* entirely to myself within our small group, disguising it under a mask of general mateyness. Nor of course did I allow the slightest hint of my urgent preoccupation to emerge with my rowing and rugger-playing room-mate Jeremy, or among my other good and sometimes brilliant friends like John Weston. You might have thought that the Buskins would be more tolerant of the love that still at that time was reluctant to speak its name, but even in our relaxed theatre group there was never any open reference to the subject. This after all was 1960: homosexual acts were still criminal, so that any serious or even casual prejudice against queers and queerdom was reinforced by the legal system. Moreover, psychiatrists were still defining homosexuality as a mental sickness. There were lots of reasons, in other words, for a popular, 'self-confident and stylish' young man like myself to keep his yearnings strictly to himself. Besides, I believed that this was a 'phase', and that I would soon pass through it and move smoothly into the heterosexual life to which I so much aspired. I was keen to marry and have children. I did not want to be homosexual.

For every undergraduate, their second year was the high point of enjoyment and devil-may-care. The anxiety and strangeness of being a newcomer had worn off, and the perils of final exams were far enough away in the distance to ignore. Of course for me the weekly requirement of an essay for Christopher Ricks remained, along with the continuing study of *Beowulf, Sir Gawain and the Green Knight, The Pearl* and *Piers Plowman* with David Evans, our tutor for Old and Middle English. But these – along with a handful of lectures – were still our only obligations, and I remember few details of them, nor indeed of the passing weeks and months of that whole happy time, lifted into occasional transcendence by my ripening intimacy with Roger and his friends.

Our December revue, called *Paper The Town,* went by, Christmas at Studley went by, and I was back in College for a snowy January and more high jinks as another term dragged its fast length along. As always, weeks and weeks fade from the memory, but the odd episode stands out in stark line and colour:

Over the year I had come to be friends with old Colonel

Wilkinson, who enjoyed his visits to Buskins performances, and I would be invited to his rooms with one or two other undergraduates for tea, and occasionally for a tour of his books. At one of these visits he pulled out a book and told us: "Look at this book: it is bound in camel-skin." While we felt and admired it he pulled out another book, very small and chunky: "This one is bound in elephant-skin." And then he pulled out a third, a book of old sepia photographs: "And this one," he said, rubbing his hand over its smooth surface, " is bound... in human skin." He handed it to us, and reluctantly we took it and opened it up. The photographs, he told us, were of atrocities committed by the Germans in the First World War. None of us had the nerve to inquire further: there was an odd glint in the old soldier's eye which discouraged questioning. It was a sinister moment.

At the end of Hilary Term I received a note from the Wilk asking me whether I would call in on him. I did so.

"What are you doing next Tuesday?" he asked me.

"Nothing very much, sir, "I answered.

"Good," he said. "I would like you to go up to London for me, go to Christie's, and bid on two little things which are coming up for auction, and which I would dearly like to possess. Would you do that for me?"

"Certainly, sir," I replied, pleased and flattered by the commission, and excited at the prospect.

"Good," he said again. "Come to my rooms at eight in the morning, and I will give you the money."

When I showed up at his rooms the following Tuesday morning he handed me three hundred guineas – £315 – in cash, counted out in those big and handsome white five pound notes which really used to look as though they were each a personal promissory note from the Governor of the Bank of England. He told me of the upper limit he wanted me to bid for each item, and insisted that I telephone him from London the moment the sale was through. And so off I trotted over the Canal to the station, having stuffed the notes carefully into a briefcase I had brought for the purpose.

The Wilk's main target was a copy of the rare 1655 edition of *Silex Scintillans*, a collection of poems by the Welsh religious poet Henry Vaughan. The other was a modest curiosity: a poem by Oliver Goldsmith, separately printed in 1776 and entitled *The Haunch of Venison*.

In the event I successfully bid for both items for well below his limit, and rang him to let him know.

"When are you coming back?" he asked impatiently.

"On the 4.45," I told him.

Around half past six I knocked at his door, took out my briefcase, and handed him his change, and a parcel wrapped up by Christie's – tied neatly with string in the old way.

"First, have a sherry," he said, and poured out a couple of glasses. Then with fumbling hands he unwrapped the parcel, and picked out Vaughan's poems. He caressed the cover greedily. "I have wanted this book all my life," he said. He sat down, motioning to me to do the same, and took a sip of his sherry. Then carefully opening the old volume he began to read in a loud voice:

"My soul, there is a country
Far beyond the stars
Where stands a winged sentry
All skillful in the wars ..."

A week or two later in that Easter vacation I was heading down to Southampton to work with Chris Ellis for a weekend on *Theodora*, back now from its transatlantic voyage and much in need of refurbishing. Hearing from me that I would be in the area, Wilkinson had invited me over to his family house, beautifully named 'Salt Grass' and facing over the Solent to the Isle of Wight, with Henry VIII's Hurst Castle visible to the west where it guarded the Solent's entrance. After a simple lunch, served by an aged housekeeper, I returned to *Theodora* (Chris had lent me a car), and after another day or two's scraping and painting I took the train back home.

Three weeks later we heard that the Colonel had suffered a stroke. He was brought back to Oxford by ambulance, and died a few days later at the Acland Nursing Home.

I wrote a poem:

I have found through life
said the book-collecting colonel
that I always regret my economies
and never my extravagances
the remark was made possible
not only by his brutal need to possess
but by a handsome private income

I remember him grasping
a first edition of vaughans poetry
bought too dearly at an auction
all my life I have wanted this he said
reading aloud in a bellow
my soul there is a country
far beyond the stars
six weeks later
he suffered a ravaging stroke

I saw the scarlet bookman
keel like an ox
 among his lifes treasures
himself the prize
the one extravagance
he did not live not to regret

Reading the poem over, I am puzzled by its lack of affection. I liked the Wilk, and was moved to attend his funeral in Worcester College chapel, with the Provost giving the farewell address to his old friend.

Memory scuttles on to the summer term, which I remember now only as a long round of punting on the Cherwell, and parties at one College garden or another, drinking Pimms No.1 and a great deal of champagne or punch. This of course was in addition to the Friday night pub crawl, where I am ashamed to say I became known for my powerful consumption: I once put down a total of 15 pints of bitter beer in an evening. 'Friday night is Bawters night', my friends used to say. My drinking friends included Roger Mills and John Weston, and sometimes Roger French and Malcolm Booth. The Gloucester Arms behind the Playhouse was our local, but we spread our custom around town – especially if there was a dartboard or snooker table to be had. I like to think – we liked to think – that the beer simply brightened and sharpened our conversation and our wit, and this may well have been true in the earlier stages of the evening. We certainly never became rowdy, although I do remember shinning up a lamp-post late at night outside the Bear, and finding it had just been painted green.

The Buskins outdoor production chosen for that second summer was *Two Gentlemen of Verona*. It was directed by graduate student Richard Proudfoot, who cast me as Launce, the clownish servant to Proteus – played by Richard Hooper, by this time Buskins' president. Launce's scenes involved his dog Crab, and the obvious casting for him was Sooty, our family's ten-year-old black spaniel of dubious parentage and lubricious habits, but of sweetly good temper. He was brought into the city from Studley for this great theatrical opportunity, and (since dogs were *verboten* in College) he was housed by Mrs Harris, the wife of our scout. I believe my double act with Sooty was the hit of the evening, if only because it is written that way: Crab's part in the play has been described as "the most scene-stealing non-speaking role in the canon". Sooty on stage behaved impeccably, or rather as peccably as the part required. And a photograph of the two of us even made it to the *Oxford Mail*.

The moment that summer term was over we began rehearsing our second Regatta revue, called (for some reason I don't remember) *Next Time Yes*, to be performed for a week at the Oxford Playhouse before proceeding to Henley A certain amount of material was recycled from the previous year, but we also produced some new sketch material and new musical numbers. The cast included my partner from the Commemoration Ball, Caroline Seebohm, Caroline's current boyfriend Roger Smith, Derek Wood, and a bright young woman from Somerville College called Esther Rantzen. But even more ambitious plans were afoot: while we were preparing the show, Iain Mackintosh had been quietly working to bring it to the Lyric Theatre, Hammersmith, for a week in September. Never mind that folk didn't go to theatre during the summer holidays. Never mind that our intimate cabaret had already been inflated to fit the Playhouse, then reduced for the smaller Kenton Theatre space, and would now have to be expanded again for a much grander stage and auditorium in London. Never mind that we could not be considered more than reasonably gifted amateurs. Iain's confidence was unstoppable. He told us he had even managed to persuade Rex Nettleford to join us again as our choreographer, and was also bringing our old colleague Neil Bratton back into the show. This cheered us up a lot.

Once the Regatta performances (reasonably well reviewed and attended) were over, we dispersed until the end of August. I had been invited to spend some days with Roger French and his family at a summer cottage they rented on the island of Guernsey. Roger and I were to follow this with just the two of us travelling on to Brittany. I looked forward to this swooningly, but first I had to earn some money. I can't remember the circumstances, but on my return from Henley I applied to Tuckwell's, the Oxford builder's merchant, and was hired as a driver for one of their lorries. The following Monday I reported for work in Cowley at 7 am, and for the next few weeks I could be spotted in my blue lorry delivering bricks, bags of cement and gravel to building sites all over Oxford and area. It was the first labourer's job I had ever taken on, and I enjoyed it. I remember earning something like £8 a week after deductions, which was the most basic working wage, but enough to help me pay both for my trip to Guernsey, where the French family welcomed me handsomely, and later to Brittany.

We took bicycles and a small pup tent over to France, and spent just two or three days exploring the coast around the Golfe du Morbihan, with a night on Ile-aux-Moines (Monks' Island) in the middle of the Bay. I was happy beyond words to be alone with the loved Roger, but once again never gave any sign throughout the brief trip of my strong sexual attraction to him. I remember even now how grindingly difficult this was, and the emotional pain it cost me, as I continued to act the cheerful, matey friend. Monks' Island indeed.

Back in England it was time to assemble for a week of rehearsals before our opening in Hammersmith. Those of us without a place in London were billeted in someone's house, and since the Lyric was dark that week we were able to rehearse on stage. Time has blotted out all memory of those days, and indeed of the week of performance, though I still remember Christopher Ricks' cheeky telegram of good wishes: 'BEST OF LUCK FOR FIRST NIGHT. HOPE IT WONT BE YOUR LAST.' The joke was not exactly prophetic, but it was not far out: the auditorium remained cavernously unfilled for our whole run. We had been able to land only one brief advance article about the show in the Evening Standard before we opened (I remember it referred to me as 'intellectual beefcake', whatever that meant); and since theatre critics were either still on holiday or loth to take the tube to Hammersmith we received only one laconic and unloving press notice, which brought us few theatrecomers. That said, I have nothing but praise and admiration for the sheer nerve which propelled Iain Mackintosh into organizing the whole project. His experience and *chutzpah* were to stand him in good stead when a year or two later he launched into the creation of a professional theatre company, Prospect Productions.

I believe that one other reason for our lack of success was that the style of our show, based on the light and frothy musical entertainments from before the war, had become stale and unprofitable. That very same month of August 1960 in fact saw the first appearance at the Edinburgh Festival of a very different kind of revue. It was *Beyond the Fringe*, and most of the material for it was written by my old Radley friend Peter Cook. *Beyond the Fringe* had none of the wicked bite, none of the anger, of American satirists like Lenny Bruce and Mort Sahl, but it took aim at some untouchables like the Royal Family, Prime Minister Harold Macmillan, the Church of England, and reverential attitudes to the

Second World War. It also had no trouble being openly rude to people, and hurting their feelings. Our own revue included some gently mocking sketches, amidst one or two seriously intended love songs, and 'sweet' numbers like my perennial '*Share My Tea*': its whole premiss was to offer jocular light entertainment to a middle class audience, without upsetting their prejudices or their politics. Sweetness and jocularity played no part in the more unforgiving world of *Beyond The Fringe*, which has been seen as launching the whole 'satirical' movement of the 1960s.

Roger Mills and I continued to be drinking pals in London during the run of *Next Time Yes*: after two years of work and play together we were now the closest of friends. But I was very much astonished, after the show was over and we had gone our separate ways, to receive a passionate letter from him, saying how deeply he loved me: how he had always wanted to attach himself to someone like me: 'someone to die for.' How could I forget the phrase?

Roger's steady girlfriend was Katie (whom he later married), a highly studious, diminutive and bespectacled classical scholar of great brilliance, and being with Roger a great deal I also spent time with her: we were all three of us close, and all continued to write letters to one another for months and even years afterwards. But here was one of my hearty heterosexual friends, girlfriend in tow, declaring his deathless love for me! Naturally I wrote a loving letter back saying how honoured I was by what he had told me, that I loved him as a friend and would always love him, but that I was simply not that way inclined. As I look back on it I think how complicated and even Shakespearean it all was: while in love with a Roger to whom I felt I could not declare – let alone express – my love, I was rejecting the advances of another Roger, to whom I protested my indifference to the very idea. I was clearly hanging on for dear life to the vision of myself as a normal heterosexual young man who was having a hard time growing out of his adolescent male crushes. The social strictures of those days, especially within the heavily male and woman-fearing institutions in which I had been brought up, created such wretchedness for those ensnared in them.

The completion of my second year at Oxford in fact tied off many of the strands of my life up to that time. Many of my good Buskins friends had gone down from the University having completed their degrees: Iain Mackintosh, Roger Mills and Ron Heapy had all left. And sadly I had to move out of College, out of the elegant Somerset rooms which had briefly placed Jeremy and myself in the pulsing heart of College life. Already, before the summer term had been over, we had had to start the search for digs for our third and last year.

I was lucky again. My old Radley friend Richard Latham had also gone down from Oxford that summer, and before he left he had introduced me to his landlady, Catherine Brown. Catherine owned a creaky old house, with two rooms on each floor, above a shop on Broad Street. It was number 14A, and was reached through an alleyway beside the shop. Catherine, now in her seventies, was one of Oxford's most celebrated characters. Her father had been Mayor of the city when she was a young woman some time in the early 'twenties, and since her mother had already died Catherine had carried out the duties of the Mayoress of Oxford. She later opened a café in the Covered Market, known as Ma Brown's, and from then on she was referred to by everyone as Ma Brown. Our mother and we children (not Father, of course) had been eating at Ma Brown's cafe since early Studley days, and my mother used to enjoy the menu, typed out by Catherine with idiosyncratic spelling, many xxx-ed mistakes and jumps of line, startling changes of colour from blue to red and back again, and spattered with comments and exclamation marks like:

Rabbit Stew (beware small bones!!!)
Chicken Soup (rich and nourishing!!!)

Catherine rented out rooms to undergraduates, each of whom had to come with references and be subjected to an interview over tea and cake before being accepted as one of 'my boys'. I was able to pass muster, and was given the room at the top of the house, overlooking Broad Street and opposite the main gate of Balliol College. It was a prime spot in the centre of the city, with close access to College, to the Bodleian Library and to the lecture halls in Schools.

I had also decided, after my joyous but frustrated days in Brittany, to review this whole business of being enamoured of Roger French. 'Grow up!' I said to myself: 'Find yourself a girlfriend.' And soon the opportunity came my way. Invited over for tennis that September by the family who lived in Boarstall Towers (a bike-ride from Studley Priory) I met a radiantly beautiful young woman called Emma. Her tennis was a great deal better than mine (whose wasn't?), but we got talking over drinks, and found we had much in common: an interest both in literature and the theatre. She lived in Derbyshire, but was studying in Scotland at St. Andrew's University. We met two or three more times before she drove back up north and on to Scotland, but we soon started a correspondence which kept up all through the autumn and the following spring, and at least twice she drove all the way down to Oxford for us to spend the weekend together. This was serious business: I even took her to Studley to meet my parents, who were suitably charmed. She was a lovely, lively and intelligent person, and we laughed a lot.

Studley Priory Country House Hotel was now in the final year of the 14-year lease signed by the 'the Props' in 1947, and all three of them were beginning to count the days to March 1st, 1961. But some time late that summer of 1960 Captain Henderson came to my father and made a proposition: he offered him the whole of the Priory and its 10-acre gardens for the sum of £10,000. It turned out, in fact, that the Hendersons had made the decision to sell their entire estate with its sixty tied cottages and their own farm, along with the Priory. Father told me of the offer, and I was enthusiastic, even insistent, that he should accept. I still had £1000 or more squirrelled away from my legacy, and told him I was happy to contribute it. Surely we could put together a loan or a short-term mortgage to purchase the place? And having purchased it we could set about finding a buyer for the whole hotel business, with the house and grounds as part of the deal. Without ownership of the house, it was clear that there would nothing to show for their fourteen years of slogging work and sacrifice. I even told him I would be prepared, the moment I had finished at Oxford, to join him in organizing the affair and become a partner.

Nothing indicated more clearly to me that my father was no businessman than his point-blank refusal even to consider the idea. I pleaded with him, but he was so clearly worn out and dispirited that the prospect of taking on new liabilities and extending his anxieties beyond the following March was simply unbearable. And he saw my offer to become a partner as simply a step towards enmeshing his son in his own agonies.

I believe now, in fact, that my father had no concept of the practice of borrowing money in order to start or sustain a business. He saw a mortgage as an evil, and any large loan from a bank as nothing more than an invitation to default and eventual bankruptcy. And bankruptcy was for him, as I have already noted, a fate almost worse than death. Too much reading of Dickens? Maybe. In any case, nothing could move him, and I went back to Oxford for my last year frustrated by his failure to grasp this one possibility for his financial redemption.

I had already decided, with the encouragement of Christopher – who had patiently put up with my doing less than my best for my first two years because I had been so involved in the theatre – to drop all connections with the Buskins, and to see if I couldn't get myself ready to aim for a first class degree. I began to be a regular at the Bodleian Library, for the first time finding a genuine pleasure in the discipline of full-time study. And my weekly essays for Christopher became more ambitious and I think more accomplished.

The pattern of my social life also changed, with the good friends of my own year now scattered all over town. Although we continued to turn up at the dining hall and sit together for our daily dinner, the old custom of repairing to someone's rooms afterwards for coffee and music and talk was now more difficult. My links with Roger French and his circle began to weaken as we saw less of one another, though I made a new friend and drinking pal in a young Worcester man, Robin Grove-White, who was clever, well-read, anarchic and very funny.

My new home at 14A The Broad also put me in touch with new friends further afield. The undergraduates sharing Ma Brown's digs were both serious sportsmen from other colleges. Colin Payne was to win a blue for rugby that year, and David Veit another for field hockey. We did our own weekend drinking together, and they invited me several times to Vincent's Club, the hallowed home of Oxford sporting types, where I must have pulled my weight because before the end of the year they had put me up for membership and

I was elected – I who never touched an oar or a rugger ball, let alone a hockey stick, in my whole time at the University. At the end of the year I was even urged to become a life member. The fee for this, if I remember, was £1. It was a deal. I forked out.

As a scholar of Worcester John Weston enjoyed the privilege of having rooms in College for three years, and his room now became a familiar stopping point for a group of us. We talked of everything. Having achieved a First in classical Moderations John was now settling down to Greats with its concentration on logic and philosophy, so it was natural for our more serious chat to revolve around the latest problems he had been studying, and I found myself intrigued by the questions which I would have been dealing with myself had I stuck to the classics. I relished hearing, for example, the old story of the question asked in a Logic paper a few years earlier:

'Is this a fair question?'

(It was said that the wag who responded simply 'Yes, if this is a fair answer' was summarily failed.)

I also became friendly with some of John's friends, chief among them James Cogan from Corpus Christi, who like me had shifted from the classics into English, and brought his quizzical and pessimistic view of life into the mix of our conversations: we used to tease him that his favourite quotation in all literature was Wordsworth's '*Each day dawns, but dawns to disappear...*'

Some time that term a debate was organized between two of Oxford's philosophers: John Simopoulos of St. Catherine's Society (soon to be St. Catherine's College) and Michael Hinton of Worcester. The question to be debated was this:

"You are seeing one of your students off on the train as he goes down from Oxford at the end of his time here. You have a final piece of advice for him, to be compressed into no more than one sentence. What would you say?"

The debate was well attended by philosophy students and others. And the two philosophers – as was perhaps foreseen – came to the question from very different angles. John Simopoulos' advice was: "Live a beautiful life." Michael Hinton's was: "Be kind."

The question and its two very different responses generated hours of talk amongst us. I found Hinton's 'Be kind' a rather namby-pamby motto to be branded on my forehead: "Love is lubrication," I protested, "not the machine." On the other hand, 'Live a beautiful life' had its own problems. We had all recently read *Justine*, the first volume of Lawrence Durrell's *Alexandria Quartet*, and discussed at length the morality of Durrell's finding beauty in the sight of the child prostitutes in a brothel. Living 'a beautiful life' seemed to leave out altogether the question of morality, of kindness, of caring about our neighbour. Was this a Christian versus Pagan argument? Or at least a moral versus an amoral view of life? Perhaps. I have no doubt of course that John Simopoulos was being provocative – and that Michael Hinton was not. And then again, as so often at Oxford, one had to consider the meaning of words: could beauty be consistent with immorality? Depends what you mean by 'beauty', and 'immorality' – and even 'consistent'. Etc... The talk went on.

I suppose that our discussions were given an extra edge because we were nearing the end of our own university days, and the task of finding an overarching shape and direction for our own future lives was drawing ever closer. But it's interesting to me now that we seemed much more concerned about the quality of life we were setting out to live than any particular career. This was certainly true of myself: I don't believe that forging a successful career for myself was even remotely on my agenda at this time, and anyway there were no Careers Offices around as there would be now. 'Something in the arts' was I suppose a kind of goal, though for all my enjoyment of acting I never imagined myself as a professional actor. Nor did I have any thought of becoming an academic. If there was anything more definite in my imaginings, it was to be 'a writer'; and if anything excited me at this time it was 'adventure'. I wanted to travel, and to experience new things. I found myself endlessly stimulated by the words Tennyson puts into the mouth of Ulysses:

Yet all experience is an arch wherethro'
Gleams that untravelled world whose margin fades
For ever and for ever when I move.

Meanwhile, there was work to do. I stayed in Oxford until just before Christmas, living at Catherine Brown's and studying every day. And it was around this time that I met up with a graduate student, Christopher Hogg. Chris had approached his English exams the previous summer in an extremely businesslike manner, analysing the papers set in former years and calculating the most likely questions to be asked of him in his finals. He had taken voluminous notes at the lectures he had calculated to be worth attending, and had memorised them all with meticulous attention to detail. He had also memorised quotable quotes from every writer in the canon. Not surprisingly, he had gained his first-class degree.

Chris in fact had understood early on that doing well in an exam had not so much to do with native intelligence and erudition as with careful planning and technique. This was an entirely foreign world for me. My old reluctance to believe that you could get any better at something by working at it, or by employing techniques, was still encouraging me simply to rely on my own instinctive abilities, and to wing it. But Chris convinced me. Not only that, but he kindly passed on to me all the notes he had taken during his three years of study. With some reluctance, and with even a sense that I was somehow cheating, I began to add canniness and guile to my intellectual qualities. I had my own notes of course. But those that Chris handed on to me gave me another whole *tranche* of useful information, which I did my best to absorb.

(Chris went from Oxford into the world of business, where unsurprisingly he shone, becoming among other things CEO of Courtaulds and boss of Reuters and Glaxo. Knighted for services to industry, he has been described as 'a principled industrialist.')

The last Christmas and New Year's Eve at Studley Priory were still busy with guests and meals, but 'the Props' were no doubt happy to put these *festas* behind them: they would never again have to spend Christmas breaking their backs in looking after other people. And from the beginning of the new year they were starting to close things down, as they entered what were in any case the worst two months of the year for business. The cows were sold, and plans were being made for a sale of the furniture we would not need again, and for storage of our own meagre possessions. It was a depressing time, but there was also elation. For Father of course there was the glum fact to be faced that while you are still in business your creditors will be patient, but that when you wind things up for the last time their bills all at once become pressingly due. He knew now that when it was all over he would still be heavily in debt. The prospect gave him more sleepless nights, the poor fellow.

I must admit that I was only too happy to climb on to my little Velocette and tootle back to the comfort and ease of 14A Broad Street, and to the loved life of Worcester College and all my many friends. Oxford by this time had in fact become so layered with my acquaintances of Radley, the Regiment, Studley and the University that I could now hardly walk five yards without bumping into someone I knew: a schoolmaster, a soldier from my platoon, a hotel guest or one of my College friends.

As an added pleasure, the relationship that we senior students had with Christopher Ricks had ripened into a warm relationship with him and his wife Kirsten, and I think I can say without immodesty that I was becoming a 'particular friend', sometimes baby-sitting, and sometimes having meals with them in their house across the way from the College. I made him laugh, he made me laugh: how much we laughed in those days! He also seemed to have some respect for my intelligence: he once said that he tended to wince at my judgements – an admission which I must say I prized. I certainly winced at his.

During those last winter weekends I would often drive out to Studley on Sundays. There would be beer in the bar beforehand, and then for lunch Mother's roast beef and Yorkshire pudding, with roast potatoes and brussels sprouts, all superbly cooked, and to be followed by her lemon and meringue pie with Jersey cream. It was a wonderful respite from the spartan meals at College, or the fried eggs and toast thrown together in Catherine Brown's kitchen.

But then came March 1st, and Studley was finally abandoned. Wilma went off to stay with her sister, kindly giving my parents the loan of the Morris Oxford which she had recently bought with family money. But Mother and Father had nowhere to go. They had been invited by two or three kind friends in the area to come and stay with them until they could see their next move. But Father would not hear of it: "I won't accept charity," he said.

Which is why, on the sunny Sunday of March 5th, 1961, I drove my motorbike *not* out through Headington, past Stanton St. John, down Waterperry Hill, along the Straight Mile, up the hill and through the gates of that beautiful Elizabethan mansion Studley Priory; *but* to the village of Elsfield, reached off the Oxford Bypass. I had been given directions, and found myself soon nosing up a track and into the floor of an old quarry.

It was a picture I will never forget. There at the far side stood our shabby old army bell tent, used for camping holidays in days gone by. In front of it was a blazing camp fire, my mother in trousers sitting on a stool beside it, with vegetables boiling and some chops and tomatoes ready for the frying pan. High on the ridge above I caught sight of my father, his grey hair flying in the wind, and with a pile of firewood over his shoulder which he was bringing down into the quarry. In the back of the open tent sat my sister Jenny, reading an Aldous Huxley novel.

We had an excellent lunch. After it I tentatively asked my father if he was all right. "Never happier in my life," he snapped back. It was astonishing how unaware he was that his refusal to accept charity had not only propelled him out on to the heath under the open sky, but that his pride had dragged his wife and daughter along for the ride. Mother insisted that she found it 'fun'. She was forever a trooper.

Both of them were of course immensely relieved at being shot of the long and weary burden of Studley Priory, and Dad was behaving like a little boy on a camping holiday. But he also knew that when he left the hotel he personally owed something over £5,000, some in trade debts, some in personal loans. He had in fact already written to one or two former guests of the Priory asking them whether they could forward him a loan to pay off the tradesmen who were beginning to threaten him with small claims court.

It was a warm March that year, and the family were still camping in the quarry when I visited them again a week or two later. I found them buoyant. Dad had just received a letter from Sir Bruce and Lady Richmond (frequent Studley guests), expressing their concern that my parents had been reduced to camping in a tent, and enclosing a cheque for a thousand guineas: £1,050. This would go a long way towards paying down his most unforgiving creditors.

Sixty years later, on a whim, I searched my father's name on Google, and to my surprise the search led me to Lady Richmond's papers, now in the archives of the University of Leeds. What I eventually tracked down was the letter that Father had written to the Richmonds following receipt of the gift, and dated 21st March, 1961:

Dear Lady Richmond,

You would hardly believe the happiness and relief that your letter and cheque for one thousand and fifty pounds brought to our camp this morning. I don't mean an irresponsible sort of happiness for we are very deeply aware of our responsibility to repay this sum to you in full in addition to the earlier loans, but what your great kindness has done is to remove the horrible threat of bankruptcy proceedings – a threat that has been hanging over us for months or even years. In our most hopeful moments we did not expect to receive such a generous loan by return of post, but thought that there would inevitably be some delay, even if you were kind enough to make the loan at all. As it is, I am going to Oxford this very afternoon, to pay this cheque into my bank, and to visit my patient tradesmen to discharge my liabilities to them. I cannot emphasize too much the relief that this will bring to me.

Another great joy is that I shall be able to go at once and order a suit of clothes. I have not had a suit for many years, even an old one, and I have had to limit my activities to what can be suitably covered by a sports coat and trousers or a very well-made suit of tails of some antiquity. But it has long worried me that neither of these outfits is really suitable for being interviewed by prospective employers, and I am sure that, careful as we must be, a good suit is a sound investment. The boost to my morale will be very great indeed.

Now there is one thing I want to make very clear: we are camping, mostly because it is the cheapest way to live, but also because we wish to be independent. We are experienced campers and it is no hardship to us. We are far happier here than we should be in some third-rate boarding house in Oxford. Thank you for your very kind offer of assistance in the case of illness but we are in splendid health, and, thanks to your kindness, face the future with much confidence. So please don't worry about us.

Yours very sincerely,
Raymond F. Bawtree

The letter points up my father's fear of bankruptcy but also his astonishing resilience. It reveals too that this was not the first time he had asked the kind Richmonds for a loan. As I have noted, over the years he had in fact approached a number of friendly Studley regulars for funds in the form of an 'investment': one of the perks being to be able to stay at Studley with full board for two weeks every year free of charge. Whether any of them got their money back in the end is doubtful – though I remember that Charles Wrinch, whom I had drawn in a year or two before on Father's behalf, was always impressed that Father had at least paid back half the loan I had negotiated. There was no alternative for me, either, but to hand over the remainder of my own precious legacy to what Mother used to call 'the blotting paper fund.'

Three weeks into the family camp-out in the quarry, the weather turned cold and it began to snow. At that point Father's pride finally had to buckle, if only for Mother's sake, and he struck camp and accepted the offer of friends (former Studley guests) who put them up in their large house on Cumnor Hill for several weeks.

There was still the future to consider. After taking an unsuccessful shot (in his new suit) at the vacant position of Domestic Bursar at Merton College, he decided all at once to go back to pig-farming. He took a crash course somewhere or other to bring his twenty-year-old expertise up to date, and then applied for a job as manager of a pig farm at the home of Lord Winterbottom: Lilford Hall, Lilford, Northamptonshire. To his amazement he was hired by His Lordship, and that summer the parents moved into a semi-detached stone-built farmhand's cottage on the estate, next door to the Hall's ancient game-keeper. Mother was hired at the same time to collect monthly rents from the tenantry on the estate. Their salaries were no doubt very modest indeed, but so were their needs. They had no car, but bought second-hand bicycles, and I won't forget the sight of the two of them pedalling gently off to the local pub of a Sunday, with Sooty trotting behind. Father on a bicycle!

The Landrace pig herd which Father had taken over had been utterly neglected and was in a more or less feral state. Father took it in hand, and within a year had turned the whole pig farm around. Winterbottom was a lucky man.

That year of 1961 marked a change too in the life of my two sisters. Jenny had taken the entrance exams for Oxford and Cambridge the previous December, and was awarded an Exhibition to Cambridge, but she decided to plump for Oxford, and was accepted into Somerville College. She had now left Wycombe Abbey, and spent the spring and summer teaching little boys at a prep school – a job she enjoyed so much that for a while she thought seriously of giving up the whole idea of university. Meanwhile Jo had left FAO in Rome, and had gone down to Sicily to work as a volunteer with the social activist Danilo Dolci, 'the Gandhi of Europe' as he was called by Aldous Huxley. The Bawtree family were all over the map.

Except for myself, of course, stuck into the books for the last lap of preparations for my final exams – known in Oxford as 'Schools.' The marathon of nine three-hour papers took place around the second week of June, to be followed by a 'viva' in July, where the candidate has to face the five or six examiners who have read and marked the exams. I acquitted myself in front of them with reasonable facility, but I knew that Old and Middle English were my weak areas, and I finished up with what they call 'a good Second': some *alphas*, but one or two too many *betas*. Since I did not plan to go further in the academic field, my result presented no great difficulty, though I did feel I had not quite done justice to my own potential. Christopher was reasonably pleased, though he too would have been happier if I had followed in his footsteps and gained a First.

On the 20th of June a small Worcester College dining club of which I was a member held a fine dinner, I think at the Mitre Hotel. There were no more than ten or twelve at table, and the wine flowed freely. A group of us stayed together and wandered back up the Turl to Broad Street in our dinner jackets some time after midnight, continuing to drink our whisky, and holding on as long as we could to one of the last nights of the summer term. It was about three in the morning when we made the sudden, probably semi-drunken decision to head down to Stonehenge to watch the sun rise at the summer solstice. We changed into warm clothes and rode out of the sleeping city, south through the dark over the Berkshire Downs and Salisbury Plain, on two motorcycles: my own, with John Weston up behind, and the other belonging to a recent friend of mine, Nick Bruford, with Jeremy Twynam behind him on pillion.

We arrived in plenty of time to witness the dawn, only to find the monument wreathed in morning mist, and the rising sun entirely obscured. We wandered through and around, and sat damply on what we reckoned was the altar-stone on which the dawning sun would have shone had it had a fighting chance.

Disappointing, but this was still an escapade to remember. And what is amazing to me now is that we could just walk right across from the road and into the ring of stones. Perhaps we climbed through a perfunctory barbed-wire fence, but there was no security of any kind. More amazing still, when I think of the thousands of neo-Druids who besiege the place every summer solstice these days, there was only one other person there, a solitary man in a raincoat. We still lived in an ostensibly Christian country.

There was also another Commemoration Ball at the end of term, in Brasenose College I think, and I had arranged with Emma that she would come down to Oxford and be my partner. We had made another compact too. Up to this time we had kissed and snuggled, but we had never made love. We agreed that this night would be the night.

And so it happened. We went back to Catherine Brown's, crept upstairs, undressed, and lay down together. I have no idea whether it was Emma's first time, but it was certainly mine. All things considered it was successful, but it was a messy business, as first times usually are, and after it was over I felt wretched. Indeed, I found myself wanting to get away, wanting never to see this lovely girl again. She did not stay the night, and when I saw her next day I was distant. I couldn't help myself. She was dismayed. I told her it was nothing she had done – that it was my fault. But it was the end of our romance. She left the city in tears, and I felt deeply guilty. But I felt – I still feel – that something had happened to me over which I had no control.

Everything now at Oxford was for the last time. The last drinks before dinner in the Buttery, the last dinner in the dining-hall, the farewell party with Christopher, the last walk with friends down and around Worcester's lovely lake, the last drinks at the Gloc. The three happiest years of my life were drawing to an end.

But as so often with these things, it was not really the end. That summer the Buskins had produced *Ring Round The Moon* (Christopher Fry's adaptation of Anouilh's *L'Invitation au Château*) in the College gardens, with Richard Hooper both directing the play and also playing the hefty double lead role of the twin brothers Hugo and Frederick. Richard had decided to make this the Buskins offering for Regatta Week at the Kenton Theatre. But at some point he felt that he should hand over the acting to someone else, and he invited me to take over the Hugo and Frederick double act. I had been away from the boards for over a year, and this was an offer I eagerly snapped up.

So once again at the end of June I took the road down the Thames Valley to Henley. I was so busy learning the part that I remember little of where we stayed. I was also a little out of step with the new young members of the Buskins and somewhat missed the dear friends of past years. But it was a splendid opportunity. Hugo has to leave the stage and re-appear as his brother – and then vice versa – sometimes with only a few seconds to spare. I was nervous: though I had now quite a few shows behind me, I had never received a single acting lesson, and a modicum of natural ability will take you only so far – as I observed later on in life. Our Buskins revues had called for some clever but superficial comic characterisations, quickly donned and as quickly discarded. But Hugo and Frederick were rounded characters developed through the course of a play. Not since I was a schoolboy had I been faced with this kind of challenge. I'm not at all sure how well I pulled it off. But at least I knew my lines.

(The lovely Emma [not her real name] later married, and died of cancer in her fifties. We had an affectionate reunion a few years after our affair.

Richard Hooper went on to a career in the converging worlds of media and communications. He headed up the British Government's recent review of the Post Office, and has been made a Commander of the British Empire.)

Even now my time at Oxford was not entirely over. I returned from Henley to my rooms at Catherine Brown's, and decided to apply once more for my old driving and delivery job at Tuckwell's. They took me on again, and for the rest of July I was once again lugging cement bags and tipping gravel and ballast of various grades round the neighbourhood: I once had to drive their three-tonner as far as Cheltenham.

But all this activity after the end of my Oxford dream-time was simply postponing a fateful question: what was I going to do with my life? Since I still had no answer, I decided to apply for a position as a teacher in France. I would spend a year learning French and in my spare moments would embark on my immortal first novel. I wrote to an address on the boulevard Raspail in Paris, enclosing my credentials. But I was also advised by someone that if I turned up in person my chances of getting a position were considerably greater.

Earlier in the summer, I think through Vincent's Club, I had become friendly with an American undergraduate from Oriel College named Harrell Smith, who it turned out was engaged to the daughter of the serving American Minister in Paris, Mr Herbert Fales. Harrell was heading over to Paris to spend some weeks with his fiancée, but because of her father's position the proprieties had to be respected and he would have to find his own accommodation. We decided to travel over in early August and room together. The day we reached Paris we found a place in rue Madame on the south bank, close to Le Jardin du Luxembourg. It was a single room in an apartment above a Baptist church, and our motherly landlady was the widow of the former pastor. The place was small, but comfortable and clean, and we soon made ourselves at home.

Paris in 1961 still retained for us its allure as the city of art, philosophy and romance. We all knew the songs of Charles Trenet and Edith Piaf, which seemed to talk about love in a way which no one in English quite matched. *'Sous les Ponts de Paris'*, *'La Mer'*, *'Je Ne Regrette Rien'* and the rest, all in their ways conveyed the idea that love was not simply a feeling but the most important thing in the world. Intellectually, of course, Paris was the home of the Existentialists, a very different philosophical school from Oxford's, and seeming in our eyes to be linked more closely to the experience of life than the dry dissections of meaning urged on us by the Oxford choppers of logic. Jean-Paul Sartre and Simone de Beauvoir were still writing, and Albert Camus (who I think had lived on our own street, rue Madame) had been killed in a car accident only two or three years before. Though Sartre was more or less impenetrable and de Beauvoir simply unread by my male contemporaries, Camus' *L'Etranger* and *La Peste* had circulated among us, and conveyed an idea of living quite at odds with the cautious certainties of our English middle class upbringings. The idea that we had no essential nature, and that our existence could only be defined by the sum of our acts: all this was a voyage into new territory.

Paris that year was also seething with tension. De Gaulle's France was coping with a crisis of identity and empire, as the nation faced losing its North African territories. Algeria's National Liberation Front was taking a more and more threatening stance in the heart of the capital. Every day we walked past intersections guarded by police or even military vehicles, their occupants fully armed and waiting for trouble. It was no more than two months later that the police, under the directions of ex-Vichy collaborator Maurice Papon, attacked a 30,000 strong demonstration of pro-FLN Algerians, killing as many as 200 of them in what became known as the Paris Massacre. The ironies of love and war were alive and well in the City of Light.

But trouble about to happen is often trouble ignored. It was not long before Harrell and I sauntered along to *Les Deux Magots*, the reputed hang-out of Sartre, looking in vain for him and his friends. No sign of *le maître*. But young people were sitting over glasses of wine and beer and Pernod, talking excitedly around us and no doubt discussing the finer points of philosophy. I cursed myself that my French was still not good enough for me to be able to understand a word of what they were saying.

I also took the first opportunity to look in at the government offices at 96 boulevard Raspail (why do I still remember the number?) and even to have an interview with the man responsible for handing out teaching positions. He was pessimistic about my chances because I had applied so late, and in any case I would be unlikely to hear anything before the first days of September.

I had come over to France with very little money, and now had to stick around in Paris for several more weeks. Harrell must have mentioned this to Mr and Mrs Fales, because on the first occasion that he invited me over to meet them at their palatial official residence in the XIVth Arrondissement, Mrs Fales asked me whether I would like to do odd jobs for them around the house, for which they would be glad to pay me. I was happy to accept and for the next weeks turned up every day, donned my French worker's apron, and set about polishing silver, constructing a tray holder, piling firewood in the basement, and so on. When it came to meals, of course, I ate with the family, and I think that Mrs Fales, a middle-aged southern belle, took a shine to me; so that when she invited the wives of her Embassy to tea – they all came wearing white gloves – I was asked to take off my apron and help to entertain them. And once, when the Fales were invited to attend a reception given at a nearby hotel by the American Ambassador General Gavin, I was lent the Minister's second tuxedo and asked to be one of the party.

Incidentally, these were the high days of the Cold War, and I can remember being told to speak very discreetly when I was in the Fales' living-room, because just over the high wall of their back garden was the Russian Embassy, and our conversation was almost certainly being heard and recorded.

Harrell and his fiancée Willa and I went on several expeditions around Paris, visiting Chartres, and Versailles, and St. Cloud; and once we took her Morris Mini Minor and travelled to Normandy. I persuaded them to visit Pegasus Bridge, and was excited to see the spot where my old army friends Tod Sweeney, Denis Fox and David Wood had had their moment of glory. We then drove on to Mont St. Michel, where we stayed the night before returning to Paris.

A few days into September I received a letter at rue Madame requesting me to call once again at boulevard Raspail. To my delight I was offered a teaching position in Toulouse at a *Centre Pédagogique Régional*, a kind of Teachers' College. I was told that my Oxford credentials had earned me the job, since it would require me to hold conversation classes with teachers who had taken a term or two off school in order to improve or brush up their knowledge of the language: "*L'anglais d'Oxford, c'est le meilleur*," he advised me. As I explained it to my friends, I was being called upon 'to teach teachers of English English.' I was given a one-way ticket to Toulouse, and a few days later took the train to the south-west.

I was to spend seven months in *La Ville Rose*, and my memories of it are predominantly sad, chiefly because I was homesick for the high happiness of Oxford. I was extremely lucky though in the position I had been given. My students were aged between 25 and

45. They were mature teachers from all over the South of France, who were studying because they wanted to be there. They were polite, friendly and cooperative.

Unfortunately, the money I was paid was hardly enough for subsistence. I began by staying in the attic of the Henri IV Hotel, but eventually rented a small and scrappy apartment with another *lecteur d'anglais*, a perky graduate from the University of Bangor. To help pay my share of the rent I took on a job teaching a class once a week in a Technical College. My class of young men – learning to be plumbers, electricians and gas fitters – had not the slightest interest in their compulsory English lesson, and used it as a heaven-sent opportunity to drive their teacher mad. They wrote and drew obscenities on the blackboard to greet me when I walked in. They threw chalk and paper pellets and darts. They made faces or fought each other behind my back. And once, when under extreme frustration I made the motion of cuffing their ringleader on the side of the head, barely touching him, he fell off his bench and lay senseless on the floor. He was clearly playing a joke, but he was inert for minutes, until I had to call in the Principal. After six weeks of this I fled. I heard that I had stuck it for longer than most.

Some time before Christmas I was lucky enough to fall in with an engineer called Henri, employed by the aeroplane manufacturer Avions Breguet and working out of Toulouse Airport, which was even then a major centre for the aeroplane industry. The company was developing an aircraft which they hoped to sell to the American market, and Henri, who had become aware of my poverty, hired me to translate US Civil Aircraft regulations into French, at five (old) francs a word. He lent me an English–French Aeronautics Dictionary, and before long I was steeped in the arcane world of *ailerons* and *hélices* and *carburants*. Naturally I was only able to furnish a very literal version, and Henri took on the job of turning my text into acceptable French. I often wonder whether any planes went down as a result of my mistranslation.

Henri and his wife invited me to their home several times for dinner. In fact theirs was the only French home I ever stepped inside during the eight months I spent in Toulouse. I was told that the French family, at least there in Languedoc, keeps itself to itself. I was also introduced before long to the *comme il faut* manners of the French bourgeoisie. One of my teacher students of especial propriety would be walking towards me in the town around lunch-time, and the exchange was always the same. "*Bonjour, Michel,*" she would say beamingly, "*Est-ce que tu as mangé?*" If I said, "*Non, pas encore,*" she would respond, "*Alors, bon appétit!*" If I replied, "*Oui, j'ai mangé déjà,*" she would come back with, "*Alors, bon après-midi!*" Another of my students, a left-wing cynic from Corsica, was devastatingly scornful of this kind of formulaic politesse. In fact he was scornful of Toulouse in general, seeing it as the very worst of provincial cities, and mocking the Toulousains who went around in enormous floppy berets, referred to as '*champignons.*' The most exotic feature of the place was the number of exiles there from Franco's Spain: poets and artists, many of them veterans of the Republican army, and still actively passionate in their hatred for Franco's Fascist regime.

My own mood was not helped by what seemed to be incessant rain, and, having so little money and being so very lonely, I embarked on that first novel for which I had been preparing myself for so long. I completed almost three chapters in careful longhand, working hard to incorporate some of my inmost thoughts and feelings from Oxford. It included a drunken motorbike ride with Roger, I remember, and the style of it all probably owed much to Hemingway. It was at least a muffled burst of creativity, and served to remind me that making something out of nothing was what I wanted to do. But I eventually lost confidence or hit some kind of a block, and I put the manuscript aside. With one thing and another I never took it up again, but it stayed with me for many years as a token of my long dream, before being stolen in Canada, along with the other contents of a locked closet. Maybe just as well.

Two expeditions stick in the mind. The first was to the Principality of Andorra for a long weekend. A group of us British exiles drove in someone's car, leaving after work on Friday at the end of October and heading due south up into the Pyrenees. We reached Andorra la Vella and found our simple and beautiful old whitewashed inn well after dark. We awoke in the morning to a cloudless sky, surrounded by the ancient town, which was at that point untouched by mass tourism. I can remember not much more, except for a walk I took by myself that afternoon, starting off down a track leading over a cow pasture into the rocky woods, the yellow and russet colours of autumn magical against the blue. I realized that in Toulouse I had been starved too long of beauty, and absorbed all this greedily. Wanting to take a photograph of the view across the valley, I climbed a pinnacle of rock and took a lovely shot – then realized that the way down was terrifyingly steep. I froze. If I fell and broke a leg no one could possibly know where I was. After five or ten minutes I managed to get moving again, and clambered down inch by inch. It had been a major fright.

In the early spring the same group of us took off past the massive walls of Carcassonne, past Perpignan and then down along the coast and across the border into Spain, where we spent a couple of nights by the sea at Torre del Mar, on the Costa del Sol. Again I was delighted to be away from the gloomy streets of Toulouse and in the sunshine of the south. A brilliant Spanish guitarist played in the dining-room, and kept us awake and rapt until the small hours.

Between these two outings was Christmas, and my parents,

anxious for me to be with them and aware of my unhappiness in France, sent me money for a return train ticket. I was overjoyed to be back in England, and we celebrated the first Christmas as a private family (Jenny was there but Jo couldn't make it) since I had been nine years old. Mother had by this time decorated and furnished the little house to her satisfaction, and it shone with her love and care. We had our own Christmas tree, we swapped presents, we ate our own turkey, we played our own games, we went out to parties at neighbouring houses, we walked to the nearest pub for drinks. I had never seen all of us so contented.

Soon after the New Year I returned refreshed to my two jobs in Toulouse, and was beginning to find at last that though I had a hard time understanding French when spoken to me, I was speaking it now with greater fluency than ever before. And one particular day – it must have been in February or March – the miracle happened: suddenly when people spoke to me I could understand! It was as though my familiarity with words and phrases and intonations had been slowly building up, to the point where the words and phrases I could understand outnumbered those I still had trouble with – which I could then guess at. It was like a deaf person suddenly being able to hear. I have never forgotten that first delighted sensation.

My contract ended in April, and I took the first train up to Paris, staying a few days I no longer remember where. But I took the opportunity of going back to *Les Deux Magots*, where once again those bright young things were in animated discussion. Now at last I would be able to follow their philosophical arguments, and perhaps even to join in. It took a while to tune into what they were saying, but before long it was clear they were talking about the same things all young people talk about: boyfriends, girlfriends, money, cars and vacations. I was dashed.

Back in England, and at home with my family in Lilford, I was once again facing the overwhelming question: what next? My friend John Weston had completed his fourth year at Oxford, and was now one of those rare beings who had achieved a Double First in 'Mods and Greats'. He applied to enter the Foreign Office, and was duly accepted, heading the list of successful candidates. Was this my future too? I wrote away for the application forms, filled them out and sent them off with a ten shilling fee. I was even given a date for my written examination. But a few days before I was due to show up, I reneged. I suppose I felt that I was not, in the words of Henry Wotton, suited to be 'an honest gentleman sent to lie abroad for the good of his country'. Perhaps the problem was not so much the lying as the honesty. Since the ending of my affair with Emma a year earlier, and all through my time in France, my sexual life had been on hold. I admired both handsome men and beautiful women, but from a distance. I continued to dissemble good spirits and happy assurance through this confusion, but I knew I was not being entirely honest either with myself or with other people. It was no state of mind or heart with which to enter government service.

But I was also very reluctant to enter yet another large institution where you were required to obey orders, often regardless of your own opinions. And I was as eager as ever on the idea of adventuring: "*all experience is an arch…*" My sister Jo was setting the pace. She had accompanied Danilo Dolci as his interpreter on a speaking tour of the eastern United States, and stayed behind when he left in order to put together a Danilo Dolci fundraising committee. To keep herself she had accepted a short contract at the Iranian Mission to the UN, where one of her first tasks had been to write a speech for the Foreign Minister to deliver in English at the General Assembly. (It was there too that she was wooed by an Iranian diplomat who was also a poet, and had been described as the 'Omar Khayyam of the Twentieth Century'. She turned him down, writing to me: 'I don't mind the Bread and the Wine, but am not so keen on the Thou.') When her contract expired she had decided to live in Mexico for a year, but her money ran out after four months and she returned to New York, where she had accepted an invitation to join the UN Mission of the United Arab Republic – politically much more in her line. All this sounded a lot more exciting than settling down into the long and narrowly British groove of the Foreign Office.

I looked around at some of my other friends. Jonathan Harlow, who had gained a First in History at Cambridge, had been accepted into the former Colonial Service (by then known as the Department of Commonwealth Relations) and would soon be shipping out to become an administrative officer in the Bechuanaland Protectorate. Jeremy Twynam had joined an advertising agency in London. David Kimball was studying for a graduate degree in music and would before long be a distinguished professor at the University of St. Andrew's.

I had written to Bill Glassco and had casually let him know of my quandary. Bill had married his fiancée Jane the previous year, and they had just produced a son, Benjamin. Bill was working for his PhD in English and teaching at the University of Toronto. In his letter back to me, he told me that there were exciting things going on in Canada at that time. There was a Toronto theatre company called The Crest, producing good work. There was a lot of drama being created on television by the Canadian Broadcasting Corporation. And of course there was the Canadian Stratford which every summer was presenting Shakespeare productions of international quality. Bill made the suggestion: why not come out to Canada for a year, and see what might happen?

Canada. The country had been at the outer edge of my

consciousness since early childhood. There were the Canadian stamps passed down to me by my father. There were Canada's National Film Board documentaries which I had first watched at my preparatory school. There was my Radley schoolfriend Chris Dobson, who had returned from his summer in Canada with his red plaid shirt and Indian leather jacket, and with exciting stories of canoeing in Northern Ontario. And now there was my good friend Bill and his wife Jane, who offered to give me a bed in Toronto for a while if I got there, and who would put me in touch with some of the people they knew in the entertainment business. I was even offered introductions by Roger French's father, who did some purchasing for Eaton's Seven Seas Giftshop in their flagship Toronto store, and knew its manager well. And I had just spent a year in France learning at least the Toulouse version of Canada's other official language. The country was certainly sending out its siren call.

What were the alternatives? I was wary of anything which involved me becoming a part of the London scene, though Peter Cook's star was now in the ascendant, with *Beyond the Fringe* selling out at the Fortune Theatre. I much enjoyed my times staying with him in London that summer, but as I have noted already I always felt like an outsider in the capital, and disliked the whole business of pushing myself forward through charm and connections. I also found that Peter's increasingly caustic and ridiculing view of the world was simply not mine, and I felt out of place in what were becoming London's 'satirical sixties'. Then again, I had no desire to teach in a school: I had seen enough of school. My Worcester friend Roger Mills had joined the BBC, and was to become a noted documentary producer, but I suppose I rebelled at the whole thought of 'working my way up' which such jobs entailed: and the BBC was just another vast institution. Ron Heapy was soon to launch a distinguished career working for Oxford University Press, and through my connection with Pippa Norrington's father I played with the same idea. But I had always dreamed of being published rather than being a publisher. As for the British Council, Charles Wrinch had long ago set my mind against it. I was reminded of his words: "People who work for the Council just… well, they just disappear."

I spent a happy few days staying with Christopher and Kirsten Ricks at the idyllic cottage they had just bought in Gloucestershire, and I shared my dilemma. Christopher heard me out, and strongly encouraged me to head out to Canada and try my fortune there for a year. Not only that, but he offered to lend me the money for the voyage – "strictly a one-way ticket, of course," he stipulated.

My parents had already resigned themselves to my sister Jo's international adventures, and would obviously have been happier if I were to remain in England. But they had long ago made clear that once our education was completed we were free to do as we wished. After all, Father himself had taken ship for Australia at the age of twenty: who was he to resist my wandering?

And so it was decided. Early in September I found that there was a Greek Lines boat leaving for Canada from Tilbury Docks towards the end of the month. I booked my passage, cabin class, on the *SS Arkadia*, for the modest sum of £74. I then applied to the Canadian Consulate for 'landed immigrant' status. I had to fill out forms and have a chest X-ray, and amazingly the whole business was completed in four days.

There were farewells to arrange. I took a last trip up to Northamptonshire for a few days with the parents: I was delighted to see them busily ensconced in their new life, which was much improved by the gift of a car from my sister Jo, bought second-hand from my uncle's garage in Cobham. Of course they had their aggravations. Mother was finding the routine of collecting rents a tiresome business, with some of the tenants (a handful of whom were American servicemen's families) unable to pay up, or asking for extra time, or complaining of this or that. Father continued to do wonders with his herd, having culled the least promising sows, getting rid of an unproductive boar, and keeping the pig sheds clean as a whistle, often mucking out himself. Sales at the market in Northampton were even beginning to make their owner some money. Winterbottom, though, was giving him some trouble. Like Father, Winterbottom, an unlikely Labour peer, was used to having his own way, and the two of them did not always agree ("two queen bees," as my mother used to say). But these were minor problems. The little garden enclosing the house was full of flowers and vegetables, and birds were crowded round Dad's bird-table outside the kitchen window. Mother had joined the local Women's Institute, and had already been elected president; she was heavily involved in the steady round of the Institute's workshops and competitions. So I was saying goodbye to a happy household.

I packed and labelled my suitcases and took the train to Oxford (I had sold my Velocette motorbike to my friend Robin for £5), where I picked up some more of my belongings which had been stored with Catherine Brown. I then took another train to London. I stayed for a few more days, I think with Jeremy and John, who with a couple of other friends had leased a flat in South Audley Street. On my last night a group was got together for a drink to bid me farewell. And the next morning, September 19th, I rode the train to the docks at Tilbury, embarking at 8.30 am. Love of the sea was in my blood, and I could scarcely contain my excitement to be on board.

The *SS Arkadia* had sailed to London across the North Sea from Bremerhaven, where it had already picked up hundreds of continental Europeans emigrating to Canada. They were now joined by several hundred more Britishers, including myself. I shared my cabin with a Polish trumpeter who spoke little English, but was full of good spirits. In fact throughout the ship there was a sense of excited anticipation, with many of the passengers beginning the greatest adventure of their lives. Sailing down the English Channel along the south coast of England I was keenly aware of crossing the paths of my old troopship *Asturias* and of the beloved *Theodora*.

We steamed out past Land's End and over the Irish Sea, dropping anchor in the early morning off Cobh to pick up some last immigrants from the Irish Republic. Then we were away again, this time headed across the heaving waters of the North Atlantic: Canada bound.

INDEX

Any titles and ranks are listed here as they stood at the time. One or two names are incomplete and irretrievable. The author's name is abbreviated to MB.